LABOR DIVIDED

LABOR DIVIDED

Austerity and Working-Class Politics in Contemporary Italy

MIRIAM GOLDEN

Cornell University Press

ITHACA AND LONDON

First published 1988 by Cornell University Press.

International Standard Book Number 0-8014-2200-0
Library of Congress Catalog Card Number 88-47726
Printed in the United States of America
Librarians: Library of Congress cataloging information appears on the last page of the book.

The paper in this book is acid-free and meets the guidelines for permanence and durability of the Committee on Production Guidelines for Book Longevity of the Council on Library Resources.

Contents

Preface

Why do the policy orientations of labor movements in contemporary capitalism differ? Why do some trade unions and working-class political parties embrace moderation whereas others exhibit radicalism? These questions acquired new political salience in the years after the first oil shock of 1973, as policies of wage moderation became the goal of governments across the advanced capitalist world. Incomes policies could not be enacted, however, without the consent of organized labor, which was too powerful to be excluded from policy considerations. But whether union confederations would accede to policies of wage moderation was at first an open question. Although the market did its work everywhere by the 1980s, forcing wages down in most advanced capitalist countries, the reactions of organized labor were critical in deciding whether such adjustments would be, in a political sense, orderly or not.

Unions could resist policies of wage moderation or accede to them. This book tries to account for the choice—radicalism or moderation—that would characterize labor's responses to the economic and political pressures of the 1970s and 1980s. I examine a union movement that offered visibly divided responses to these pressures, one where radicals and moderates repeatedly battled each other in a struggle to determine national union policy. Although the moderates won, their victory came with a price: Italian wage policies incorporated compromises from the outset in the form of concessions made by moderates to their radical opponents.

In examining the policy orientations of different groups in the Italian labor movement, I start with what union officials said they were trying to do and with how they explained their own intentions, beliefs, and ideological leanings. I ground their strategic preferences in the material opportunities afforded by organizational structures, and I show how different patterns of organizational reproduction characterized different parts of the union movement. By focusing on what I call labor's divergent logics of organizational behavior, I offer an account of union policies and politics that unites attention to the goals officials held, the historical circumstances that initially established those goals in the pattern-setting commitments of the Italian "hot autumn" of 1969, and the material conditions that perpetuated them into the 1980s. Using a dozen interlocked case studies at both the national and the local level, I demonstrate that labor organizations responded to the new political and economic pressures of the late 1970s and early 1980s according to their established repertoires of action, that their responses were routinized and predictable, and thus that (except in unusual circumstances) strategies and structures persist over time.

Among political scientists, empathy is a largely unspoken research technique, but it is critical to the kind of fieldwork required by the problem at hand. Those from the heartland of Italian radicalism and resistance to income policies permitted me the luxury of empathy, and it gives me great pleasure to thank the officials and activists associated with the metalworking unions in Turin. Like all the union and Communist party officials who made my research possible, the specific individuals must remain anonymous. These are, however, among the least anonymous, most distinctive, and most courageous people I have had the privilege to know. As specialists in the division of labor they will, I trust, forgive me for having done my job even when it led to conclusions they will not agree with.

In my research I called on many others in the Italian labor movement, and their helpfulness was uniformly impressive. I thank the national offices of the Italian metalworking unions, as well as their offices in Cuneo, Modena, Pordenone, and Milan; the national labor confederations and their offices in the same four provinces as well as in Turin; and the offices of the Italian Communist party in Rome, Cuneo, Modena, Pordenone, and Turin.

Although empathy is crucial to understanding, it is not sufficient. For having instructed me initially in the requisite critical distance, I thank Sidney Tarrow for his imagination, generosity, and expertise. Peter Katzenstein's ability to untangle complicated intellectual problems is already well-known but should not for that reason go unrecorded. Gianfranco Pasquino's help was a stroke of good luck, and I was also fortunate to have Isaac Kramnick's contributions. Finally, Steven Jackson made the statistical work fun through his skill and good humor.

A number of other people very generously read all or part of my manuscript. I thank David Cameron, Anthony Daley, Stephen Hellman, Margaret Keck, Peter Lange, J. Donald Moon, George Ross, Ian Shapiro, Stephen Skowronek, Rogers Smith, and George Tsebelis. They have been patient, encouraging, and skillful critics.

Various Italian institutions made unpublished data available. I thank the Industrial Relations Office of Fiat, S.p.A.; the president of the Federmeccanica, Felice Mortillaro; the national offices of the Istituto Centrale di Statistica; and the statistical offices of the Italian Communist party. The CGIL's library and archives in Rome opened its doors to me, as did the Centro Studi CISL in Florence and the Istituto Gramsci Piemontese. In Turin I was fortunate to enjoy the hospitality of the Fondazione Luigi Einaudi, whose director, Mario Einaudi, has been a special friend to foreign researchers. When I was in Rome, Gino Giugni offered me a desk in his already crowded offices. For help with unionization data, I thank Guido Romagnoli. For teaching me to work with ISTAT's data, I am grateful to Fabrizio Carmignani for his generosity. Finally, this research allowed me to talk to a large number of Italian scholars in the social sciences. Their encouragement and hospitality make those of us from abroad who study Italy extremely fortunate.

Financial support for the research reported here was provided by the Social Science Research Council in conjunction with the American Council of Learned Societies, the Fulbright-Hays Commission, the Danforth Foundation, Sigma Xi (the Scientific Research Society), the Fondazione Luigi Einaudi, Cornell University, the University of New Mexico, and Wesleyan University. None of these institutions is responsible for the final product.

Finally, it gives me deep pleasure to thank the person who taught me that it is impossible to sever empathy from criticial distance. I remain unsure if this is what he intended. Aris Accornero's continuing lack of success in repudiating his own political history, coupled with his scholarly expertise and generosity, has inspired and guided a generation of both American and Italian scholars. I am honored to be among them.

I have been extremely fortunate to work with John Ackerman of Cornell University Press. He has been the editor authors dream of but rarely find.

MIRIAM GOLDEN

New Haven, Connecticut

Abbreviations

AI	Associazione Industriale
API	Associazione Piccole Industrie
ASAP	Associazione Sindacale per le Aziende Petrochimiche e Collegate a Partecipazione Statale
AUSI	Agenzia Unitaria Sindacale
CCNL	*contratto collettivo nazionale di lavoro*
CD	Comitato Direttivo
CdA	*consiglio di azienda*
CdF	*consiglio di fabbrica*
CeSPE	Centro Studi di Politica Economica
CGIL	Confederazione Generale Italiana del Lavoro
CGU	Consiglio Generale Unitario
CI	*commissione interna*
CIG	*cassa integrazione guadagni*
CISL	Confederazione Italiana Sindacati Lavoratori
CNA	Confederazione Nazionale Artigianato
Coldiretti	Confederazione Nazionale Coltivatori Diretti
Confindustria	Confederazione Generale dell'Industria Italiana
CVS	Cotonifici Valle di Susa
DC	Democrazia Cristiana
DP	Democrazia Proletaria
ENI	Ente Nazionale Idrocarburi
Federbraccianti	Federazione Nazionale Braccianti, Salariati, Tecnici
Federmeccanica	Federazione delle Industrie Meccaniche
FGCI	Federazione Giovanile Comunista Italiana
FIM-CISL	Federazione Italiana Metallurgici
FIOM-CGIL	Federazione Impiegati Operai Metallurgici

FLM	Federazione Lavoratori Metalmeccanici
FULTA	Federazione Unitaria Lavoratori Tessili Abbigliamento
INAIL	Istituto Nazionale Assicurazione Italiano del Lavoro
ISTAT	Istituto Centrale di Statistica
Intersind	Associazione Sindacale Intersind
ISVET	Istituto per gli Studi dello Sviluppo ed il Progresso Tecnico
IU	*inquadramento unico*
OECD	Organization for Economic Cooperation and Development
PCI	Partito Comunista Italiano
PSI	Partito Socialista Italiano
PSIUP	Partito Socialista Italiano di Unità Proletario
RSA	*rappresentante sindacale aziendale*
SIDA	Sindacato Italiano dell'Automobile
SNS	Sindacato Nazionale Scuola
SSA	*sezione sindacale aziendale*
SSC	*senza scelta confederale*
UIL	Unione Italiana del Lavoro
UILM-UIL	Unione Italiana dei Lavoratori-Metallurgici

LABOR DIVIDED

I

Policy, Purpose, and the Internal Politics of Labor Movements

It is commonplace to observe that trade unions are organizations and that organizations have interests. But how does interest come to be defined? Interests are not given but made; they are the ways organizational officials come to define their collective purposes in relation to the world they perceive around them. How do the people who staff complex organizations such as trade unions decide that specific policy positions, ideological orientations, and strategic trajectories correspond to and will further their interests? How do union officials know what they ought to do?

Labor organizations have displayed substantial differences in their policy orientations across the advanced capitalist countries in the decades since World War II. Some trade unions have appeared largely reconciled to the capitalist order, integrated into the democratic polity, pragmatic in their bargaining stance, and typically moderate. The behavior of organized labor elsewhere has been more unpredictable, often considerably more militant, and occasionally even taken on the appearance of radical anticapitalism. Different countries have seen different mixtures of strategies and policies at different times. Moderation and militancy, quiescence and contestation, radicalism and reformism—all have characterized organized labor in one or another of the advanced capitalist countries since 1945, and in a few countries labor has passed through periods exemplifying each. In short, there has been considerable variation in how trade unions have determined their organizational interests and policies under contemporary capitalism. What accounts for such variations? Why do unions differ in their policy orientations?

To investigate such questions, this book presents materials drawn from an intensive examination of the Italian labor movement in the late 1970s and early 1980s. For reasons explained below, I focus on the varying policy orientations exhibited by the three Italian union confederations and the joint metalworkers' federation both nationally and in four northern localities. I also pay particular attention to the Italian Communist party, at both the national and the local levels, and examine its role in Italian labor politics. I investigate factional conflicts within the labor movement over issues of wage control and incomes policies, issues that constituted the focus of national policy debate during these years. Using multiple case studies of divergent policy orientations—studies framed by national context and policy decision—I offer a theoretically grounded account of union policy orientations in general and Italian labor politics in particular.

The Problem: Explaining Union Policy Orientations

Empirical studies have advanced a plethora of variables to account for the observable differences in the policy orientations of organized labor under contemporary capitalism. One convenient grouping distinguishes political, sociological, economic-industrial, and organizational explanations.

Various political explanations of union policy orientations exist. It is commonly argued that the partisan affiliations union officials bring with them into their organizations are important determinants of their policy orientations: that Communist unionists tend to differ systematically from their social democratic counterparts, for instance, and that union officials drawn from socialist subcultures differ from those with Catholic backgrounds. Similarly, regular contact or shared partisanship with state officials is said to render union functionaries politically more docile and more likely to cooperate in government policy-making endeavors. Finally, left-wing governments are frequently assumed to induce policy and wage moderation on the part of organized labor whereas centrist, conservative, and labor-exclusionary governments are said to engender labor opposition. At the extreme, a repressive and antilabor state is thought to induce radical trade unionism.[1]

1. Leo Panitch, "The Development of Corporatism in Liberal Democracies," *Comparative Political Studies* 10 (April 1977), 61–90; Robert Michels, *Political Parties: A Sociological Study of the Oligarchical Tendencies of Modern Democracy* (New York: Free Press, 1962); David Cameron, "Social Democracy, Corporatism, Labour Quiescence, and the Representation of Economic Interest in Advanced Capitalist Society," in *Order and Conflict in Contemporary Capitalism: Studies in the Political Economy of Western European Nations*, ed. John H. Goldthorpe (New York: Oxford University Press, 1984); Walter Korpi and Michael Shalev, "Strikes, Power and Politics in the Western Nations, 1900–1976," in *Political Power and Social Theory: A Research Annual*, ed. Maurice Zeitlin, I

Sociological variables customarily deemed important in determining the policy positions of union officials include class background—officials drawn from middle class backgrounds are typically assumed to be more moderate, less ideological, and more pragmatic than their genuinely working class counterparts—educational attainments, and generational cohort, with the young presumably more likely to embrace intransigence than their older colleagues. Similarly, the sociology of the work force is often considered an important external determinant of union policy: generational cohort, skill level, work experience, and occupational, class, and status identity have all been viewed as possible explanations of rank-and-file militancy and subsequent union response. The unskilled, the semiskilled, and their official representatives have frequently been seen, for instance, as carriers of values that are more democratic, egalitarian, and participatory than the skilled and their union representatives (historically construed as one or another version of an "aristocracy of labor," albeit a well-organized and often militant one). At the same time, however, the contemporary semiskilled production worker has also come to be viewed as both privatized and instrumental in his sociopolitical orientations and increasingly likely to support predominantly service- rather than class-oriented trade unionism. Finally, the sociology of labor's counterpart has often been seen as an important determinant of union policy orientations. Repressive and authoritarian management is said to breed militant and radical unions, for instance.[2]

Economic and industrial variables, too, have been used to explain differences in the policy orientations of labor organizations. Well-paid work-

---

(Greenwich, Conn.: JAI Press, 1980); Seymour Martin Lipset, "Radicalism or Reformism: The Sources of Working-Class Politics," *American Political Science Review* 77 (March 1983), 1–18; Edward Shorter and Charles Tilly, *Strikes in France, 1830–1968* (London: Cambridge University Press, 1974); Douglas A. Hibbs, Jr., "On the Political Economy of Long-Run Trends in Strike Activity," *British Journal of Political Science* 8 (April 1978), 153–75, and idem, "Industrial Conflict in Advanced Industrial Societies," *American Political Science Review* 70 (December 1976), 1033–58.

2. Michels, *Political Parties*; Colin Crouch and Alessandro Pizzorno, eds., *The Resurgence of Class Conflict in Western Europe since 1968*, 2 vols. (New York: Holmes & Meier, 1978); Dick Geary, *European Labor Protest, 1848–1939* (New York: St. Martin's, 1981); Eric J. Hobsbawm, *Labouring Men: Studies in the History of Labour* (London: Weidenfeld & Nicolson, 1964); John H. Goldthorpe, "The Current Inflation: Towards a Sociological Account," in *The Political Economy of Inflation*, ed. Fred Hirsch and John H. Goldthorpe (Oxford: Martin Robertson, 1978); John H. Goldthorpe et al., *The Affluent Worker in the Class Structure* (London: Cambridge University Press, 1969); Charles F. Sabel, *Work and Politics: The Division of Labor in Industry* (Cambridge: Cambridge University Press, 1982).

ers and their representatives have been assumed to be more attached to pure wage militancy and more likely to define their self-interest in relatively narrow, instrumental terms, whereas poorly paid workers have often been viewed as more egalitarian and solidaristic. Similar differences have been ascribed to craft versus industrial unions. The external economy has also been viewed as important in determining union policy, though with contradictory results: economic downturn is said to breed either increased discontent or mass quiescence, boom conditions are almost uniformly thought to engender greater industrial militancy. Plant size, industrial concentration, and productive technologies have also been considered important determinants of workers' attitudes and hence union policy, though also with contradictory results.[3]

Organizational variables, finally have been used with considerable effect to explain union policy differences. Most frequently considered have been the extent of union centralization and concentration. National officials are customarily assumed to be more moderate but also less particularistic and parochial than their tendentially more militant local or shopfloor colleagues. Organizational centralization is thus deemed important in ensuring the triumph of moderate, pragmatic policy orientations. Similarly, large, encompassing organizations are often seen as less particularistic, more moderate, and more effective than their smaller and more fragmented counterparts, making the degree of internal organizational concentration important in determining the tenor of policy likely to prevail nationally. At least by implication, both arguments ascribe militancy and radicalism to workers and moderation (if not outright conservatism) to full-time officials; they suggest that union policy orientations reflect the degree of organizational exposure and porousness to the influence exercised by the rank and file. Organizational radicalism is thereby thought to characterize subnational officials and shopfloor union representatives in their power struggles with national elites.[4]

We are thus confronted with an embarrassment of explanatory riches, a dazzling array of competing and often contradictory explanations for union policy, all of them analytically plausible and each apparently cor-

3. Hibbs, "Industrial Conflict in Advanced Industrial Societies"; Peter Lange, "Unions, Workers, and Wage Regulation: The Rational Bases of Consent," in Goldthorpe, *Order and Conflict in Contemporary Capitalism*; Crouch and Pizzorno, *Resurgence of Class Conflict in Western Europe*; Robert Blauner, *Alienation and Freedom: The Factory Worker and His Industry* (Chicago: University of Chicago Press, 1964).

4. Michels, *Political Parties*; Claus Offe and Helmut Wiesenthal, "Two Logics of Collective Action: Theoretical Notes on Social Class and Organizational Form," in Zeitlin, *Political Power and Social Theory*; Mancur Olson, *The Rise and Decline of Nations:*

roborated in one or another empirical study. This book offers two different responses to this dilemma.

First, I designed my research to test some of the most important of these hypotheses against one another. Although the empirical materials I present are all drawn from a single national setting during a relatively short period of time, they involve three central confederations, one national industrial union, the same four organizations in four localities, and two separate policy decisions. These cases allowed me to work on twelve sets of comparisons simultaneously and to test multiple competing hypotheses across them. In particular, I look at the partisan affiliations and sociological backgrounds of union officials, some aspects of the market and industrial environment, external economic and political pressures and opportunities, and a number of attributes of the organizations in question in what was designed as a systematic sorting through of competing causal hypotheses. None of these conventional hypotheses accounts adequately for the divergent policy orientations found in the Italian labor movement in the years under consideration, and some of the superficially more plausible turn out to be patently inaccurate.

I therefore offer a second kind of response to the dilemma of multiple, competing hypotheses: I supplement them with another strategy of inquiry and type of explanation. I thereby reject what is perhaps the dominant type of explanation advanced in the literature and characteristic, for instance, of cross-national, aggregate statistical studies of strikes and industrial militancy. The empirical research on trade unions noted above is predominantly causal, attempting to explain union policy–relevant behavior as determined by various political, sociological, economic, or organizational variables. This kind of explanation posits trade unions as little more than organizational black boxes that, given basic organizational attributes, transform inputs—business conditions, political pressures, rank-and-file demands—into outputs such as strikes, wage rates, and incomes policies.

In this book, I argue that a more adequate account of union policy orientations should instead be actor-centered, focused on union officials, themselves conscious agents who evaluate situations and issues according to their goals and preferences and on that basis respond to structural

---

Economic Growth, Stagflation, and Social Rigidities (New Haven: Yale University Press, 1982); Wolfgang Streeck, *Industrial Relations in West Germany: A Case Study of the Car Industry* (New York: St. Martin's, 1984); Charles F. Sabel, "The Internal Politics of Trade Unions," in *Organizing Interests in Western Europe: Pluralism, Corporatism, and the Transformation of Politics*, ed. Suzanne D. Berger (Cambridge: Cambridge University Press, 1981); Crouch and Pizzorno, *Resurgence of Class Conflict in Western Europe*.

constraints—business conditions, the extent of organizational centralization, the pressures from friendly or unfriendly political parties and governments. This perspective builds on the findings of recent empirical work on the strategic responses of trade unions in a number of Western European countries to the economic pressures generated by the oil shocks of 1973 and 1979. A five-country comparative study concluded, for instance, that "each union is likely . . . to respond to outside stimuli toward change in a different way," depending on its particular history and established patterns of behavior.[5] I extend this line of research to show how patterns of behavior and organizational preferences get established and are then institutionally perpetuated; in other words, I specify the mechanisms by which policy orientations become organizationally encoded, embedded in relatively autonomous institutional structures.

Such an endeavor requires explicit attention to the complex internal workings of the organizations in question: to the setting of goals and agendas, to internal factionalism and conflicts, to the processes and procedures of decision making, and to rules governing organizational form. Although the external environment and organizational design set parameters for union policy, trade union officials act as relatively autonomous decision-making agents within those parameters. Both external economic and political pressures and internal organizational arrangements offer constraints and opportunities to union officials, but neither can explain official policy choices. To do so, we must incorporate the intentions of the actors themselves into analysis. We must look at what they thought they were doing and why, and we must evaluate their behavior both in relation to the material pressures and opportunities coming from their environment and in relation to their own goals.

In this book, then, I move between and coordinate methods of empathic, interpretive, intentional understanding (*Verstehen*) with conventional causal explanation in order to make sense both of the meaning and of the external determinants of the phenomena under investigation.[6] I look at

5. George Ross and Peter Gourevitch, "Conclusion," in *Unions and Economic Crisis: Britain, West Germany, and Sweden*, by Peter Gourevitch et al. (London: Allen & Unwin, 1984), 362. The companion volume, which develops an actor-centered framework, is Peter Lange, George Ross, and Maurizio Vannicelli, *Unions, Change and Crisis: French and Italian Union Strategy and the Political Economy, 1945–1980* (London: Allen & Unwin, 1982).

6. On empathic understanding, see Max Weber, *Economy and Society: An Outline of Interpretive Sociology*, ed. Guenther Roth and Claus Wittich, 2 vols. (Berkeley: University of California Press, 1978), vol. I, pt. 1, chap. 1. For the distinction between intentional and causal analysis, see Jon Elster, *Explaining Technical Change: A Case Study in the Philosophy of Science* (Cambridge: Cambridge University Press, 1983), chaps. 1 and 3.

how the actors themselves understood and explained their own policy-relevant behavior, and I use this information to discriminate among competing causal explanations of union policy choices on the assumption that an a priori justification may be made for privileging those that correspond best to the subjective intentions and understandings of the actors themselves. Although such an approach would be inappropriate for investigating problems of unintended outcomes, it is perfectly suitable for examining the kinds of decision-making processes and overt policy conflicts of concern here. This book demonstrates that the impact of political, economic, sociological, and organizational variables on union strategies and policies varies according to the existing pattern of intentional, goal-oriented behavior characteristic of the organization. It shows, too, that organizational preferences and goals, while generated by material circumstances, are neither reducible to them nor random.

The Logic of Organizational Behavior

Modern trade unions are relatively autonomous from their environments. Their policies are not mere functions of the external pressures exercised by their constituents, the sociology of their officials, or the claims of their counterparts. Autonomy is a function of the intentionality of the agents and may be developed using what I call the "logic of organizational behavior," a concept I employ to characterize the interweaving of strategy, policy, and institutional design typical of highly structured, modern organizations. In later chapters, I refine this concept operationally by showing that different logics may be distinguished according to the daily priorities established for organizational reproduction: the principal mechanisms used to attract members, militants, and officials. But if organizational logics are fundamentally rooted in issues of organizational reproduction, they also permeate organizational life as a whole, characterizing strategic priorities and goals, patterns of exchanges with other actors, types of linkages with the rank and file, and organizational identity and ideology.

Theoretically, the notion of an organizational logic coincides with and draws on the intellectual tradition represented, for example, by Philip Selznick's classic study *Leadership in Administration* and in general by organizational studies sensitive to issues of bounded rationality. Describing the process of what he calls institutionalization, Selznick writes: "to the extent that they are natural communities, organizations have a history; and their history is compounded of discernible and repetitive modes of responding to internal and external pressures. As these responses crystallize into definite patterns, a social structure emerges. The more fully developed its social structure, the more will the organization become valued for itself, not as a tool but as an institutional fulfillment of group integrity and aspiration."[7] Selznick distinguishes "routine" from "critical" organizational decisions, in a formulation similar to that developed by James March and Herbert Simon in their work on routinized decision making.[8] For Selznick, critical decisions encompass "'character-defining' commitments, which affect the organization's capacity to control its own future behavior." They generate pattern-setting choices for organizations, "choices which fix the assumptions of policymaking as to the nature of the enterprise—its distinctive aims, methods, and role in the community."[9] Once its character has been stabilized, the organization tends to make subsequent decisions as matters of routine, working within the assumptions laid down initially and behaving in ways consistent with its established identity, distinctive competence, defined mission, and set role. Most organizational decisions are not, therefore, rationally calculated responses to visible, external stimuli but rather arise predictably out of the organization's established repertoire of action; most decisions, in short, reflect organizational "givens."[10] Officials, rather than recalculate their policies from the top at every opportunity, deliberately avoid questioning the established routines and integrity of their organization, in a perfectly (if bounded) rational allocation of intellectual and organizational resources. Only catastrophic organizational failure or suddenly successful innovation makes it likely that the organization will reconsider the parameters of its established identity.

One empirical implication of these theoretical considerations is that organizational behavior is unlikely to coincide fully and systematically with contemporary external economic, political, and social variables. It is not surprising that union policy orientations fail to correspond necessarily to business conditions or the sociology of the rank and file. Organizations embody their own histories and established pattern-setting commitments as much as they respond to and reflect current pressures and opportunities. Policies and decisions emerge as an organization seeks to respond to new

7. Philip Selznick, *Leadership in Administration: A Sociological Interpretation* (Evanston, Ill.: Row, Peterson, 1957), 16. On bounded rationality see, for instance, Herbert A. Simon, *Administrative Behavior* (New York: Macmillan, 1947).

8. James G. March and Herbert A. Simon, *Organizations* (New York: Wiley, 1958), chap. 6.

9. Selznick, *Leadership in Administration*, 35, 55.

10. March and Simon, *Organizations*, 169.

external pressures and opportunities in ways consistent with its distinctive, historically defined, and relatively coherent internal logic of behavior, or what Selznick calls "character" and March and Simon organizational "structure." But as organizations may develop varying logics of organizational behavior, attention to these internal processes is required to account adequately for policy orientations and behavior.

It is in these terms that I frame this analysis of the wage policies of the Italian union movement in the late 1970s and early 1980s. The policy orientations of various components of the union movement were, I show, predictable and routinized. They reflected different internal logics of organizational behavior, themselves grounded in the critical, pattern-setting decisions made in the closing years of the 1960s during the wave of rank-and-file militancy that swept Western Europe in general and Italy with particular severity. I demonstrate that conventional causal accounts of variations in the policy orientations of different components of the union movement are largely inaccurate: Communist union officials did not distinguish themselves as a group from other union officials in their responses to incomes policies, for instance, nor were national union elites necessarily in conflict with local officials and shop-floor representatives. Conventional explanations fail because of their insensitivity to the perceptions and intentions of union officials themselves, and I detail the mechanisms by which the pattern-setting commitments of the Italian "hot autumn" in 1969 were perpetuated in two quite distinct logics of organizational behavior.

The two logics I identify in the Italian union movement were discovered inductively but could plausibly enrich our understanding of organized labor across the advanced capitalist world. Studies of trade unions customarily assume that organizational survival depends critically on the recruitment of members and that the core priority of the organization lies with related activities.[11] I show that this assumption may be descriptively inaccurate, and I detail the conditions required to establish alternative procedures for what is commonly referred to as organizational maintenance. This second logic of organizational behavior focuses attention and resources not on members but on militants, and in particular on the staffing and operation of the union's shop-floor representative body. In doing

11. I take this as an axiom of such incentive theorists as James Q. Wilson, *Political Organizations* (New York: Basic Books, 1973), chap. 7. The issue has been central to the collective action literature, although I do not believe it has yet been successful in explaining why people join unions when they do not have to; see Mancur Olson, *The Logic of Collective Action: Public Goods and the Theory of Groups* (Cambridge: Harvard University Press, 1965).

so, it may systematically and deliberately discourage the recruitment of new members, regardless of the relative size of the organization. Although this second logic may be relatively uncommon, it carries with it specific consequences for union policy, strategy, and ideology. It represents such a challenge to established theories of union goals that consideration of it may allow us to review some of the assumptions we typically bring to the study of trade unions.

Studying the Internal Politics of Labor Organizations

To pay attention to the perceptions and intentions of union officials is to assume that the complex world of labor movements speaks not in a single tongue but in many. To know why labor movements endorse different policy orientations, we must know what officials hear when they listen to their world. And we must therefore listen to them.

To understand how the Italian labor movement has engaged in strategic choice and to assess its policy orientations, I investigate the intentions, beliefs, and reasoning of the various actors involved: I look at what union officials thought they were doing and how they justified their choices. I concentrate my attention on those participants whose ideas and intentions are most susceptible to external analysis because of the wealth of public speech and written records they generate: unpaid (shop-floor) activists and militants, paid intermediate (provincial) officials, and paid national elites. Occasionally I use indirect (behavioral) evidence to get at the ideas and intentions of the rank and file, but such evidence is most fruitful in ruling out certain interpretations and not especially good for making compelling positive claims about rank-and-file beliefs.

I employ a multidimensional methodology, one rooted in the classic tradition of Anglo-American labor scholarship, endorsed by such organizational analysts as Selznick, and perhaps best labeled "organizational ethnography." In their examination of the British union movement, *Industrial Democracy*, Beatrice and Sidney Webb dissect their own procedures for the study of trade unionism. The purpose of such work, they argue, is to discover "the actual structure and function of the organisation about which [one] is interested." To do so, the investigator must "cherish all the hypotheses he can lay his hands on," taking care, however, not to begin with "only a single hypothesis, for this inevitably biasses the selection of facts" one will encounter.[12] Working hypotheses may be culled from a

12. Sidney Webb and Beatrice Webb, *Industrial Democracy* (London: Longmans, Green, 1920), xxiii, xxiv.

variety of sources, including a thorough examination of the available literature (presumably rather less existed in the Webbs' day than in our own). And they may be initially examined by recourse to government documents and statistics, including those on employment, wages, strikes, elections, and so forth, all of which I used in my research.

For the actual fieldwork, which I carried out between September 1979 and April 1981, during the summer of 1983, and between December of that year and January of the next,[13] the Webbs recommend using "three good instruments of discovery: the Document, Personal Observation, and the Interview." The document may include "cash accounts, minutes of private meetings, internal statistics, rules, and reports of societies of all kinds"—all of which I gathered. I have followed their injunction to "collect every document, however unimportant, that [one] can acquire," including a good many that proved of no subsequent use whatever.[14] I use evidence drawn from minutes of union meetings, regulations regarding rules and procedures, written communications between union offices, and internal statistics both as already available and as union offices compiled them for me.

A second instrument I employed was personal observation: "a continued watching, from inside the machine, of the actual decisions of the human agents concerned." The Webbs suggest two ways to carry out this procedure: either by infiltrating the organization in question—a potentially successful approach only if the investigator is able to integrate fully, and thus not possible in this case—or by "gaining the intimacy and confidence of persons and organisations, so as to obtain the privilege of admission to their establishments, offices, and private meetings." In conducting this research, I attended nearly four dozen meetings, from factory assemblies and union meetings closed to the public to city council sessions. Average meeting time was two days, and though the information I collected was directly pertinent to what follows only occasionally, the procedure was invaluable for sorting "hypotheses of classification and sequence, for [subsequent] verification by an exhaustive scrutiny of documents or by the wider-reaching method of the Interview." Following the Webbs' advice, I also sought to spend as much time as possible in union offices observing the daily operation of "the machine." In this I was perhaps fortunate; as the Webbs note, "in this passive observation the woman, we think, is specially well-adapted for sociological inquiry; not merely because she is accustomed silently to watch motives, but also because she gains access and confidence which are instinctively refused to

13. For details, see appendix A.
14. Webb and Webb, *Industrial Democracy*, xxv, xxvi.

possible commercial competitors or political opponents."[15] Women may be rather less silent in our own day, but to the degree that female investigators successfully exploit their invisibility, they still enjoy some advantages in observing predominantly male organizations. More than once I was mistaken for a secretary, an impression I did nothing to correct.

Finally, the Webbs advise using the open-ended interview: "something more than the preliminary talks and social friendliness which form, so to speak, the antechamber to obtaining documents and opportunities for personal observation of processes." The interview, they write:

> is the skilled interrogation of a competent witness as to facts within his personal experience. As the witness is under no compulsion, the interviewer will have to listen sympathetically to much that is not evidence, namely to personal opinions, current tradition, and hearsay reports of facts, all of which may be useful in suggesting new sources of inquiry and revealing bias. But the real business of the Interview is to ascertain facts actually seen by the person interviewed. Thus, the expert interviewer, like the bedside physician, agrees straightway with all the assumptions and generalisations of his patient, and uses his detective skill to sift, by tactful cross-examination, the grain of fact from the bushel of sentiment, self-interest, and theory. Hence, though it is of the utmost importance to make friends with the head of any organisation, we have generally got much more actual information from his subordinates who are personally occupied with the facts in detail. But in no case can any Interview be taken as conclusive evidence, even in matters of fact. . . . Consequently, the fullest advantage of the Interview can be obtained only at the later stages of an inquiry, when the student has so far progressed in his analysis that he knows exactly what to ask for.[16]

To the Webbs' endorsement of open-ended interviewing I would add only that the procedure is required as well for getting at the intentions, goals, and agendas of union officials. Documents provide formal policy statements; national statistics tell us much about collective bargaining and industrial militancy; but we have to actually talk to union officials to discover the reasoning behind the policy statements and the intentions that guided collective bargaining. As the Webbs point out, interview materials nonetheless cannot be used unreflectively: as a matter of methodological caution, I normally sought the same information from several individuals and as often as possible from officials affiliated with each of the three union confederations. I conducted nearly a hundred interviews in 1979–81, excluding numerous repeats, and another three dozen in 1983–84.

15. Ibid., xxvi, xxvii.
16. Ibid., xxvii–xxviii.

What follows is thus based on an eclectic mixture of government and union statistics, union documents, minutes of meetings, and unstructured interviews: a blend of the quantitative and the qualitative. Any one of these techniques would be insufficient, but combined they allow organizational study from many directions. They provide different kinds of information with which to examine how different components of labor movements work, what they do, and how they think about what they are doing. If we listen long and carefully enough, labor movements themselves can tell us why they choose different policy orientations.

The Setting: Italy, National and Provincial

That the kind of research techniques discussed above can be applied by a single person only in an extremely small number of national cases is obvious. However, practical considerations are not the only justification for limiting the analysis to a single country. Theory suggests the same conclusion.

In designing this research, I wanted both to test some conventional causal hypotheses for union policy and to get inside the workings of the organizations in question in order to supplement causal with intentional analysis. Multiple case studies in a single national setting offered the most economical strategy of inquiry. It made sense, too, to select a country with an especially complex and internally heterogeneous labor movement, one that would automatically offer many cases within a single national setting. In this regard, the Italian seemed the most appropriate case in the advanced capitalist world. Its union movement is organizationally fragmented, its labor movement politically divided, and its geography especially variegated both electorally and industrially. Policy orientations within the labor movement were heterogeneous in the years under consideration, with moderates pitted against radicals over issues of wage restraint. The Italian labor movement, in short, housed divergent policy and strategic orientations in a variety of organizational, political, social, and economic contexts.

To maximize the number of settings in which to examine Italy's labor movement, I selected both national and provincial sites for research. At the national level, I examine the policy orientations of the three central confederations and compare them with the national metalworkers' union. At the provincial level, I focus on these same agents in four localities. Research sites were initially selected on the basis of their policy outcomes (understood as moderate or radical). The logic of comparison for two types of outcomes across six settings involves sorting through causal hypotheses and rejecting those that do not systematically fit the same outcome in different settings. This procedure generates a series of empirical correlations linking policy outcomes to industrial, political, and organizational variables. A second type of analysis is then introduced, one that transforms the correlations into explanations by focusing on the intentions, goals, and beliefs of the relevant agents. This second kind of analysis shows how the effects of external opportunities and pressures are filtered through the organization and how officials construct historically grounded and ongoing patterns of behavior and organizational reproduction.

The Issues: Wage Regulation Policies, 1978 and 1982

Research in what I have labeled the "black box tradition" of union studies posits that political and economic pressures constitute fundamental determinants of union policy and strategy. Organizational studies, by contrast, argue that institutional design is critical in accounting for policy. This book shows that neither view is necessarily the case, that attention to the intentions, goals, perceptions, and habits of the actors themselves is also required to account for policy orientations. To investigate this claim requires us to fix our attention on specific policy decisions. Because of their intrinsic political and economic importance, as well as their public and organizational visibility and salience at the time, I have chosen to examine wage and incomes policy issues in the late 1970s and early 1980s. These issues are generally of such centrality to labor organizations that policy orientations on them may be taken as indicative of overall strategic propensities.

This book examines two major policy decisions. The first occurred in early 1978, when organized labor approved what is called the "EUR line," a policy calling for wage restraint and greater labor productivity. The second took place in late 1982, when the union movement recommended altering Italy's system of wage indexation; these recommendations led to a tripartite agreement some months later. These two sets of events are the major instances of formal union commitments to wage restraint in Italy in the years under consideration. Using a variety of indicators, I classify policy outcomes on these issues as reconciled or opposed, moderate or radical.

These policy decisions were not uncharacteristic of what confronted labor movements across the advanced capitalist world in those years. The conjunction of the increases in commodity prices that began in the early

1970s and the effects of the industrial militancy that had rolled across Western Europe in the late 1960s had put incomes policies on the political agenda everywhere while also introducing questions about their political feasibility. Unions were powerful enough in almost all of the advanced capitalist countries that their consent was required for incomes policies to be enacted.[17] The Italian context was especially problematic because of the combination of particularly acute economic problems with the country's historically high rate of industrial conflict and the degree of wage militancy characteristic since the "hot autumn," as the wage round of 1969 is known. In Italy, union consent to incomes policies was thus vital but less likely to be forthcoming than elsewhere.

By the standards of the twenty-four member countries of the Organization for Economic Cooperation and Development (OECD), Italy's economy called for especially adept macroeconomic management. Italian inflation and unemployment rates were higher than those in virtually any other OECD member country. Between 1964 and 1981, for example, consumer prices in Italy rose at an annual average rate of 10.6 percent, compared with 6.6 percent in the United States, 4.3 percent in West Germany, and 10.4 percent in the United Kingdom. Between 1979 and 1981 Italy's relative position worsened: her consumer prices rose on average by 18.5 percent each year, whereas in the United States prices increased 11.7 percent and in West Germany and the United Kingdom they rose 5.2 and 14.4 percent, respectively.[18] Unemployment was also relatively high in Italy: the average annual unemployment rate between 1974 and 1980 was 6.7 percent, compared with 3.2 percent in West Germany, 5.6 percent in the United Kingdom, and 6.7 in the United States.[19] Overall, Italy in the 1970s had the worst "misery index"—as the combination of inflation and unemployment rates came to called—of any of eighteen of the world's most advanced capitalist democracies.[20]

At the same time, Italian levels of industrial militancy were extremely high. One analysis of postwar strike trends in eighteen advanced capitalist democracies found, for example, that relative strike involvement (the

17. Robert J. Flanagan, David W. Soskice, and Lloyd Ulman, *Unionism, Economic Stabilization, and Incomes Policies: European Experience* (Washington, D.C.: Brookings, 1983), chap. 1.

18. Reported in David R. Cameron, "Does Government Cause Inflation? Taxes, Spending, and Deficits," in *The Politics of Inflation and Economic Stagnation: Theoretical Approaches and International Case Studies*, ed. Leon N. Lindberg and Charles S. Maier (Washington, D.C.: Brookings, 1985), 244, table 9.4.

19. Reported in Charles S. Maier, "Inflation and Stagnation as Politics and History," in ibid., 12, table 1.3.

20. See Cameron, "Social Democracy, Corporatism, Labour Quiescence," 150, figure 7.1.

number of persons involved in strikes per thousand in the nonagricultural labor force) was higher in Italy than in any other country examined. This was the case for the postwar period as a whole (1946–82)and for each subperiod examined since then.[21] Other studies have replicated these findings while showing that the relative number of strikes and strike days has been higher in Italy than in almost any other advanced capitalist democracy.[22] Given this record of industrial militancy, organized labor's agreement to policies of wage restraint could hardly be taken for granted.

Finally, wage militancy has been especially pronounced in Italy. Real hourly wage rates in manufacturing, for instance, rose at an average annual rate of 15 percent between 1960 and 1980 in Italy, compared with 8 percent in the Federal Republic of Germany, 6 percent in the United States, and 13 percent in Japan. From 1973 until 1980, the same figures were 22 percent for Italy, 7 percent for West Germany, 9 percent for the United States, 11 percent for Japan, and 12 percent for all twenty-four member countries of the OECD.[23] Labor costs per unit of output rose by an average of 19.4 percent in Italy for each year between 1972 and 1976, compared with 11.9 percent in France, 5.5 percent in West Germany, and 17.6 percent in the United Kingdom.[24] Both unions and workers, then, were accustomed to rapidly increasing wage rates, and any turn to moderation was unlikely to come easily.

Despite these apparently unpropitious circumstances, some degree of genuine wage restraint was achieved in Italy in the 1970s and 1980s. Incomes policy effects were present in 1976, 1978, 1979, and probably for some years of the early 1980s as well.[25] Economic performance im-

21. Michael Shalev, "Strikes and the Crisis: Industrial Conflict and Unemployment in the Western Nations," *Economic and Industrial Democracy* 4 (November 1983), 440–41, table 2.

22. See for instance Martin Paldam and Peder H. Pedersen, "The Macroeconomic Strike Model: A Study of Seventeen Countries, 1948–1975," *Industrial and Labor Relations Review* 35 (July 1982), 519, table A1. Italy ranked second on number of conflicts (after Australia), first on strike days, and first on workers involved.

23. Reported in Paolo Garonna and Elena Pisani, "Italian Unions in Transition: The Crisis of Political Unionism," in *Unions in Crisis and Beyond: Perspectives from Six Countries*, ed. Richard Edwards, Paolo Garonna, and Franz Tödtling (Dover, Mass.: Auburn House, 1986), 123, table 4.

24. Reported in Michele Salvati, "The Italian Inflation," in Lindberg and Maier, *Politics of Inflation*, 510, table 15.1.

25. Annual "gap" calculations—defined as the extent to which growth in real wages exceeded or fell short of growth in productivity—for 1970–1979 have been calculated by Flanagan, Soskice, and Ulman, *Unionism, Economic Stabilization, and Incomes Policies*, 528, table 9.4. The technical construction of indicators radically affects the conclusions one draws; calculations for the 1980s differ among economists.

proved, strike rates fell, and a measure of wage moderation was implemented. But of course such transformations could not occur painlessly. Union power, labor militancy, and wage regulation were among the most hotly debated public issues of the period. Within the labor movement, the turn to moderation was effected only against substantial internal opposition and in a general climate of dismay and defeat.

The Empirical Puzzle: Policy Conflicts in the Labor Movement

At least two empirical curiosities stand out in this story. First, though the external pressures for wage moderation altered between the 1970s and the 1980s, union responses across all levels of organization remained constant. Second, the pattern of union responses does not appear systematically related either to the partisanship or sociology of union officials or to pressures from the rank and file. Conventional accounts of the determinants of union policy orientations, in short, appear inadequate to address the Italian case.

Economists have faced difficulties in untangling the causes of the wage moderation enforced in Italy in the 1970s and 1980s. Nevertheless, the external pressures on organized labor to endorse wage restraint were relatively transparent. These pressures were largely political in the 1970s and overwhelmingly market-based by the 1980s, as I shall show in greater detail in chapter 3. During the period of "national solidarity," from 1976 through 1979, the Italian Communist party collaborated with the Christian Democratic government in attempting to sort out Italy's pressing economic problems. As part of this endeavor, the Communists endorsed a policy of austerity and pressed organized labor to do the same. The Communists returned to full opposition at the end of the decade, and labor markets worsened; the external pressure on the union movement for wage restraint then shifted from the Communists to the market, in conjunction now with the ruling Christian Democratic–Socialist coalition. Yet despite these different external sources of pressure, the policy responses of different components of organized labor remained constant. Those groups initially reconciled to moderation remained so; opponents continued their resistance.

These outcomes surprised observers even at the time. In particular, the continued support for wage moderation shown by the national confederations even after the Communists returned to political opposition was unexpected. That a tripartite incomes policy could be achieved in the absence of a pro-labor government flew in the face of conventional accounts of the partisan determinants of union policy. It suggested that a full explanation of union policy would have to incorporate additional factors.

Policy orientations in organized labor also appeared unsystematically related to partisanship in another way. As I shall document in later chapters, the partisanship of union officials was not an accurate predictor of their policy orientations. Communist unionists did not necessarily embrace austerity even when their party told them to, nor did they necessarily oppose austerity after their party returned to opposition. Similarly, the sociology of union officials did not accurately predict their responses to policies of wage moderation. Younger officials recruited during the wave of mobilization known as the hot autumn were not necessarily opponents of wage moderation in the 1970s and 1980s. Finally, overt rank-and-file wage rebellion was not part of the story at all, and opponents of wage moderation did not necessarily represent more radical, more militant, or better paid groups of workers. In the face of such evidence conventional explanations for union policy orientations again fail. These empirical puzzles are core problems for analysis in this book.

I stress that I am concerned not with explaining actual wage moderation but rather with the policy positions different union offices took on these issues. The causes and consequences of wage moderation are tricky to untangle. As of 1976, for instance, wage drift—defined for Italy as the difference between increases in nationally contracted wages and increases in actual wages—fell, but it is unclear whether this "should be attributed to . . . union political design or to the deterioration of business conditions."[26] Events in the 1980s sparked even greater debate: some argue that largely identical economic outcomes would have occurred even in the absence of the political agreements enacted; others believe that these agreements were crucial to generating incomes policy effects.[27] Such disagreements are not uncharacteristic of the kinds of political and analytic problems posed by incomes policies. In their comparative study of incomes policies in the earlier postwar era, Murray Edelman and R. W. Fleming noted:

> Private and public wage-price pronouncements, acts, gestures, and programs not only have economic consequences, but also wide and deep implications

26. Salvati, "The Italian Inflation," 538. See also Flanagan, Soskice, and Ulman, *Unionism, Economic Stabilization, and Incomes Policies*, 553–54.

27. For a sense of the debate, see Mimmo Carrieri and Paolo Perulli, eds., *Il teorema sindacale: flessibilità e competizione nelle relazioni industriali* (Bologna: Il Mulino, 1985). In English see, for instance, Gian Primo Cella and Tiziano Treu, "Collective and Political Bargaining," and Mario Dal Co and Paolo Perulli, "The Trilateral Agreement of 1983: Social Pact or Political Truce?" both in *Economic Crisis, Trade Unions and the State*, ed. Otto Jacobi et al. (London: Croom Helm, 1986).

> for social stability. Because this policy area is viewed with widespread and profound concern, the wage-price actions men read about and hear about become sensitive triggers of political unrest or of quiescence. Wage and price talk and action is typically tailored to this fact of political life. It often has considerable impact upon political and organizational loyalties, although its direct impact upon economic trends is more doubtful.[28]

This book is concerned less with the economics of wage moderation than with its politics, with how union officials come to endorse these kinds of policies or their grounds for opposition, and with what these divergent policy orientations tell us about union politics in general.

The Actors: Unions and Parties

Policy orientations within the Italian labor movement were divided both in 1978 and in 1982. Whereas some workers accepted recommendations for restraint, others resisted. Moderates and radicals within organized labor fought each other at every step. The center of moderation lay with the three national confederal offices, which set the policy agenda for labor as a whole. The national center of resistance and radicalism was the metalworkers. The inclusion of both the confederations and the metalworkers' federation in this analysis allows us to explore divergent policy positions at the national level. Policy is also examined in four provinces, two of which exhibited moderate orientations similar to those characteristic of the confederations, two of which engaged in resistance akin to that of the national metalworkers' federation. Finally, an analysis of the political pressures for wage restraint policies requires explicit attention to the Italian Communist party and an examination of its links to organized labor, both nationally and in the four provinces.

The Partito Comunista Italiano (PCI) generally receives about a third of the popular vote, making it Italy's second-largest party after the Democrazia Cristiana (DC). The PCI is also considerably larger than its left-wing rival, the Partito Socialista Italiano (PSI), which wins from 10 percent to at most 15 percent. Strongly class-identified, the PCI is the country's major working-class party, with historically close ties to organized labor and a solid core of working-class voters. Because of the party's importance in national politics—especially its inclusion in the

28. Murray Edelman and R. W. Fleming, *The Politics of Wage-Price Decisions: A Four-Country Analysis* (Urbana: University of Illinois Press, 1965), 321.

governing majority during the period of national solidarity—as well as its direct ties to the labor movement, I have paid particular attention to the role of the party and the partisanship of union officials in determining policy orientations.

Although this book contains much material on the PCI, its major focus is organized labor. The Italian union movement is divided into three confederations, the Confederazione Generale Italiana del Lavoro (CGIL), the Confederazione Italiana Sindacati Lavoratori (CISL), and the Unione Italiana del Lavoro (UIL). At the end of World War II the three were united in the CGIL, but by 1950 the confederation had split into three ideologically competitive camps. The CGIL remained affiliated with the Communist and Socialist parties, the CISL with the ruling Christian Democrats, and the UIL with the minor Republican and Social Democratic parties. The three confederations severed their formal links to political parties around 1970, and during that decade and into the following they generally worked through the Federazione Unitaria, an umbrella federated body established in 1972. The confederations remained partisan-oriented, however, as was apparent in their leadership composition: the CGIL toward the Socialist and especially the Communist party; the CISL toward both the DC and the independent Catholic Left; and the UIL largely toward the Socialists. Despite organizational and political fragmentation, the confederations constituted the locus of support for moderate wage policies during the period under consideration.

Each of the three confederations houses parallel industrial unions, what are called the "vertical" structures of Italian labor. In 1982, for instance, the CGIL was composed of nineteen category unions, or national federations, ranging from the Federazione Impiegati Operai Metallurgici (FIOM), organizing the metalworking industries, to that organizing farmhands (the Federazione Nazionale Braccianti, Salariati, Tecnici, known as the Federbraccianti) and that for teachers (the Sindacato Nazionale Scuola, the SNS). Category unions are in principle responsible for their own sectoral activities, although the confederations seek to coordinate them. Of particular importance are the collective bargaining activities of the various federations, especially the renewals of the generally triennial *contratti collettivi nazionali di lavoro* (CCNLs), industrywide agreements that set wage minima and establish a variety of other conditions (working hours, job classification systems, etc.), though most have to be implemented at the firm or plant level. The CCNLs make national category unions the pinnacle of regularized wage bargaining in Italy. The confederal role in wage determination, on the other hand, is somewhat irregular. The three confederations may sign economywide agreements with employer organizations or the government, or both, but they exercise no formal or official role in the process of wage determination.

The three metalworking federations—the Federazione Impiegati Operai Metallurgici (FIOM-CGIL), the Federazione Italiana Metallurgici (FIM-CISL), and the Unione Italiana dei Lavoratori-Metallurgici (UILM-UIL)—have long been Italy's largest and most important industrial unions. Together they constituted the heart of anti-austerity opposition in the labor movement. Traditionally the metalworkers have served as labor's pattern setters, acting as strategic innovators and guides for other industrial unions and often even for the three confederations. In collective bargaining in the 1970s, for instance, the sector was used to spearhead agreements for other industries, especially wage agreements.[29] In the 1970s and 1980s, the joint metalworking federation—the Federazione Lavoratori Metalmeccanici (FLM)—constituted the single most radical union in the country, wedded to egalitarianism, participatory democracy, militancy, and dreams of social revolution generated by direct action.[30] Why this was the case and how radicalism was perpetuated in the FLM are important empirical concerns of this study.

Radicalism and resistance were not, of course, only national. Neither were they products of grass-roots rebellion. To demonstrate this point and to investigate policy orientations in additional settings, I examine union organizations in four highly industrialized northern provinces. Two—Turin and Pordenone—were centers of radical anti-austerity opposition, two—Modena and Cuneo—were more moderate in their reactions to wage restraint.

The importance of local and provincial offices in the Italian union movement derives from their relative independence in wage bargaining. Geographically, category unions maintain provincial and occasionally local offices, and these offices are directly tied to the factory councils operating in firms in their sectors. The three confederations are also organized geographically, along what are called horizontal lines. Until 1979 the major geographic units were provincial, occasionally supplemented by communal offices. In 1979 the Federazione Unitaria officially abolished its provincial offices and substituted regional and ward offices (*comprensori*) in their stead. Reorganization proceeded with some delay, however,

29. See the evidence presented by Paolo Santi, "I differenziali retributivi occupazionali nell'industria italiana e la politica sindacale negli anni '70," *Rivista Internazionale di Scienze Sociali* 89 (1981), 634–70.

30. See Aris Accornero, "Sindacato e rivoluzione sociale: il caso italiano degli anni '70," *Laboratorio Politico* 1 (July–August 1981), 5–34.

and the geographic analysis involved in this book was conducted at the extant provincial level, although by the end of my fieldwork regions and comprensori had largely replaced the provinces for both horizontal and vertical union structures. Horizontal offices are entrusted with coordinating activities and with representing labor in dealings with local governments; they have no independent role in wage determination.

Finally, the shop-floor body in Italy is the *consiglio di fabbrica* (CdF), or factory council, adopted by the Federazione Unitaria upon its formation in 1972 as its official workplace organ. The CdF replaced a variety of other workplace bargaining and union structures, most notably the *commissione interna* (C.I.), or internal commission. The CdF is atypical in that it is a triorganizational union body, the only genuinely joint union structure that exists in Italy. It is, moreover, elected by all employees, including workers who are not members of any of the unions. CdFs are simultaneously the union's lowest representative structures and also its bargaining agents, recognized (in slightly different language) by the Statuto dei Lavoratori, Italy's major piece of labor legislation, passed by Parliament in 1970. In nonindustrial settings, the CdFs may be referred to as *consigli di aziende* (CdAs), or firm councils, though these are considerably less diffused in the tertiary sector than are CdFs in industry. Factory councils bargain over an extremely wide range of issues, including wages; their task is to raise earnings above the legally recognized minima established by the CCNLs. Chart 1 offers an abbreviated overview of Italian union organization.

During the 1970s and into the 1980s, Italian wage determination was tripolar, because at least three distinct union levels were able to bargain wages and to call strikes without having to seek the formal approval of any other level. The central confederations were important for the negotiations they conducted with other political actors—especially the prime minister's office—and with the country's business associations, especially the largest, the Confederazione Generale dell'Industria Italiana, known as the Confindustria. Italy's system of wage indexation (the *scala mobile*) was, for instance, established through confederal agreements. During this period, the Federazione Unitaria also attempted to exercise increasing control over the collective bargaining conducted by the various national federations. But the national federations also exercised their own powers and influence, particularly in the renewals of national labor contracts. Finally, the CdFs themselves engaged extensively in collective bargaining, raising wages above the minima established in the CCNLs and also negotiating a wide range of work and safety conditions. Provincial union officials in the relevant category unions generally acted to coordinate and guide the activities of CdFs; little collective bargaining was actually prov-

Chart 1. Levels of Decision Making in Italian Union Organization, 1980

Vertical Structures/Category Unions (Federations)	Horizonal Stuctures/Confederations
National Level	
Segreteria nazionale FIM, FIOM, or UILM	Segreteria confederale CGIL, CISL, or UIL
Comitato Esecutivo	Comitato Esecutivo
Consiglio Generale	Consiglio Generale
Provincial Level	
Provincial category union office	Camera del Lavoro or equivalent
Secretariat	Secretariat
Apparatus	Apparatus
Factory Level	
Factory Council	
Executive	
Union members and nonmembers	

incewide. Rather, provincial category unions offered external support and direction to firm, plant, and shop bargaining.

Union strategy was thereby worked out at three distinct sites: at the national confederal level, at the national federation level, and by the CdFs in conjunction with the provincial union offices of their relevant category unions. No one level could authoritatively set strategy for the union movement as a whole, because no one level could authoritatively restrict wage bargaining or strikes for any other level. In consequence, open conflicts were always possible among the various structures in the attempt to define strategy and policy. Because each level exercised some independence in policy implementation, divergent policy orientations could appear within Italy's union movement. These differences, and the conflicts they engendered, are the subjects of this book.

Outline of the Book

The next chapter introduces readers to the major organizational actors, especially the Communist party and the three union confederations, and to the general parameters of policy orientations characteristic of these organizations in the decades since World War II. Chapters 3 and 4 then detail the policy orientations of the PCI, the three confederations, and the metalworkers' federation regarding the approval of the EUR policy and subsequent recommendations to alter Italy's system of wage indexation. These chapters offer an initial explanation of the different policy positions of these actors at the national level. With chapter 5 the analysis moves to the provinces. Three chapters describe the policy orientations of the labor movement in the four provinces in 1978 and 1982 and then provide a full explanation of these orientations. Given the kind of analysis I employ in this book, it is not until chapter 7 that readers will have the complete explanation before them. Each chapter builds cumulatively on those before it. Only in chapter 7 is the movement between correlational analysis and intentional understanding complete. Readers already familiar with the events described and the actors in question and who wish to get immediately to the heart of my arguments are therefore advised to proceed to chapter 7 first and then to read the earlier chapters. Readers who follow the order of the chapters as they appear will gradually acquire the full analysis as they read. Finally, chapter 8 synthesizes some of the most important empirical findings of the study and offers some analytic conclusions.

2

Policy Orientations in the Italian Labor Movement

Policy orientations reflect organizational interest; interest, in turn, is historically embedded. This chapter outlines the organizational and historical parameters of policy orientation in the Italian labor movement since World War II, tracing changes in their broad structural determinants for the PCI and organized labor. I concentrate on the organizational and political resources held by each, resources that set boundaries for the range of policy options feasible for each type of organization. Drawing on analytic formulations developed by Adam Przeworski, in his work on labor politics, I detail the relationship between the overlapping social bases of Italian unions and parties and their general strategic and ideological propensities.[1]

Like other modern labor-affiliated political parties, the PCI since World War II has pursued what Przeworski has described as a supraclass strategy, one aimed at attracting both working-class votes and the electoral support of allied social groups. This has produced a largely moderate policy orientation in the party. However, because the party has also been excluded from governing since 1947, continued internal pressures for radicalism have never been eradicated. This internal tension between moderation and radicalism has had consequences for the party's relationship with organized labor. The union movement has replaced the party as the most important shop-floor institution, and this situation has rendered the party increasingly dependent on its electoral, organizational, and policy ties to organized labor, particularly since the party can no longer count on orthodox "transmission belt" mechanisms of direct control over union

1. See Adam Przeworski, *Capitalism and Social Democracy* (Cambridge: Cambridge University Press, 1985), chap. 1.

affairs. At the same time, however, the autonomy of the trade unions from the PCI began to expand dramatically in the 1960s. Italian unions were offered opportunities to construct new organizational forms capable of carrying radical strategies with the unprecedented levels of militancy that obtained between 1968 and 1972. Labor's internal transformations included alterations in its ties to the political parties, its structure of collective bargaining, the internal distribution of influence, levels of unionization, and the construction of new shop-floor organs. Cumulatively, these changes meant that relations between organized labor and the PCI were rendered competitive yet remained symbiotic. Union cooperation with the party became politically vital yet organizationally dubious.

Reformist Strategy and the Communist Party

The Italian Communist party, founded in 1921, emerged as Italy's most important resistance organization during the fall of fascism. For this and other reasons, it was included in the first Italian government following the end of World War II, and it was during this period that the party began staking out the clearly reformist orientation that was to guide it for the next forty years. It collaborated in drawing up the new Italian constitution, thereby demonstrating its commitment to political cooperation with the other antifascist parties, and in a host of other ways sought to establish social alliances. It soon converted from a cadre to a mass party, expanding its membership among a variety of social groups. Although the core of the PCI's membership and electoral following was to remain working class, the party—in part because of its initial postwar political inclusion, in part thanks to its local electoral successes—launched itself almost immediately on a supraclass electoral strategy whose thrust has remained largely unaltered since then.

The PCI was, however, expelled from government in 1947 and has not since reentered the executive. Political exclusion interrupted the party's moderate orientation but has never entirely undermined it. Its general strategic propensity continued to be reformist and classically social democratic, while it used radicalism to short term advantage at opportune moments. During those periods of most severe political exclusion—much of the 1950s and 1960s as well as the 1980s—the party argued that working-class collective action and militancy would be necessary if its reformist strategy was to succeed, since social unrest would verify the political indispensability of the Communists. When social and industrial conflict finally surged in the 1960s and 1970s, the PCI sought to take advantage of it—but mainly with the aim of transforming direct action into electoral gains and legislative initiatives. Its claims to political legitimacy thus ironically resided with its calls for social order and the demobilization of militancy. Determined to be more than a protest party, the PCI increasingly came to resemble a modern social democratic party, both in its class composition and in its strategic orientation.

Who Votes Communist?

The Communist party consistently increased its share of the popular vote in every postwar election through 1979, when for the first time it suffered a slight reversal. In fact, however, this setback was less important than it might appear. Of considerably more significance was the party's sharp increase in the 1976 elections—when its share of the vote peaked at 34 percent, compared with the 27 percent it had received in 1972 and the 30 percent it would garner in 1979—and in general the greater volatility of the Italian electorate in the 1970s.[2] For the PCI this volatility has meant a broadening of its class appeal, especially into middle-class strata, along with an improved ability to appeal to workers of Catholic backgrounds.[3] The increasing secularization of the Italian electorate has freed many of Catholic extraction to vote on the basis of class rather than religious identity.[4]

This said, it is nonetheless difficult to assess the precise class composition of the PCI's electorate, if only because of the high proportion of nonresponses in pertinent sample surveys. One recent sample, for example, elicited nonresponses regarding partisan preference from fully a third of those questioned,[5] and such a level is not atypical. Additionally, the usual difficulties obtain in comparing survey results based on different

2. See Renato Mannheimer, "Il voto comunista negli anni '70," *Studi e Ricerche*, supplement to *Politica ed Economia*, no. 2 (February 1986), 33–43; of conceptual and empirical importance is Arturo Parisi and Gianfranco Pasquino, "Changes in Italian Electoral Behaviour: The Relationships between Parties and Voters," in *Italy in Transition: Conflict and Consensus*, ed. Peter Lange and Sidney Tarrow (London: Frank Cass, 1980).

3. See Marcello Fedele, *Classi e partiti negli anni '70* (Rome: Editori Riuniti, 1979), especially chap. 3, as well as Paolo Farneti, *The Italian Party System (1945–1980)*, ed. S. E. Finer and Alfio Mastropaolo (London: Frances Pinter, 1985), 97–98.

4. On the traditional importance of religious identity in outweighing class in Italy, see Samuel Barnes, "Italy: Religion and Class in Electoral Behavior," in *Electoral Behavior: A Comparative Handbook*, ed. Richard Rose (New York: Free Press, 1974). On increasing secularization, see Roberto Biorcio and Renato Mannheimer, "Elettorato e fratture culturali," *Studi e Ricerche*, supplement to *Politica ed Economia*, no. 3 (March 1985), 33–45.

5. Biorcio and Mannheimer, "Elettorato e fratture culturali," 40, table 4.

definitions of class and varying wording of similar questions. The most precise empirical research, conducted by Giacomo Sani in the mid-1970s, found that some 10 percent of the party's electorate was composed of managers, businesspeople, and other professionals; 21 percent was drawn from various white-collar strata; 22 percent from skilled and technical workers; 5 percent from peasants and other agricultural strata; and slightly more than 40 percent from manual and white collar workers, farmhands, and other working class groups.[6] Nearly half of the PCI's electorate identified themselves as working class, a mere 15 percent as middle or upper class, and the remainder did not know.[7] However the data are analyzed, they show a high degree of class heterogeneity in the Communist party's electorate, not more than half of which could be considered working class. By the mid-1970s, the PCI had proved itself adept in generating a supraclass electoral appeal.

Communist Working-Class Electoral Appeal

As Przeworski has argued with respect to other Western European, labor-affiliated parties,[8] the PCI too is a party of workers and yet not only of workers. Its increasing electoral support as of the mid-1970s expanded the party's appeal simultaneously on both fronts. Evidence indicates that the PCI's share of the working class vote has risen over the postwar period so that by the mid-1970s the party received a plurality of working-class votes. Historically deeply divided in its electoral allegiances, the Italian working class has nonetheless turned in greater proportions toward the PCI, itself the party most strongly identified in public opinion with trade unionism and working-class interests.[9]

Few studies of working-class electoral behavior in Italy have been conducted, and its history since World War II can only be pieced together using a variety of not strictly compatible sources. The only relevant data that span the full postwar period are the PCI's own ecological analyses of working-class communes. Electoral results for 172 predominantly work-

6. Giacomo Sani, "La composizione degli elettorati comunista e democristiano," in *La politica nell'Italia che cambia*, ed. Alberto Martinelli and Gianfranco Pasquino (Milan: Feltrinelli, 1978), 108, table 2.

7. Ibid., 109, table 4.

8. Przeworski, *Capitalism and Social Democracy*, chap. 1.

9. Giacomo Sani, "L'immagine dei partiti nell'elettorato," in *Un sistema politico alla prova: studi sulle elezioni politiche italiane del 1972*, ed. Mario Caciagli and Alberto Spreafico (Bologna: Il Mulino, 1975); Alberto Marradi, "Immagini di massa della DC e del PCI," in Martinelli and Pasquino, *Politica nell'Italia che cambia*.

Table 1. Communist Vote in 172 Working-Class Communes Compared with National Results, 1946–83 (Percentages)

	Working-Class Communes		National Results	
Year	PCI	DC	PCI	DC
1946	26	34	19	35
1948	32[a]	46	31[a]	48
1953	25	40	23	40
1958	25	40	23	42
1963	28	36	25	38
1968	31	37	27	39
1972	31	36	27	39
1976	39	36	34	39
1979	35	35	30	38
1983	34	29	30	33

Sources: PCI, Ufficio elettorale e statistica, ed., *Ricerca sul voto operaio tramite i risultati delle elezioni politiche dal 1946 al 1976 (nonchè delle elezioni regionali del 1970 e 1975), di 172 comuni* (Rome: PCI, 1977); PCI, Sezione Elettorale e di Statistica, ed., *Ricerca sul voto operaio tramite i risultati delle elezioni politiche dal 1968 al 1979 e del Parlamento europeo del 10 giugno 1979 di 172 Comuni operai,* vol. 2 (Rome: PCI, 1980); and untitled equivalent third volume (ca. 1983), all internal documents courtesy of PCI, Rome.

Note: Refers to electoral results for the Chamber of Deputies.

[a]In 1948, the PCI ran on a joint list with the PSI.

ing-class communes have been compiled for every national election since 1946. The data show that the PCI's share of the vote has been persistently (though not dramatically) higher in predominantly working class communes than in Italy as a whole. And though variations from one election to the next in working-class communes follow national trends, the former exhibit somewhat greater stability than the latter,[10] as table 1 indicates. More to the point, the PCI's share of the vote in these working-class communes has surpassed that garnered by the DC for all three elections since 1976, although nationally the DC still manages to collect more votes than the Communists.

Other estimates differ from the PCI's ecological analyses. Mattei Dogan, for instance, calculated that the PCI received 38 percent of the

10. Fedele, *Classi e partiti negli anni '70,* 107–11.

working-class vote in 1958, or 13 percent more than the PCI's estimate.[11] Ten years later, Paolo Sylos Labini found that 40 percent of Italian wage earners voted for either the PCI or the PSIUP.[12] Samuel Barnes, in a study also conducted in 1968, found that only 18 percent of industrial manual workers (a narrower classification than Sylos Labini's) supported the PCI when questioned about party preference.[13] In the study already mentioned, Sani estimated that among blue- and white-collar industrial and tertiary employees, hired farmhands, and other types of manual workers, 41 percent formed part of the PCI's electorate.[14] In a more recent study, Sani and Renato Mannheimer report that about 40 percent of manual industrial workers voted for the PCI in the mid-1980s.[15] Finally, in response to the question, "What parties or existing political movements do you think best defend the interests of your class?" asked in a 1971 sample survey of blue- and white-collar workers in the manufacturing industries, only 18 percent chose the PCI.[16] When the same question was asked in a parallel study conducted in 1982, the PCI's share of support among manual workers and white-collar employees had risen to 25 percent.[17]

The evidence thus shows that the Italian working class remains divided in its electoral allegiance, but as the importance of religious practices

11. Mattei Dogan, "Political Cleavage and Social Stratification in France and Italy," in *Party Systems and Voter Alignments: Cross-National Perspectives,* ed. Seymour M. Lipset and Stein Rokkan (New York: Free Press, 1967), 140.

12. Paolo Sylos Labini, *Saggio sulle classi sociali*, 4th ed. (Bari: Laterza, 1975), table 7.4. The Partito Socialista Italiano di Unità Proletario (PSIUP) was a small party formed when left-wing elements broke away from the PSI after the latter's entry into a coalition government with the DC in 1962.

13. Calculated from Samuel H. Barnes, *Representation in Italy: Institutionalized Tradition and Electoral Choice* (Chicago: University of Chicago Press, 1977), 60. The figure has undoubtedly been depressed because of the usual underreporting of support for the left-wing parties by working-class respondents in sample surveys.

14. Sani, "Composizione degli elettorati," 108, table 2.

15. Renato Mannheimer and Giacomo Sani, *Il mercato elettorale: identikit dell'elettore italiano* (Bologna: Il Mulino, 1987), 68, table 4.2.

16. The largest proportion—39 percent—responded either "all," "none," or "don't know," again indicating severe underreporting of support for the PCI. Among blue collar workers alone, the PCI's share was 21 percent. Reported in Domenico De Masi, Giuseppe Fevola, et al., *I lavoratori nell'industria italiana*, 2 vols. (Milan: F. Angeli, 1974), vol. 1, book 3, chap. 23, and 2:414.

17. Responses of "all or none," on the other hand, had fallen to less than a third (31 percent). Reported in Gustavo De Santis, "Il sindacato nella visione dei lavoratori: risultati dell'indagine ISVET," opening address presented at a conference on "Lavoratori e sindacato nell'Italia in mutamento," Iafe, Castelgandolfo, 5 May 1983, 21. The PCI's working class expansion is confirmed, too, by the finding that among workers enrolled in the traditionally Catholic CISL, a slightly higher proportion reported favoring the PCI over the DC.

wanes the salience of class in determining voter behavior has increased. Although the working class is far from compact in its vote, the PCI's appeal outweighs the DC's. Even so, only somewhere between one-third and half—at a rough estimate—of the industrial working class votes Communist. The PCI is a party of workers, but not all workers—perhaps not even an absolute majority—support the PCI.

One of the main determinants of the PCI's expanding appeal to working-class voters lies with the growth of the union movement in the past few decades. Vittorio Capecchi and Giorgio Galli, for instance, found a correlation of +.718 between the Communist vote in the provinces and provincial CGIL membership in 1953 and a correlation of +.722 between the same variables in 1963.[18] Sani's work corroborates these findings. PCI voters are more likely to be union members than are supporters of the DC, and most unionized PCI supporters are members of the CGIL.[19] Finally, the correlation coefficient between the PCI's share of the national vote and industrial unionization for the CGIL and the CISL for the years from 1953 through 1979 was +.511. It was +.906 for the years from 1960 through 1979, when unionization was expanding.[20] Union growth is thus positively related to the electoral expansion of the PCI. Although statistical evidence alone cannot tell us whether unionization causes voting behavior or vice versa, in the analysis of double militancy below I argue that other sorts of evidence make it likely that the PCI's growing appeal to working-class voters is principally a function of the expansion of union membership since the 1960s. If this is the case, it corroborates the argument that the PCI has become increasingly dependent on the union movement for its cooperation, and specifically for an indirect electoral mobilization of the industrial working class.

Communist Subcultural Networks and Class Appeal

Like other labor-affiliated political parties, the Italian Communist party is not merely class based but also supraclass in its electoral appeal. In the

18. Vittorio Capecchi and Giorgio Galli, "Determinants of Voting Behavior in Italy: A Linear Causal Model of Analysis," in *Social Ecology*, ed. Mattei Dogan and Stein Rokkan (Cambridge: MIT Press, 1969), 236–37.

19. Sani, "Composizione degli elettorati," 118.

20. For the sources of the data, see appendix B. The results of multiple regressions that attempted to take the time trend into account in the relationship between unionization and the PCI's electoral support were inconclusive. For the longer period, only time was significant at the .05 level; for the shorter period, neither time nor unionization was significantly related to the PCI's share of the vote.

1970s, as I have already noted, the PCI began increasingly to appeal to the more volatile and typically middle-class opinion voter. At the same time, the party has also exercised a traditional type of supraclass appeal, one rooted in Italy's long-standing socialist subculture. Italian political subcultures may be defined, according to Paolo Farneti, as "those geographic areas (one or more regions) in which a party (such as the Catholics) or two ideologically affiliated parties (such as the PCI and the PSI in the period 1948–58) obtain, for several decades, a clear relative majority, for example at or above 40 percent."[21] These high and persistent levels of electoral consensus are, in turn, grounded in an area's century-old political tradition—either Catholic or Socialist-Communist—and sustained through a multiplicity of collateral associations.[22] The PCI's subcultural strength is concentrated in the center of the country, in the so-called red zone, which includes most of Emilia Romagna, Tuscany, and Umbria,[23] all characterized by small industry and fewer industrial employees than the country's major industrial centers in the Milan-Turin-Genoa triangle.[24] In 1981 nearly a third of the party's members were concentrated in the three red regions,[25] and in the 1983 national elections the party drew a quarter of its vote here,[26] although the three regions together accounted for only 15 percent of the Italian population.[27]

The political strength of the PCI in the red zone testifies to the historical nature of the party's supraclass composition. Since the end of World War II, the PCI has successfully mobilized a socially heterogeneous electorate

21. Paolo Farneti, *Il sistema dei partiti in Italia, 1946–1979* (Bologna: Il Mulino, 1983), 100. Because the English translation of this book (see n. 3) is poor, I have translated the definition myself.

22. On the institutionalization of political subcultures, see Barnes, *Representation in Italy*.

23. See Barbara Bartolini, "Insediamento subculturale e distribuzione dei suffragi," in *Continuità e mutamento elettorale in Italia: le elezioni del 20 giugno 1976 e il sistema politico italiano*, ed. Arturo Parisi and Gianfranco Pasquino (Bologna: Il Mulino, 1977), 105.

24. On the relation between subcultures and small industry, see Arnaldo Bagnasco, *Tre Italie: la problematica territoriale dello sviluppo italiano* (Bologna: Il Mulino, 1977).

25. Calculated from PCI, sezione centrale di organizzazione, *Organizzazione dati statistiche*, XVI Congresso nazionale (Rome: PCI, 1983), 9–12, internal document courtesy of PCI, Rome.

26. Calculated from PCI, sezione elettorale, ed., *I risultati della elezione della Camera dei Deputati (relativi alle province) del 26 giugno 1983* (Rome: PCI, 1983), internal document courtesy of PCI, Rome.

27. Calculated using the 1981 national census; ISTAT, *Primi risultati provinciali e comunali sulla popolazione e sulle abitazioni: dati provvisori*, vol. 1 of *Dodicesimo censimento generale della popolazione: 25 ottobre 1981* (Rome: ISTAT, 1982), 8, table 7.

in these areas of the country. In the past few decades, moreover, the party has increasingly consolidated its hold in its traditional areas of strength, in contrast to the DC's diminishing appeal in the historically Catholic northeast.[28] There are, of course, many reasons for this, but one certainly lies with the PCI's explicit "strategy of alliances," articulated as early as the opening years of the 1950s, a classically reformist supraclass electoral strategy aimed at the middle class and small businesspeople.[29] The result has been that the PCI's postwar electorate has probably always been less working class than those of the strongest of the Western European social democratic parties. If a reformist strategic orientation derives from the ability of a labor-affiliated party to construct cross-class alliances,[30] the PCI's electorate makes it as reformist as any other European socialist party.

Party Organization in the Workplace

Like those of other labor-affiliated parties, the PCI's electoral following is simultaneously class based and supraclass; the PCI is a party of workers, but not only of workers. In moving to attract other social groups, it has consciously chosen to downplay the direct organization of workers in the workplace. But it has never done so without hesitation: it has sought to retain class specificity without indulging in extreme forms of workerism (*operaismo*). The organizational predicament caused by the party's ambiguous class identity is best understood by tracing the fate of its shop-floor structures. Since the end of the 1940s, the most accurate characteriz-

28. See Arnaldo Bagnasco and Carlo Triglia, eds., *Società e politica nelle aree di piccola impresa: il caso di Bassano* (Venice: Arsenale, 1984), and idem, *Società e politica nelle aree di piccola impresa: il caso della Valdelsa* (Milan: F. Angeli, 1985).

29. See Stephen Hellman, "The PCI's Alliance Strategy and the Case of the Middle Classes," in *Communism in Italy and France*, ed. Donald L. M. Blackmer and Sidney Tarrow (Princeton: Princeton University Press, 1975). Other analyses of Italian geography, party organization, and voting behavior include his "Militanti e politica nel Triangolo industriale," in *L'identità comunista: i militanti, le strutture, la cultura del Pci*, ed. Aris Accornero, Renato Mannheimer, and Chiara Sebastiani (Rome: Editori Riuniti, 1983); Fausto Anderlini, "Militanti e società nelle zone bianche e rosse," in Accornero, Mannheimer, and Sebastiani, *Identità comunista*; Marcello Fedele, "La dinamica elettorale del PCI 1946/1979," in *Il partito comunista italiano: struttura e storia dell'organizzazione 1921/1979*, vol. 21 of *Annali Fondazione G. Feltrinelli, 1981*, ed. Massimo Ilardi and Aris Accornero (Milan: Feltrinelli, 1982); Arturo Parisi and Gianfranco Pasquino, "Relazioni partiti-elettori e tipi di voto," in *Il sistema politico italiano*, ed. Gianfranco Pasquino (Bari: Laterza, 1985); and, in English, Parisi and Pasquino, "Changes in Italian Electoral Behavior."

30. Przeworski, *Capitalism and Social Democracy*, chap. 1.

ation of the PCI's factory organization is captured by the notion of the "unionization" (*sindacalizzazione*) of the party in the workplace. The party's decision to place its factory resources at the disposal of the union movement—namely, the CGIL—shows that union gains have long been perceived by the PCI's leaders as crucial to the party's own electoral and political goals. But the results have included an endemic weakness in the PCI's factory organizations, when these have not been entirely abandoned. This weakness in turn has meant that the CGIL has increasingly tended to mediate the PCI's relations with the working class. The party has become ever more dependent on its ties to the union movement for oganizational as well as electoral resources.

The party's ability to enroll working-class members has steadily diminished since World War II. In 1945, 53 percent of the PCI's membership was composed of blue-collar workers; by 1947 this had fallen to 45 percent, and by 1952 it was 40 percent, where it has hovered ever since.[31] Although this still renders the party's composition relatively class specific, it does not make the working class very Communist. In 1950, 31 percent of the employed working class had party cards. A decade later the figure had fallen to 12 percent, and a decade after that it was a mere 7 percent.[32] The PCI's organized working-class presence is shallow and selective.

The data on the fate of Communist factory bodies since World War II also testify to a demise in the party's direct links with the working class.[33] In 1950 just over 6,500 factories and another 4,500 nonindustrial workplaces contained party cells. By 1964 the same figures had been halved: approximately 3,000 factories and 1,500 nonindustrial workplaces had PCI units in situ.[34] In 1982, out of some 12,500 party sections in Italy, a

31. Figures for 1945 through 1977 reported in Celso Ghini, "Gli iscritti al partito e alla FGCI," in Ilardi and Accornero, *Partito comunista italiano*, 287. The PCI's definition of "manual workers" is relatively stringent, covering only industry (and therefore excluding manual workers in the service sector, including transportation).

32. Figures for 1950 through 1964 reported in [Aris Accornero], *I comunisti in fabbrica*, Documenti delle lotte operaie, no. 1, ed. "Centro Giovanni Francovich" (Milan: Feltrinelli, 1967), 9. Figures for 1968 through 1976 in Marzio Barbagli and Piergiorgio Corbetta, "Partito e movimento: aspetti e rinnovamento del PCI," *Inchiesta* 8 (January–February 1978), 26. Seven percent was reported for 1971; 1970 is unreported.

33. This discussion of the PCI's factory organizations is based on developments in large industry. The situation in small firms differed considerably, as revealed by evidence presented by Renato Mannheimer, Mario Rodriguez, and Chiara Sebastiani, *Gli operai comunisti* (Rome: Editori Riuniti, 1979).

34. Figures on factory cells between 1950 and 1964 from Fausto Anderlini, "La cellula," in Ilardi and Accornero, *Partito comunista italiano*, 207. Figures on the total number of workplace cells from [Accornero], *Comunisti in fabbrica*, 9. While the source of the figures in the latter is not given, the text indicates these are official PCI data.

scant 700 were in industrial plants and another 500 in nonindustrial workplaces.[35] The PCI's organizational presence in the workplace, though still of considerable political importance for the party, has become relatively marginal compared both with the predominantly geographically based party organization and with union penetration of the workplace.

The postwar decline of the Communist party's independent organization of the working class has been a function of both party strategy and material difficulty. The latter, a product of the conjunction of widespread anti-Communism in a context of rapid industrialization in the 1950s, is less interesting for present purposes than the party's own organizational strategy vis-à-vis the working class. Since the early 1950s the PCI has pursued organizational objectives that inevitably entailed the "unionization" of the party in the workplace, and in fact the very concept dates back to that era. Between 1947—when the party was expelled from the national government—and 1950, the PCI had placed great weight on its factory cell, responsible for virtually all rank-and-file mobilization in large industry. By 1951, however, the PCI had shifted its attention from its own factory organization to the unions: "The task of the [factory] cell," enjoined the PCI's general secretary at the party's seventh Congress in 1951, "is that of making Communists the best parts of the union."[36] The PCI placed its workplace resources at the disposal of the CGIL in order to prop up the union as the cold war intensified, because the CGIL—itself composed of both Communists and Socialists—was potentially capable of reaching a broader mass base than the evermore isolated party, and as part of the party's distinctive strategy of alliances. Cadres were shifted, often more or less against their will, from the party to the union, and the party's own organization was weakened as a result.[37] More or less the same process was under way across all the PCI's flanking organizations. The party was moving resources from its own organization to the social associations affiliated with it. This strategy provided the Italian context for the notion of a "transmission belt": the creation and expansion of affiliated but nominally independent mass organizations, open to non-Communists but in which party members and party ends were expected to dominate.

35. Figures reported in PCI, *Organizzazione dati statistiche*, 81.

36. Palmiro Togliatti, at the seventh PCI congress (1951), quoted in Massimo Ilardi, "Sistema di potere e ideologia nel PCI: le conferenze nazionali d'organizzazione," in Ilardi and Accornero, *Partito comunista italiano*, 22. On the period between 1948 and 1951, see ibid., 21–22 and [Accornero], *Comunisti in fabbrica*, 30.

37. [Accornero], *Comunisti in fabbrica*, 35–37. For studies of the eventual consequences of the "unionization" of the party, see Romano Alquati, "Torino: il partito nella città-fabbrica" (1965), and idem, "I militanti comunisti tra la fabbrica e il partito" (1966), both reprinted in Romano Alquati, *Sulla FIAT e altri scritti* (Milan: Feltrinelli, 1975).

With respect to the unions, however, the term "unionization" of the party is more accurate because it better captures the extent to which the party's own resources were depleted with the strengthening of collateral organizations.

The impetus for "unionization" lay with the dual notions that only social conflict would undo the PCI's political isolation and that social conflict itself would not arise spontaneously but would come only with the reinforcement of politically inspired shop-floor organizations. Not surprisingly, the PCI officially announced the end of the "transmission belt" between union and party at its eighth congress in 1956,[38] the same congress that again articulated the party's commitment to mass membership in place of an organization of militants and cadres. The factory cell was officially abandoned as the party's "normal" and "fundamental" organizational unit, while the geographic section assumed preeminence[39] as the party attempted to broaden its social appeal and to move out of the factories into society as a whole.

Since then, however, the role of the PCI in the workplace has been the object of considerable confusion. The party's own decision to reinforce its affiliated voluntary associations contributed to the demise of the factory cell. Nevertheless, the PCI has repeatedly called for the reestablishment of its own organizations on the shop floor without, however, clearly defining the nonunion tasks these units should perform. The party's leadership has consistently maintained that "without the constant work of orientation practiced by the party's organizations, the workers' struggle is blind, tends to fold in on itself and to remain confined to the factory; it is incapable of politically evolving."[40] Without the party, the working class and the unions remain prepolitical, incapable of elaborating a general, national strategy. Despite this reiteration of the need for the party to lead shop-floor action into the political realm, the tasks involved have remained vague. In 1957 party leader Giorgio Amendola had complained of an "ever more evident insufficiency of our organization in the factory," while admitting that "the factory cell has not always succeeded in assuming a general political function," since it "has . . . too often assumed tasks that are predominantly paraunion."[41] Six years later a factory militant lamented, "The action of the party should not consist solely or prevalently

38. See Cesare Pillon, *I comunisti e il sindacato* (Milan: Palazzi Editore, 1972), 454–56.

39. See [Accornero], *Comunisti in fabbrica,* 38, and Anderlini, "Cellula," 197–201.

40. Such is the interpretation of Giuseppe Berta, "Le conferenze operaie," in Ilardi and Accornero, *Partito comunista italiano,* 724.

41. Giorgio Amendola, "Il partito comunista nelle fabbriche," *Rinascita* 14 (July–August 1957), 337, 339.

in the distribution of leaflets."[42] The party has been unable to define a full range of activities for factory cells that do not largely duplicate those already undertaken by the union movement.

In 1969, when the rank-and-file militancy for which the PCI had been waiting twenty years finally exploded, the party confessed, "We acutely feel the need for a qualitative improvement and a rapid development of Communist organization in the workplace in order to render it adequate to today's tasks,"[43] an open admission of the persistent weakness of Communist shop-floor presence. The party proposed the creation of provincial Federation commissions devoted to factory issues, which would function "as an instrument for the construction of the party in the factory and for a more organic and direct relationship between comrades operating in the union, in the party, [and] in the *commissioni interne*," and also recommended recreating the factory cell as the party's factory unit, even where party sections already existed.[44] Four years later the party was still calling for "a new, great reestablishment of the work of building and developing Communist organization in every workplace."[45] But in 1977 militants complained that the preceding decade, rather than rectifying the party's problems, had witnessed "a flattening of political militancy and its reduction to union activism and local administration, on the one hand, and on the other to propaganda, membership recruitment, preparation for *Festival dell'Unità*."[46] In 1980 local functionaries were still calling for the development of an autonomous party presence in the workplace, arguing that "the relationship between the party and the masses, between the party and the workers, cannot be entrusted to union mediation,"[47] despite the fact that in 1979 the PCI had proudly announced the creation of four hundred new factory and enterprise sections in the past two years.[48] After thirty

42. "L'organizzazione comunista nelle fabbriche di Torino," *Rinascita* 20 (7 December 1963), 22.

43. Ugo Pecchioli, quoted in "Un grande rilancio del partito in fabbrica," *Rinascita* 26 (21 November 1969), 3. See also Pietro Ingrao, "Partito e movimento," *Rinascita* 27 (30 January 1970), 6–7.

44. Alessandro Natta, "Relazione sulle conclusioni della commissione di organizzazione," in PCI, *Atti e risoluzioni,* XII Congresso del Partito comunista italiano, Bologna, 5–8 febbraio 1969 (Rome: Editori Riuniti, 1969), 730.

45. Ugo Pecchioli, "Politica e organizzazione nel PCI," *Critica Marxista* 11 (May–August 1973), 33.

46. Angiolo Dionelli and Massimo Baldacci, "I problemi del partito in fabbrica," *Rinascita* 34 (2 September 1977), 15.

47. Rocco Larizza, "Il Pci in fabbrica visto da Mirafiori," *Rinascita* 37 (28 November 1980), 12.

48. Enrico Berlinguer, "Avanzare verso il socialismo nella pace e nella democrazia: unità delle forze operaie, popolari e democratiche per una direzione politica nuova dell'Ital-

years, the specific, nonunion tasks of the PCI's factory organizations remained unclear. If anything, it had become even more difficult to block out the "topics and areas of intervention" that should distinguish the party from the union movement, since "for a long time the principal job of [factory] Communists has been that of reconstructing and strengthening the union."[49] The practice of "unionization"—of using party militants for union work—had left the party without an autonomous identity in the workplace and dependent on the union for an active daily involvement in factory life. The party's factory organization had become a victim of its own success in helping consolidate the union.

These problems were exacerbated by the adoption of the so-called incompatibility norms in the 1970s, which prohibited union functionaries from also holding party positions. Incompatibility, along with a provision in the 1970 Statuto dei Lavoratori that allows employees to take temporary leaves from their jobs while on union staff, disrupted the PCI's traditional pattern of shifting cadres between union and party while ensuring that their primary commitment remained with the party. Cadres could still be moved back and forth, but not without relinquishing formal organizational positions each time or, in the case of unionists on leave, actually having to quit their original jobs when assigned a full-time party position. Thus the ability of the unions to recruit and train their own functionaries expanded considerably, much to the PCI's satisfaction, since this freed party resources from union activities.[50] Nonetheless, in 1975 the PCI reported that "the autonomy of the union, after the the adoption of the 'incompatibility' norms . . . poses new and difficult problems for the participation of working-class cadres in the life of the party. . . . It is a fact that the consequences of this weigh heavily even today and may weigh even more heavily in the future."[51]

Incompatibility raised at least two problems for the party. First, it objectively put the party into competition with the union for recruiting working-class leaders, a goal that has always figured prominently on the

---

ia e per il rinnovamento della Comunità europea," in PCI, *Atti e risoluzioni*, XV Congresso del Partito comunista italiano, Roma, 30 marzo–3 aprile 1979, 2 vols. (Rome: Editori Riuniti, 1979), 1:100.

49. Larizza, "Pci in fabbrica," 11–12.

50. Since 1951, the PCI had called for increased union involvement in training cadres. See Pillon, *Comunisti e il sindacato*, 454–56, and Tatiana Pipan, "I sindacalisti," in Accornero, Mannheimer, and Sebastiani, *Identità comunista*, 280.

51. Armando Cossuta, "Relazione sui problemi di organizzazione e le modifiche allo statuto del partito," in PCI, *Atti e risoluzioni*, XIV Congresso del Partito comunista italiano, Roma, 18–23 marzo 1975 (Rome: Editori Riuniti, 1975), 667.

PCI's organizational agenda. This was especially serious for a party that has experienced increasing difficulty in promoting other than a middle-class leadership into its highest decision-making organs,[52] when Italy's union movement has remained far more working class in its leadership composition.[53] Second, and more important, direct and organic links between the union and the party had been severed. If the party was to remain an integral component of the CGIL, new mechanisms for communication and coordination would have to be created.

The eventual response, a good ten years after the fact, was the establishment of the *consulta del lavoro*, a formal party organ for the discussion of labor problems. Although merely a consultative body, and only vaguely defined in the party's statute, consulte were established both nationally and in various provinces and regions. They serve as sites for dialogue among party functionaries, Communist trade unionists, and other Communists engaged in nonparty organizations that deal with labor problems.[54] They are the party's modest answer to thirty years of moving resources to the union at the expense of the PCI's own shop-floor organization. The strategy has paid, but with a price. The union now stands directly between the party and its working-class base. If the party is to pursue a moderate strategy, the cooperation of organized labor is crucial. Organizational resources in the factory are concentrated with the union movement, not the PCI.

Communist Trade Unionists and the Problem of Double Militancy

Organizational issues such as incompatibility and the role of the party's workplace units touch directly on what is known in Communist parlance as the problem of double militancy: Communists active in both party life and nonparty associations, especially the union movement. Double militancy is far from uncommon for full-time unionists and union activists.

52. See Chiara Sebastiani, "Organi dirigenti nazionali: composizione, meccanismi di formazione e di evoluzione, 1945/1979," in Ilardi and Accornero, *Partito comunista italiano*, 400–401.

53. For the CGIL, see Eligio Biagioni, Stefania Palmieri, and Tatiana Pipan, *Indagine sul sindacato: profilo organizzativo della Cgil* (Rome: Editrice Sindacale Italiana, 1980), 246–49. Among full-time CGIL functionaries (excluding technical and secretarial staff), for instance, 48 percent held working class jobs before assuming union positions.

54. On the establishment of the consulte, see Edoardo Perna, "Relazione a nome della commissione delle strutture organizzative e dello statuto," in PCI, *Atti e risoluzioni*, 1979, 1:596, and the modification of article 36 of the party's statute, in ibid., 2:778.

Some 70 percent of the CGIL's full-time political functionaries—the term is used to distinguish union officials from technical and secretarial staff—are members of the PCI.[55] The Communist presence in joint decision-making bodies is of course far smaller. I estimate, for instance, that around 1980 only about a quarter of the Federazione Unitaria's Comitato Direttivo (the most important national joint decision-making body) was composed of Communists,[56] making it impossible for the party to control national decision making directly. While the party could conceivably control decision making in the CGIL—assuming both that the PCI issued an unambiguous policy and that unionists were prepared to follow it, assumptions that are equally dubious—its ability to influence the three confederations together is severely restricted.

As for shop-floor union activists, it is difficult to know the extent of the PCI's membership at this level, which in any case varies significantly by geographic area. One study of industrial factory delegates in Piedmont—not a scientifically selected sample, but illustrative nonetheless—found that 60 percent of the CGIL's delegates were also members of the PCI (compared with under 15 percent of the CISL's, 15 percent of the UIL's, and 21 percent of those with joint union membership). Of all delegates surveyed, half were Communist.[57] A similar study conducted in the province of Modena among a sample of metalworking delegates from all three confederations found that though 34 percent were not members of any political party, Communist party membership characterized an absolute majority, or 55 percent. Among delegates affiliated with the CGIL, 76 percent were Communist.[58] Party membership is thus highly correlated with shop-floor union activism, and it is a plausible assumption that Communists constitute a relative majority of industrial factory delegates in Italy.

Party affiliation for delegates provides important cues for political orientation and for their understanding of their own roles as union delegates.

55. Biagioni, Palmieri, and Pipan, *Indagine sul sindacato*, 278.

56. Calculated using data from Biagioni, Palmieri, and Pipan, *Indagine sul sindacato*, 278, and UIL, *Indagine conoscitiva sullo stato organizzativo delle strutture* (Rome: UIL, Servizio Organizzativo, 1979), 68, internal document courtesy of UIL, Rome.

57. IRES-CGIL Piemonte, ed., *Delegati in Piemonte: una ricerca in cento fabbriche*, Formazione e cultura FIOM-CGIL Piemonte (Milan: F. Angeli, 1986), 50, table 12, and 51, table 13. This study also found that the majority of factory delegates had first been approached with the suggestion to become a delegate by their own work groups (65 percent), whereas fewer than 1 percent had been solicited by their party; 81, table 38.

58. Maura Franchi and Vittorio Rieser, *Esperienza e cultura dei delegati: un' indagine nella realtà metalmeccanica modenese* (Reggio Emilia: Bonhoeffer, 1984), 30–31.

The Piedmontese study asked those surveyed, "What is the major task of the delegate?" Possible responses were the following:

To contribute to the workers' development in order to change society.
To contribute to the development of the workers' consciousness of their own condition of exploitation.
The daily protection of the workers in my work group.
To represent the interests of the workers in my work group.
To listen to the needs of the workers and take them to the union.
To explain the union's line to the workers.
To contribute to an improvement of relations between the workers and management.

Whereas the first two responses—which see the delegates' tasks in predominantly political terms—were given by 46 percent of all delegates questioned, this rose to 60 percent for Communist delegates who were members of the CGIL.[59]

But if party affiliation provides a general political orientation for Communist shop-floor union activists, it neither determines their behavior nor accounts for their policy positions on union affairs. For one thing, most Communist delegates—indeed, most Communist unionists—were active in union life before joining the PCI, and that initial commitment may be expected to exercise an important independent influence on their subsequent political and union decisions. The Piedmontese survey of delegates found, for instance, that 67 percent of delegates who were members of any political party had joined the union before taking out party membership, and that Communists were no different in this respect from members of other parties.[60] Among Modenese metalworking delegates, who are exposed to a dominant Communist subculture, a greater number joined the PCI before joining the union than the reverse,[61] but even so, "profound and articulated *differences* emerge on questions that are often of political relevance" among Communist delegates.[62]

Such findings are corroborated by information recently made available on the political trajectories of Communist union militants. Delegates to the party's fifteenth congress in 1979 who were classified as union activists or

59. IRES-CGIL, *Delegati in Piemonte*, 82–83.
60. Ibid., 59, table 21.
61. Franchi and Rieser, *Esperienza e cultura dei delegati*, 203.
62. Ibid., 206. Emphasis in the original.

functionaries tended to have taken out union cards before joining the PCI; more than two-thirds, in fact, had done just this. Only after 1975 had this pattern undergone a reversal as a new generation of militants emerged who more often than not joined the party before the CGIL.[63] But until then, the union provided the initial politicizing context, which only later translated into party membership.

What none of these data illuminate, however, are the genuine difficulties for those subject to the conflicting imperatives of double militancy. The Italian Communist party has never been monolithic, and its members always enjoyed a certain latitude in interpreting the claims of party loyalty. But until the 1970s the likelihood of sustained and overt conflicts between the CGIL and the party was relatively low, and what differences did occur—for there always were some, and often quite important ones—could usually be handled in private. By the mid-1970s this was no longer true, as points of conflict "multiplied," as a Communist leader of the CGIL admitted.[64] As the rest of this chapter will document, by then the union movement had acquired too many independent resources for the CGIL to trail passively in the party's wake. Asked about policy differences between the party and the union, for instance, a Communist trade union leader in Milan replied, with incredulity and abruptness, "But I, too, am the party!"[65] a response that reveals the heartfelt dilemmas of Communist unionists forced to oppose their own party.

The instinct of these unionists is to attempt loyalty to the claims made by the PCI, if only because the decision to join the party entails significant moral commitment and political identification, probably more so than joining other parties in Italy does. Communist unionists strongly prefer to conduct their union activities in ways that curry the party's favor. Only when driven by the constraints of their organizational position will they deliberately repudiate the expressed preferences of their own party, as we shall see in later chapters.

Trade Union Partisanship and Politicization

Like other modern socialist parties, the PCI has pursued a supraclass electoral strategy since World War II. This has entailed a significant

63. Pipan, "Sindacalisti," 271–73.

64. Interview no. 130, national CGIL (Secretariat), 10 January 1984. For information on the coding of interviews, see appendix A.

65. Interview no. 58, CGIL Milan (Secretariat), 23 December 1980.

downplaying of the party's direct organizational penetration of the working class. The union movement has replaced the party as the most important shop-floor institution, and this has rendered the party increasingly dependent on the union movement's cooperation, particularly since the party cannot count on double militancy as a mechanism of direct control over union decision making. At the same time, however, the political and organizational autonomy of organized labor began to expand radically in the 1960s. Union cooperation with the PCI is thus vital yet problematic: the degree of internal integration of the labor movement's two wings became variable and contingent.

Italian unions have been highly politicized throughout their existence, and union activities have invariably been conducted with an eye to their general sociopolitical consequences. Until the end of the 1960s trade unions in Italy were also officially partisan, with dual officeholding and role cumulation frequent and unionists acting as members of Parliament for their partisan delegations.[66] Formal ties between Italy's three major union confederations and political parties were abolished, however, at the turn of the decade. Regardless of their formal political status, Italian unionists remain highly aware of the depth of interaction between the industrial relations system and the political system. They have always seen themselves as political, not just partisan actors, and as vital agents in maintaining the democratic order.[67] Collective bargaining and other contractual and industrial activities are integral elements of union performance, but the ends of trade unionism transcend mere industrial relations.

Such an explicit politicization of organized labor—particularly pronounced in the largest confederation, the CGIL,[68] but also characteristic of the CISL by the 1970s—is related to the class, rather than associational, nature of these unions. Associational unionism, which involves the repre-

66. The most important analysis of the traditional partisanship and politicization of Italian unionism is Alessandro Pizzorno, "I sindacati nel sistema politico italiano: aspetti storici" (1971), reprinted in his *I soggetti del pluralismo: classi partiti sindacati* (Bologna: Il Mulino, 1980).

67. The Italian constitution contains a clause (article 39) guaranteeing the principle of union liberty and another (article 40) guaranteeing the right to strike. Article 39 also provides statutory recognition of industrywide bargaining. See Umberto Romagnoli and Tiziano Treu, *I sindacati in Italia: storia di una strategia (1943–1976)* (Bologna: Il Mulino, 1977), chap. 1, and Piero Craveri, *Sindacato e istituzioni nel dopoguerra* (Bologna: Il Mulino, 1977), chap. 1, for discussions of the constitutional status of Italian unions. In English, see Tiziano Treu, "Italy," in *International Encyclopaedia for Labour Law and Industrial Relations*, supplement no. 23 (Deventer, Netherlands: Kluwer, 1981).

68. Gian Primo Cella, Bruno Manghi, and Roberto Pasini, *La concezione sindacale della CGIL: un sindacato per la classe*, Collana Ricerche, no. 9 (Rome: ALCI, 1969).

sentation of members only, is found in the United States; class unionism, which Alessandro Pizzorno refers to as "a union system coterminous with the political system," involves union movements that work for "benefits for all employees in a country, and not merely the union's members."[69] It is found across continental Europe and configures the politicization of European labor, historically rooted in the era before the full expansion of suffrage, when union movements founded labor parties and vice versa.

From the original formation of the unified CGIL in 1944 to the schisms that rocked it at the end of the decade, the roots of postwar unionism were not merely broadly political but also explicitly partisan. Formal links existed between the unions and parties, and though organized labor was reestablished after fascism before the parties, partisan orientations heavily conditioned union activities.[70] The formal ties between unions and parties remained extremely strong for the first few decades following World War II. National union leaders invariably figured in the leadership organs of the political party with which they were affiliated; elite recruitment in the unions tended to proceed by partisan affiliation; and the most visible union leaders served in Parliament as members of their partisan delegations. Union strategies tended to be linked to the needs of the various parties.

Formal linkages ended, however, about 1970 for all three confederations. Each adopted a similar series of regulations prohibiting party and union role cumulation and the holding of political offices by trade unionists.[71] The incompatibility norms, as they are called, are extremely severe. They prohibit trade unionists who are members of secretariats at any level or who are members of any of a series of other union decision-making bodies at various levels from running for or holding any elected political office, from belonging to decision-making bodies at any level in

69. Alessandro Pizzorno, "Fra azione di classe e sistemi corporativi: osservazioni comparate sulle rappresentanze del lavoro nei paesi capitalistici avanzati," in *Problemi del movimento sindacale in Italia, 1943–1973*, vol. 26 of *Annali Fondazione G. Feltrinelli, 1974–1975*, ed. Aris Accornero (Milan: Feltrinelli, 1976), 950.

70. On the early postwar period, see Bianca [Beccalli] Salvati, "The Rebirth of Italian Trade Unionism, 1943–54," in *The Rebirth of Italy, 1943–50*, ed. S. J. Woolf (London: Longman, 1972), and Craveri, *Sindacato e istituzioni nel dopoguerra*.

71. The "incompatibility" regulations of each organization are included in their respective statutes. The statutes of the CGIL and the CISL are, in turn, published with their congressional acts. For the former, see CGIL, *IX Congresso Nazionale della CGIL*, Rimini, 6–11 giugno 1977, vol. 10 of *I Congressi della CGIL*, 2 books (Rome: Editrice Sindacale Italiana, 1978), book 1, 566–67. For the latter, see CISL, *8 Congresso confederale: atti, Roma, 14–18 giugno 1977* (Rome: Edizioni Lavoro, 1978), 616–17. The UIL's statute has been published in booklet form in UIL, *Statuto approvato dal VII Congresso Nazionale*, Bologna, 29 giugno–3 luglio 1977 (Rome: UIL, n.d.). The incompatibility regulations are found in article 41 (36–37).

political parties and political movements, and from acting in a decision-making capacity in any public body or commission except when nominated for such an office by the union itself. The regulations are so thorough that they extend all the way down to members of executive and directive organs of factory councils. If, for instance, a member of an executive of a factory council (large councils elect a smaller executive for day-to-day decision making) ran for city council, he would have to resign from the executive before the electoral campaign; similarly, his resignation would be mandatory if he accepted a position even in a local decision-making body of any political party. Formally, the severance of trade union offices from political offices was thus virtually complete.

Despite the incompatibility regulations, Communist union officials and militants continue to play active roles in party organs. The PCI's survey of delegates to its 1979 Congress found that two-thirds of the unionists were members of executive committees [*direttivi*] of party sections, a clear violation of incompatibility.[72] Comparable data for other parties are not available; every indication is that Socialists in the CGIL and the UIL are equally frequent violators of the incompatibility norms. The high level of Communist violation of incompatibility norms does not, however, necessarily mean that Communist unionists are carrying party directives to the union. Indeed, it is at least as likely that they attempt to sensitize the party to the union's position and that they see themselves as agents in what they wish would and could be a unified and compact labor movement—that they long for reconciliation while recognizing the imperatives of confrontation. All the pertinent evidence I gathered on this, including firsthand observation of closed meetings between the party and its affiliated union officials, attests to such an interpretation, as later chapters will document more fully.

The events behind the adoption of incompatibility were complex and painstaking, and the issue had been debated internally for many years before any official action. Although each of the three confederations and each political current within each confederation eventually endorsed incompatibility for different reasons, varying with ideological predispositions, two common assumptions underlay the diverse intentions of union leadership groups. First, unionists were well aware that their future strength depended on their ability to work together. But for any kind of unity of action to endure, each organization would have to offer formal concessions of trust.[73] Incompatibility introduced a measure of formal

72. Pipan, "Sindacalisti," 275.

73. For an analysis of incompatibility within the context of the development of unity among the three confederations, see Aris Accornero, ed., *Dalla rissa al dialogo*, Collana di

equality among the various partisan-defined union currents. Second, the adoption of the incompatibility norms was not generally construed as depoliticizing organized labor. Commenting in 1969 on the proposals for incompatibility, the most important Socialist leader of the CGIL remarked: "The union is not distancing itself from the political forces in order to be less active politically, but in order to maintain its own policies and to mark out its own correct role within the present context of social pluralism."[74] Or as another CGIL leader put it: "When we speak of autonomy, we in no way intend lack of commitment or political disinterest."[75] The abolition of role cumulation between organized labor and the parties freed trade unionists to indulge in greater interpretive latitude in reconciling their partisan attachments with the need to forge strategic compromises with other partisan and confederal groups in the union movement. But this alteration of the partisan status of the three organizations did not weaken trade union politicization. If anything it strengthened it, by forcing the union movement to search out direct channels into the state and political system and by formally reducing its abilities to work in and through the parties with which it was no longer formally affiliated. Incompatibility, moreover, marked the official emergence of a radical policy orientation in organized labor. Radical propensities already existed in components of the union movement, both in the CGIL and in the CISL. Incompatibility rendered radicalism a potentially enduring and self-generating strategy for labor because it cut the union movement off from its formal place in the political system and moved unionists out of Parliament and back into the factories. With the adoption of incompatibility, the Italian union movement became organizationally autonomous, free to develop its own identity and patterns of self-legitimation.

Unionization and Industrial Militancy

As a late developer, hampered moreover by internal fragmentation, the Italian labor movement has long suffered lower levels of unionization than

---

attualità sindacale (Rome: Editrice Sindacale Italiana, 1967). A summary of the moves toward unity in the late 1960s in English is Peter Lange, George Ross, and Maurizio Vannicelli, *Unions, Change and Crisis: French and Italian Union Strategy and the Political Economy, 1945–1980* (London: George Allen & Unwin, 1982), 132–35.

74. Piero Boni, "Dall'unità di azione alla realizzazione dell'unità sindacale organica," *Mondo Operaio* 22 (May 1969), 10.

75. Vittorio Foa, in Mario Didò, et al., "La parola alla CGIL," *Rinascita* 26 (9 May 1969), 4.

Table 2. CGIL-CISL Unionization in Industry, 1950–85

Year	Unionization (%)	Year	Unionization (%)
1950	47	1970	31
1955	34	1975	38
1960	19	1980	40
1965	22	1985	28

Sources: 1950–75: Guido Romagnoli, ed., *La sindacalizzazione tra ideologia e pratica: il caso italiano, 1950/1977,* Centro Studi Nazionale CISL Firenze, 2 vols. (Rome: Edizioni Lavoro, 1980), 1:81, table 9. 1980 and 1985: unpublished data courtesy of Guido Romagnoli.
Note: Refers to CGIL-CISL membership in unions covering mining, manufacturing, construction, and energy. For additional details, see appendix B.

its counterparts in most other Western European countries. During the 1960s and 1970s, however, unionization expanded dramatically, while strike rates consistently outstripped those of the other OECD countries.[76] These increased signs of organization and militancy were accompanied by significant changes in the union movement's structures and legal powers, so that by the mid-1970s Italian unions had acquired considerable independent resources and an organizational stability previously unknown. In an internationally exceptional response to the wave of industrial unrest that shook the advanced capitalist nations in the closing years of the 1960s, the Italian union movement rebuilt itself around grass-roots militancy and mobilization. In doing so, it made radicalism possible as a self-perpetuating strategy for social change.

Table 2 shows industrial unionization rates for selected years since 1950. Since the UIL has been unable to reconstruct its historical membership series, the data pertain only to members of Italy's two largest confederations, the CGIL and the CISL. Unionization fell radically during the

76. For comparisons of Italian strike rates with other OECD countries see, for instance, David R. Cameron, "Social Democracy, Corporatism, Labour Quiescence and the Representation of Economic Interest in Advanced Capitalist Society," in *Order and Conflict in Contemporary Capitalism: Studies in the Political Economy of Western European Nations,* ed. John H. Goldthorpe (Oxford: Oxford University Press, 1984), 153, table 7.3, and Michael Shalev, "Strikes and the Crisis: Industrial Conflict and Unemployment in the Western Nations," *Economic and Industrial Democracy* 4 (November 1983), 417–60.

1950s. This drop was arrested by 1959, however, and by the early 1960s the unionization rates of the two confederations began increasing. The largest single increase occurred in 1969, but as early as 1962 relations with the rank and file were clearly undergoing significant changes after what are called "the hard years" (*gli anni duri*) of the 1950s. Unionization peaked in the late 1970s, experiencing a modest drop in the 1980s. The independent organizational resources of the union movement were strengthened enormously as of the early 1960s.

Increased unionization has been largely a product of industrial militancy: when labor-market conditions and other factors propelled the Italian working class into action in the 1960s, the union movement captured and consolidated grass-roots mobilization. Industrial strike activity between 1950 and 1980 attests to the connections between unionization and mobilization. The analysis uses the four standard measures of strike behavior.[77] The data reported concern strikes in industry, composed of mining, manufacturing, construction, and energy. Volume is based on annual strike hours in these four industrial sectors divided by the number of blue- and white-collar employees in these same sectors. More succinctly, volume is the average number of hours each worker strikes over the course of the year. Size refers to the ratio of workers participating in strikes to the number of strikes in one year; it is the average number of strikers per strike. Duration is the total annual number of strike hours divided by the number of workers participating. It is thus the yearly average number of hours each striker is on strike. Frequency, finally, is the ratio between the number of strikes and the size of the relevant pool of workers. It is the average number of strikes per worker. Periodized data are presented in table 3.

The table shows that strike volume increased through the mid-1970s and then declined, though never to the depths found in the 1950s. The peak of postwar strike volume occurred in 1969, during the hot autumn, when strike volume was almost twice as great as during any other single year considered. But even in the early 1960s volume had begun to rise, and the hot autumn capped an uneven trend already under way.

The duration of Italian industrial strikes, in the meantime, had been falling erratically since the late 1950s, as the unions learned to employ more effective strike forms. This was especially important to a union movement that was without strike funds, making long strikes virtually impossible to sustain. As strikes became shorter, they also became more

77. See Charles Tilly and Edward Shorter, "The Shape of Strikes in France, 1830–1960," *Comparative Studies in Society and History* 13 (January 1971), 60–86.

Table 3. Periodized Annual Means of Strike Indicators in Industry, 1950–80

Years	Duration	Size	Frequency[a]	Volume[a]
1950–58	16.7	1,253	28.3	4.3
1959–68	37.3	765	36.3	9.5
1969–74	30.8	1,347	44.2	17.4
1975–80	12.3	3,262	25.4	9.9

Sources: Strike indicators 1950–75: ISTAT, *Sommario di statistiche storiche dell'Italia, 1861–1975* (Rome: ISTAT, 1976). Strike indicators 1975–80: ISTAT, *Annuario statistico italiano* (Rome: ISTAT, various years). Labor force 1951–58: estimated. Labor force 1959–78: ISTAT, "Una metodologia di raccordo per le series statistiche sulle forze di lavoro," *Note e Relazioni*, no. 56 (July 1979). Labor force 1979–80: ISTAT, *Annuario statistiche italiano* (Rome: ISTAT, various years). For additional details, see appendix B.
[a]Frequency and volume unavailable for 1950.

frequent, with the exception of the atypical depression after 1975. Strike size, finally, displays an erratic upward trend since the late 1950s, with a particularly large increase after 1975, indicating a union movement increasingly able to muster massive public displays of rank-and-file discontent.

Although institutional changes in the Italian industrial relations system occurred only in 1969 and 1970, clear and significant changes in labor's relations with the rank and file emerged in 1962. In that year the first real peak in the volume of postwar industrial conflict occurred, as labor won its first significant wage gains since the end of the war. Beginning in the early 1960s as well, industrial unionization began to increase, strike frequency jumped, and strike duration obtained its postwar high in 1962. The only indicator that did not change significantly until the mid-1970s was strike size, which had to await greater increases in unionization rates. By 1962 all those developments that would become institutionally irreversible in 1969 and 1970 were already in evidence.[78] Indeed, in a sense the hot autumn itself would have been impossible without the buildup of militan-

78. Most analyses emphasize the hot autumn in the reshaping of union activities. A few, however, also note that the experiences of failure earlier in the decade were critical in making the hot autumn a success. See, for instance, Mario Tronti, "Sindacato, partiti e sistema politico," in Accornero, *Problemi del movimento sindacale in Italia*, and Aris Accornero, "Le lotte operaie degli anni '60," *Quaderni di Rassegna Sindacale* 9 (July–October 1979), 113–38. In English, see Sidney Tarrow, *Democracy and Disorder: Politics and Protest in Italy, 1965–1975* (Oxford: Oxford University Press, 1988), chap. 7.

cy and organization that occurred over the course of the 1960s as the union movement gradually acquired techniques of mobilization and organization appropriate to Italy's recently developed mass manufacturing industries. Changes in working-class collective action interlocked with a union movement eager to channel militancy and transform it into more stable organizational structures.

The Structure of Bargaining and Union Organization

With the renewal of the national labor contracts in the fall of 1969, Italian labor militancy reached its postwar zenith. Significant changes also occurred in the unions' formal structures, the demands they promoted, the forms of conflict they used, and the legislative arena in which industrial relations were conducted. The most important institutional changes that came with the hot autumn were the passage of a major piece of labor legislation, the creation of new shop-floor union agents, the expansion of decentralized bargaining techniques, the adoption of the incompatibility norms, and the formalization of unity-of-action agreements among the three labor confederations.[79] These changes were but expansions of trends already evident since the early 1960s. In large part they depended on the decisions of union leadership groups to take institutional advantage of conflict rather than to repudiate it or to attempt to depress it, as occurred in most other Western European nations at the time.

The confederations had been pressing for some kind of national labor legislation for decades, as they had been working in Parliament for other reforms in social policy. The hot autumn permitted these long-standing efforts to succeed, in part because union activities were conducted jointly by the three confederations and in part because the ruling center-left government (a Christian Democratic and Socialist coalition) was determined to show some kind of reformist ability. The result was that, along with a few other important pieces of social legislation, the Statuto dei Lavoratori was finally passed into law on 20 May 1970. The bill granted a series of both individual and collective labor rights, including the right to organize, the right to hold union assemblies during working hours, and the right of shop-floor union representatives to take time off to perform union tasks. The bill thus promoted subsequent trade union stability. Most im-

79. See Gian Primo Cella, "L'azione sindacale nella crisi italiana," in *Formazione del regime repubblicano e società civile*, vol. 1 of *La crisi italiana*, ed. Luigi Graziano and Sidney Tarrow (Turin: Einaudi, 1979).

portant, it recognized the right of organized labor to act on the shop floor, finally incorporating the unions into factory life.

With the hot autumn, the unions informally relinquished the internal commissions, which until then had constituted the most important shop-floor organization of the postwar period.[80] The CIs had never been recognized union agents, and their bargaining powers had been severely restricted. Indeed, in some ways they had helped keep the union movement out of the factories by granting recognition to an alternative, officially nonunion representative organ. Their diffusion had always been quite limited and had fallen even further during the 1960s, rendering them ripe for replacement.

In their place, the three confederations adopted the consigli di fabbrica, joint bodies for which all workers, union members and not, were eligible to vote. The CdFs were composed of worker delegates (*delegati*) and became the formal and recognized union shop-floor agents. They were endowed with considerable bargaining powers and were included in the confederal decision-making process. With the passage of the Statuto dei Lavoratori, the CdFs were granted formal legal recognition; juridically, delegates were recognized as *rappresentanti sindacali aziendali* (RSAs).[81]

Factory councils have a long and illustrious history in Italy starting with their first appearance in Turin during the occupation of the factories after World War I.[82] Indeed, from that time on, the political heart of the council movement has resided in Turin, home of Italy's largest private firm, Fiat. Within a year of the CGIL's disastrous defeat in Fiat's commissioni interne elections in 1955, union and party leaders raised the possibility of establishing shop-floor factory delegates,[83] and in 1957 the Turinese met-

80. See Aris Accornero, *Gli anni cinquanta in fabbrica: con un diario di Commissione interna* (Bari: DeDonato, 1973); Guido Baglioni, "L'istituto della 'Commissione interna' e la questione della rappresentanza dei lavoratori nei luoghi di lavoro," *Studi di Sociologia* 8 (January–June 1970), 167–96; and G. Federico Mancini, "Le Commissioni interne nel sistema di relazioni industriali," *Il Mulino* 14 (December 1965), 1130–41.

81. The legal status of delegates is in fact rather complicated and varies by plant and firm. For a discussion in English, see Treu, "Italy," chap. 3.

82. In English, see Martin Clark, *Antonio Gramsci and the Revolution That Failed* (New Haven: Yale University Press, 1977).

83. See Adalberto Minucci, "La rivoluzione industriale e gli istituti di fabbrica" (1956), reprinted in *Quaderni di Rassegna Sindacale* 19 (November–December 1981), 14–18. The theme had already been introduced by the general secretary of the PCI, Palmiro Togliatti, in his visit in May 1956 to Turin, in a political criticism of the consigli di fabbrica of 1920. See Palmiro Togliatti, "Discorso all'inaugurazione della casa del Partito" (1956), reprinted in his *Discorsi di Torino*, ed. Renzo Gianotti (Turin: Gruppo Editoriale Piemontese, 1974), especially 305–8.

alworkers' union affiliated with the CGIL officially proposed the creation of CdFs during one of its radio broadcasts given in the luncheon hall of Fiat Mirafiori.[84] Only in the opening years of the 1960s, however, did the first delegates reemerge in Italy, making a temporary appearance during a strike in a Turinese metalworking plant.[85] By the middle of the decade, their establishment was under way on a sporadic and ad hoc basis, though their future remained unclear.[86] It was experiments like these that encouraged the most radical groups in Italy's union movement—especially the metalworkers' unions in Turin—to pave the way for the new, decentralized, and participatory union structure that became widespread only in 1969.[87] Organizational experiments in the 1960s were consolidated in the 1970s.

A third major institutional change following the hot autumn was the formation of the Federazione Unitaria in 1972.[88] The pact did not achieve a full merger of the three confederations. Rather, it established a series of joint decision-making bodies in a loose federated arrangement. The unitary pact codified a decade of informal and cautious unity-of-action experiments among the three confederations and the major industrial unions affiliated with them, especially the metalworkers' unions. Nonetheless, the vertical fragmentation of three ideologically divided confederations was not eradicated and continued to pose considerable problems for orga-

84. See the transcript of the broadcast by Luigi Picco given on 31 January 1957, reprinted in Piero Frasca and Giulio Sapelli, eds., *Qui FIOM: le relazioni radio alla Fiat tra repressione padronale e ripresa del sindacato in fabbrica, 1955–1961* (Bari: DeDonato, 1978), 122–25.

85. See the report on the Aspera Frigo in Paolo Frasca, "Lotte e organizzazione" (1961), *Quaderni Rossi*, no. 1 (reprinted; Milan: Sapere Edizioni, 1970), 115–26.

86. I have not been able to locate any secondary sources tracing the establishment of councils before the hot autumn. Reports attesting their existence as early as 1965 in steel and shipbuilding appear in FIOM, "Metalmeccanici e sindacato," Tavola rotonda, Desenzano sul Garda, 5–6–7 ottobre 1966, *Esperienze e Orientamenti*, Bollettino dell'ufficio organizzazione della FIOM, no. 10 (October 1966), 26, 35–36, 59. Apparently the CdFs were intended as intermediate organs linking members of the FIOM to the *sezione sindacale aziendale* (SSA). The SSAs were shop-floor union bodies established during the 1960s to work alongside the (officially nonunion) CIs; both the CGIL and the CISL had officially endorsed organs of this type.

87. On strategic innovation in Turin during this period, see Paola Agosti Ronza, "Appunti sulla contrattazione articolata: l'elaborazione della Fiom torinese (1960–1962)," *Classe* 3 (June 1971), 109–41, and idem, "Appunti sulla contrattazione articolata: la Fiom e la svolta sindacale alla Fiat (1955–1962)," *Classe* 5 (July 1973), 351–86.

88. See CGIL-CISL-UIL, "Il Patto federativo," Consigli Generali CGIL-CISL-UIL, Roma, 24 luglio 1972, *Rassegna Sindacale* 18 (30 July 1972), special insert, no pagination. The pact established the Federazione Unitaria and recognized the consiglio di fabbrica as the triorganizational shop-floor agent.

nized labor. Within the Federazione Unitaria, decision making tended to proceed slowly, and occasionally the difficulty of reaching compromises brought it to a standstill. Despite such problems, the establishment of the Federazione Unitaria meant that Italy's divided union movement was now prepared to act as an independent force for social change and that competition among the three confederations would be circumscribed in the future.

Along with the adoption of the CdFs and the federated agreement, the three confederations also adopted the incompatibility regulations discussed above. These regulations led to the resignation of trade unionists serving in Parliament and to the abandonment of official party positions held by union officials. Incompatibility constituted a precondition for unity of action: ideologically rival confederations could agree to work together only if their partisan attachments were relaxed.

Fifth, important changes in the demands promoted by the unions occurred between 1968 and 1970 as their constituency changed. During the 1950s industrial unions, especially those affiliated with the CGIL, had primarily represented skilled workers. The expansion of mass manufacturing during Italy's economic miracle in the 1950s and 1960s had transformed the composition of the working class, rendering it increasingly unskilled and semiskilled. The hot autumn signified the entry of these previously unrepresented groups onto the union stage. Demands in their favor were strongly promoted: across-the-board flat wage increases, automatic upgrading in the classificatory system, a change in job classification, and so forth.[89] Most of these new demands arose out of experiments that had been conducted in large firms in the Milan-Turin-Genoa industrial triangle in the early and mid-1960s[90] but that became widespread only during 1969. Typically, they were oriented around issues of working conditions and health and safety, particularly appropriate for shop-floor, rather than centralized, bargaining. By seizing on such demands, the Italian union movement reached industrial production workers, in a successful bid to expand unionization and representation to those previously peripheral to union strategy.

89. This aspect of the hot autumn has received considerable attention. In English see Ida Regalia, Marino Regini, and Emilio Reyneri, "Labor Conflicts and Industrial Relations in Italy," in *National Studies*, vol. 1 of *The Resurgence of Class Conflict in Western Europe since 1968*, ed. Colin Crouch and Alessandro Pizzorno (New York: Holmes and Meier, 1978), and Alessandro Pizzorno, "Political Exchange and Collective Identity in Industrial Conflict," in *Comparative Analyses*, vol. 2 of ibid.

90. For an account of those regarding work organization, especially in Milan and Turin, see Marino Regini and Emilio Reyneri, *Lotte operaie e organizzazione del lavoro*, 8th ed. (Venice: Marsilio, 1977).

As the kinds of demands promoted by the unions shifted, so too did the tactics adopted. Extremely disruptive kinds of strikes that had not been much employed since the 1940s became widespread. These were mainly short, greatly "articulated" strikes: various forms of revolving and rotating strikes that damaged production far more than they caused any single striker to lose pay. Again, the early 1960s stand out in tracing the history of the use of such strikes. The most notable case concerns a massive and extremely long conflict in 1960 at a major Turinese textile firm, the Cotonifici Valsusa (CVS). Involving eleven plants and over 10,000 employees, the 145–day strike constituted a "watershed."[91] Anticipating practices that would become widespread only in 1969, the workers at the CVS deployed two kinds of tactics for which they would be remembered: the use of open shop-floor assemblies for decision making, and the first contemporary use of checkerboard strikes since their invention by the CGIL's metalworkers' union, the FIOM, in the 1940s.[92] By the hot autumn, such strikes were regularly used across northern Italy. They were efficient and unpredictable and made extensive use of the unions' new shop-floor organization, since their implementation depended in great part on the organizing abilities of the delegates.

The thrust of all these transformations culminating in the hot autumn was to continue the massive decentralization of Italian collective bargaining that had begun about 1960. After 1969 Italian unions boasted juridically recognized shop-floor bargaining agents and rights and were making widespread use of issues and tactics appropriate for that level.[93] Decentralized bargaining—known in Italy as "articulated bargaining"—had never been wholly absent since the war but was only slowly incorporated into union strategy in the 1950s. It had first been proposed by the CISL as early as 1951, although its adoption as official policy is generally marked from the meeting of the confederation's Consiglio Generale in

91. Accornero, "Lotte operaie degli anni '60," 116.

92. Known as strikes *a scacchiera*, these constitute an extremely damaging form of articulated strike, involving short, coordinated, rotating walkouts by selected factory sections. Particularly appropriate for highly integrated productive cycles, they disrupt production continuously while asking individual employees to lose a minimum of pay. On the CVS, see Agosti Ronza, "Elaborazione," 123–26; Paolo Bolzani, "Le lotte di fabbrica dal 'luglio '60' al centro sinistra," *Classe* 10 (December 1978), especially 60–64; and Giovanni Mottura, "Cronaca delle lotte ai cotonifici Valle di Susa" (1961), *Quaderni Rossi*, no. 1 (reprinted; Milan: Sapere Edizioni, 1970), 18–52.

93. In English, see Gino Giugni, "Recent Developments in Collective Bargaining in Italy," *International Labor Review* 91 (April 1965), 273–91, and idem, "Recent Trends in Collective Bargaining in Italy," *International Labor Review* 104 (October 1971), 307–28.

February 1953 at Ladispoli.[94] The CGIL followed suit only in the middle of the decade, especially after its defeat in the CI elections in Fiat in 1955,[95] finally adopting articulated bargaining as official policy at its fifth congress in 1960.[96] Actual experiments in articulated bargaining began with the 1960 battle for an "integrated" accord for the electromechanical sector, in which the metalworkers' unions fought for the right to engage in bargaining at other than the constitutionally recognized, industrywide level. The agreement reached with the bargaining agent in the public sector, Intersind, eventually forced private business, too, to make similar concessions.[97] With these agreements, integrated bargaining received de facto recognition. De jure recognition followed in 1962 when, in response to the threat of widespread labor militancy during the delicate period just before the establishment of the first center-left government, public and private peak associations again divided. The result was the famous "Intersind-ASAP understanding," the July agreement covering the public sector in which a system of multilevel bargaining was formally recognized.[98] These trends were solidified during the hot autumn and after, when articulated bargaining became normal practice.

94. See the relevant documents available in CISL, *Documenti ufficiali dal 1950 al 1958: appendice alla Relazione della Segreteria confederale al III Congresso nazionale,* Roma, Palazzo dei Congressi, 19–22 marzo 1959 (Rome: Ufficio Studi della CISL, 1959), 73–74, 255.

95. See Vittorio Foa, "Il 'ritorno alla fabbrica' nella strategia della Cgil" (1972), reprinted in his *Per una storia del movimento operaio* (Turin: Einaudi, 1980), and Vittorio Foa and Bruno Trentin, "La CGIL di fronte alle trasformazioni tecnologiche dell'industria italiana," in *Lavoratori e sindacati di fronte alle trasformazioni del processo produttivo,* ed. Franco Momigliano, Atti del Congresso internazionale di studio sul progresso tecnologico e la società italiana promosso dal Centro Nazionale di Prevenzione e Difesa Sociale e dal Comune di Milano, sotto il patrocinio del Consiglio Nazionale delle Ricerche, Milano, 28 giugno–3 luglio 1960, vol. 1 (Milan: Feltrinelli, 1962).

96. See [Agostino] Novella, "Relazione introduttiva al Congresso," in CGIL, *V Congresso Nazionale della CGIL,* Milano, 2–7 aprile 1960, vol. 6 of *I Congressi della CGIL* (Rome: Editrice Sindacale Italiana, n.d.), especially 37–41, and CGIL, "Mozione Conclusiva del V Congresso della C.G.I.L.," in ibid., 447–54.

97. On the emergence of Intersind as a separate bargaining agent, see Ada Collidà, "L'Intersind," in Ada Collidà et al., *La politica del padronato italiano dalla ricostruzione all' 'autunno caldo,'* 2d ed. (Bari: DeDonato, 1973), and Umberto Romagnoli, "La politica sindacale dell'industria di stato," *Il Mulino* 29 (May–June 1970), 403–19. On the electromechanical battle, see Agosti Ronza, "Elaborazione"; Enzo Bartocci, "Gli elettromeccanici e la politica di settore" (1961), reprinted in his *Alle origini della contrattazione articolata* (Rome: Editrice Sindacale Italiana, 1979); and Bolzano, "Lotte di fabbrica," especially 64–70.

98. See especially Gino Giugni, "Critica e rovesciamento dell'assetto contrattuale," in Accornero, *Problemi del movimento sindacale in Italia,* 798 ff.

The Italian union movement had long been divided along ideological lines, subjecting it to competition among the three confederations. During the 1960s, however, ideological competition diminished and new lines of internal differentiation emerged around new centers of militancy, especially the national industrial federations and the newly created shop-floor factory councils. As subconfederal union bodies gained new powers, their ability to generate strategic initiatives widened. By the 1970s, patterns of rivalry and internal conflict had shifted within the union movement. The main lines of cleavage no longer divided the three confederations but rather appeared between the newly established Federazione Unitaria on the one hand and the strongest industrial federations and their factory councils on the other. It was, moreover, precisely these latter bodies that had undergone the highest degree of internal reorganization around militancy and whose structures were now attuned to its promotion. Empowered by grass-roots mobilization, they emerged as the proponents and carriers of radical policy orientations. By the latter part of the decade, their radicalism would come into increasingly direct conflict with the confederations, who felt the claims of moderation more strongly. Configured by grass-roots participatory democracy, articulated bargaining, and active shop-floor actors, however, radical union structures would prove incapable of rapid adjustment to calls for wage restraint.

The Politics of Militancy after the Hot Autumn

Scholars have advanced a variety of explanations for the burst of rank-and-file militancy that swept across Western Europe in the late 1960s. The most convincing is comparative in scope and argues that deliberate union wage restraint in the mid-1960s generated a burst of compensatory wage militancy at the end of the decade.[99] The argument applies in principle to Italy, given the notoriously poor wage gains won in the industrywide contracts in the middle of the decade, when union leaders erred in evaluating the resiliency of the Italian economy following the 1963–64 recession.[100] Pizzorno's attention to the expressive demands of previously unrepresented groups of semiskilled workers is also a useful way to think

99. David Soskice, "Strike Waves and Wage Explosions, 1968–1970: An Economic Interpretation," in Crouch and Pizzorno, *Comparative Analyses*.

100. Robert J. Flanagan, David W. Soskice, and Lloyd Ulman, *Unionism, Economic Stabilization, and Incomes Policies: European Experience* (Washington, D.C.: Brookings Institution, 1983), 518–19.

about the particularly long duration and high intensity of Italian rank-and-file mobilization after 1968.[101]

Fewer explanations have been offered for the variety of *trade union responses* to militancy. Pizzorno has argued that union movements that encouraged militancy were those that had suffered particularly deep weaknesses in the previous era. His explanation is problematic when applied cross-nationally. French trade unions, for instance, which suffered organizational and institutional weaknesses almost identical to those of their Italian counterparts, virtually refused to take up new forms of rank-and-file militancy. In consequence, the French industrial relations system remained fundamentally unaltered by May 1968.[102] Even in Italy, organizational weakness in conjunction with rank-and-file militancy did not necessarily lead to union reorganization around mobilization. Indeed, sudden bursts of rank-and-file militancy do not necessarily engender similar responses from different union organizations. Later, I shall specify more carefully the political and organizational conditions that allowed radical innovation by labor in the late 1960s. Nationally, however, I believe it was the coincidence of the PCI's essentially moderate, social democratic strategy in conjunction with a breakthrough in grass-roots militancy that empowered organized labor to pursue a strategy aimed independently at social change. But if the inherent paradoxes of political reformism in Italy made it necessary for organized labor to assume a radical stance in the search for social transformation, and if the militancy of the late 1960s made it possible, radicalism did not emerge evenly across all components of the union movement. Because the spread of militancy was itself uneven and did not everywhere engender the same response by the union movement, subsequent policy orientations differed among various components of the labor movement. For while the force of collective action may emerge more or less beyond the control of organizations, the forms it takes can be coordinated and channeled only through organizations. Without organizational reinforcement, its life tends to be brief; collective action

101. Alessandro Pizzorno, "Le due logiche dell'azione di classe," in *Lotte operaie e sindacato: il ciclo 1968–1972*, by Alessandro Pizzorno et al., vol. 6 of *Lotte operaie e sindacato in Italia 1968–1972* ed. Pizzorno (Bologna: Il Mulino, 1978).

102. Alfredo Gigliobianco and Michele Salvati, *Il maggio francese e l'autunno caldo italiano: la risposta di due borghesie* (Bologna: Il Mulino, 1980); in English, see Michele Salvati, "May 1968 and the Hot Autumn of 1969: The Responses of Two Ruling Classes," in *Organizing Interests in Western Europe: Corporatism, Pluralism and the Transformation of Politics*, ed. Suzanne D. Berger (Cambridge: Cambridge University Press, 1981), and also Lange, Ross, and Vannicelli, *Unions, Change and Crisis*, chap. 1.

can disrupt, but only organizations can create. Thanks to the hot autumn, some components of the Italian union movement found themselves equipped with new organizational resources based on the shop-floor. These subsequently provided the organizational framework for radical policy orientations in the union movement.

3

The Emergence of Moderation: The Union Confederations and the Communist Party

The organizational and historical characteristics of the Italian labor movement detailed in the previous chapter suggest that working class organizations in Italy will be potentially torn between radical and moderate policy orientations. In this chapter I begin to explore the conditions that breed and sustain these divergent ideological and strategic visions at the national level, examining strategic shifts in the PCI and the three union confederations since 1968.

Industrial Militancy and Political Stasis: 1968–75

Although the hot autumn constituted a major disruption of the Italian economy, many of its major economic consequences were delayed until the mid-1970s and the international oil crisis. Real per capita gross domestic product (GDP) continued to rise until 1975, albeit at a slower rate than between 1960 and 1968.[1] Unemployment remained relatively high and rose throughout the 1970s, while consumer price increases consistently outran the OECD's annual average as of 1972.[2] Overall economic perfor-

1. Real per capita GDP rose at an annual average of 5 percent between 1960 and 1968, 4 percent between 1968 and 1973, and only 2.1 percent between 1973 and 1979, but real growth fell below the OECD average as of 1971. See OECD, *Economic Outlook: Historical Statistics, 1960–1982* (Paris: OECD, 1984), tables 3.1 and 3.2.

2. Ibid., tables 2.15 and 8.11. For interpretations by economists, see Michele Salvati, "The Italian Inflation," in *The Politics of Inflation and Economic Stagnation*, ed. Leon N. Lindberg and Charles S. Maier (Washington, D.C.: Brookings Institution, 1985), and Robert J. Flanagan, David W. Soskice, and Lloyd Ulman, *Unionism, Economic Stabilization, and Incomes Policies: European Experience* (Washington, D.C.: Brookings Institution, 1983), chap. 9.

mance was thus fair, although it was to worsen considerably as the decade wore on.

Between 1968 and 1975, the Italian labor movement dramatically expanded its powers and influence in society. This expansion took place principally through direct action in the industrial arena. Some important legislative initiatives were also successful, but the union movement's political presence remained informal and circumscribed, while the electoral strength of the Left actually declined slightly. In response to these circumstances, organized labor sought to use industrial action to enact social change directly.

The unions pursued an extremely aggressive and highly militant strategy until 1976, aimed simultaneously at improving wages and working conditions for the employed, ameliorating social conditions for the lower classes in general, and obtaining institutional recognition. Results were won on all these fronts. At the same time, these gains for the union movement did not translate immediately into political gains for the Left. Only with the local elections in 1975 and the national elections the following year were the political shock waves of the hot autumn finally evident. Before the middle of the decade, the political resources that the PCI could offer organized labor to induce its strategic cooperation and restrain its militancy were extremely meager.

The Communist Party after the Hot Autumn: The Historic Compromise

The PCI's initial response to the hot autumn and the radical union strategy it bred was largely enthusiastic, although the party inevitably betrayed serious reservations about direct bargaining between labor and the state.[3] As early as 1970, however, the PCI began to exhibit greater caution in its dealings with radical social movements. The neofascist uprisings in Reggio Calabria in 1970 and 1971 graphically illustrated the threat of a popular reactionary backlash.[4] With the worsening of economic conditions over the next few years and the surprisingly strong showing of the DC in the 1972 elections, the PCI's caution intensified. This shifting

3. On the PCI's response to the hot autumn, see Stephen Hellman, "The Longest Campaign: Communist Party Strategy and the Elections of 1976," in *Italy at the Polls: The Parliamentary Elections of 1976*, ed. Howard R. Penniman (Washington, D.C.: American Enterprise Institute, 1977).

4. See Anna Cannizzaro, Natale Jeracitano, and Giorgio Rossetti, "Reggio Calabria: un'inchiesta preelettorale," in *Un sistema politico alla prova: studi sulle elezioni politiche italiane del 1972*, ed. Mario Caciagli and Alberto Spreafico (Bologna: Il Mulino, 1975).

combination of support for social movements and fear of popular reaction crystallized between 1972 and 1973, with the introduction of what was referred to as the historic compromise, a classically supraclass electoral strategy.[5] The historic compromise assigned primary importance to developing social and political alliances with the country's dominant political party, the Christian Democrats, which had governed Italy since 1947 through shifting coalitions with the country's minor centrist and center-left parties. Its adoption marked the end of the PCI's short-lived if potent radical enthusiasm and the party's return to its classically reformist, supraclass electoral strategy. By 1973 the PCI had recognized that the goals of social transformation could not be reached, "based on pure voluntarism and spontaneous class surges of the most combative sectors of the working masses, but arising [instead] from a vision of the possible, uniting combativeness and resolution with prudence and a capacity for maneuver."[6] The working class was thus called upon to construct alliances with other social groups and strata, alliances that would eventually be institutionalized through equally vast political convergences and collaboration.

The historic compromise was designed to confront both the political dangers and the opportunities that had arisen out of the hot autumn. Had it been successful, the strategy would have dampened the likelihood of political or popular reaction while simultaneously allowing the PCI to reap the electoral and political advantages of social and industrial unrest. It would have channeled mass militancy into electoral confines. The party continued to encourage mass mobilization to the extent that it could be used to demonstrate widespread discontent with the DC's pattern of governing. It sought to limit it severely, however, to the extent that it threat-

---

For an interpretation of the PCI's political pessimism in the early 1970s, see Gianfranco Pasquino, "Il Pci nel sistema politico italiano degli anni settanta," in *La giraffa e il liocorno: il Pci dagli anni '70 al nuovo decennio*, ed. Silvano Belligni (Milan: F. Angeli, 1983).

5. The PCI's fears of a reactionary political movement and possible political repression as responses to labor militancy and working-class gains provided much of the justification for the initial adoption of the historic compromise. See Enrico Berlinguer, "Alleanze sociali e schieramenti politici," *Rinascita* 30 (12 October 1973), 3–5, as well as his two preceding articles, "Imperialismo e coesistenza alla luce dei fatti cileni," *Rinascita* 30 (28 September 1973), 3–4, and "Via democratica e violenza reazionaria," *Rinascita* 30 (5 October 1973), 3–4. The danger of political repression and popular reaction had never been wholly absent from the PCI's thinking. It had been noticeable, for instance, even at the height of the hot autumn, though with far less emphasis than four or five years later. For an example, see Enrico Berlinguer, "La forza della democrazia è nella lotta delle masse," *Rinascita* 26 (19 December 1969), 1–3.

6. Berlinguer, "Alleanze sociali e schieramenti politici," 3.

ened to turn against partisan politics or preempt them altogether. A presumed ability to guide and control social, and particularly industrial, conflict was thus central to the strategy.

Organized Labor: The Strategy of Reforms and Industrial Militancy

Between 1967 and 1968, more or less concurrently with the resignations of trade union leaders from Parliament, the three confederations embarked on a new political strategy. They initiated a united push for specific policy reforms, ranging from traditional social policy, such as pensions and health care, to macroeconomic planning.[7] The hallmark of the "strategy of reforms," as it was known, was the extraordinary coincidence between contractual and political activities then under way, a coincidence that endured until the mid-1970s. Between 1968 and 1975 Italian unions pursued *mutually integrated* market and political strategies, seeking to employ direct action in their turn toward the state. Success in one realm made success in the other more likely.[8] Using long- and short-term goals to reinforce and consolidate one another, Aris Accornero characterizes the period as one when "not only were higher wages and increased employment demanded at the same time, but demands for social reform overlay factory bargaining 'platforms.' "[9] Thanks to the remarkable levels of collective action then manifest, the unions embarked on a radical plan for "social revolution": an attempt to fundamentally alter Italy's social and political structures through direct union initiatives backed by mass mobilization.

The strategy of reforms comprised two analytically distinct kinds of

7. See Emilio Reyneri, "Comportamento di classe e nuovo ciclo di lotte," in *Problemi del movimento sindacale in Italia, 1943–1973*, vol. 16 of *Annali Fondazione G. Feltrinelli, 1974–1975*, ed. Aris Accornero (Milan: Feltrinelli, 1976), especially 844–45, and Sergio Turone, *Storia del sindacato in Italia, 1943–1980* (Bari: Laterza, 1981), 355–62. In English, see Peter Lange, George Ross, and Maurizio Vannicelli, *Unions, Change and Crisis: French and Italian Union Strategy and the Political Economy, 1945–1980* (London: George Allen and Unwin, 1982), 131–41; Ida Regalia, Marino Regini, and Emilio Reyneri, "Labor Conflicts and Industrial Relations in Italy," in *National Studies*, vol. 1 of *The Resurgence of Class Conflict in Western Europe since 1968*, ed. Colin Crouch and Alessandro Pizzorno (New York: Holmes and Meier, 1978), 132–34; and Flanagan, Soskice, and Ulman, *Unionism, Economic Stabilization, and Incomes Policies*, chap. 9.

8. Alessandro Pizzorno, "I sindacati nel sistema politico italiano: aspetti storici" (1971), reprinted in his *I sogetti del pluralismo: classe partiti sindacati* (Bologna: Il Mulino, 1980), 146.

9. Aris Accornero, "Sindacato e rivoluzione sociale: il caso italiano degli anni '70," *Laboratorio Politico* 1 (July–August 1981), 6. Much of the argument in this section is drawn from this essay, along with that by Mariucci referred to below (n. 12).

activities. The first was something like a "unionization" of political activities and emerged in the closing years of the 1960s. Issues once considered the exclusive competence of parliamentary politics were taken up by organized labor and pursued through direct pressures on the executive. These activities betrayed a long-standing frustration with parliamentary politics: disappointed with the progressive potential of the governing Socialist–Christian Democratic coalition, labor struck out on its own. The second, which took shape in the early 1970s, involved a politicization of collective bargaining. Direct conflict with management was used to pursue more general sociopolitical goals. In both cases, organized labor used rank-and-file militancy to attempt social change without working through electoral and partisan mechanisms.

A classic example of the unionization of politics was pension reform, the issue that provoked the strike held on 14 November 1968, the first general strike called jointly by all three confederations since 1948. Using strikes to ensure massive social pressure, the confederations dealt directly with the government. Pensions were interpreted as a form of indirect wage rather than as a welfare issue, as had previously been the case.[10] After their victory, the confederations engaged in similar bilateral meetings with the government over the abolition of geographic wage differentials, health service reform, taxation policy, housing, and other problems of social service reform. These activities were generally conducted using direct consultations with the executive, mass strikes, and supportive parliamentary maneuvering by the Communist and Socialist parties. All these issues had long been part of labor's agenda: the unions were now able to pursue them with a new aggressiveness. The strategy of reforms mixed elements of moderation and militancy, radicalism and reformism: while aimed directly at the state, it depended on direct action in place of strictly electoral or partisan mobilization.

A good illustration of the politicization of market activities, on the other hand, was the attempt to influence private investment location through collective bargaining. In 1970, in the first accord of this kind, the metalworkers' unions agreed to stagger the implementation of the forty-hour workweek at Fiat (a concession won in their 1969 industrywide contract) on condition that specified corporate investments be directed to the south of the country.[11] By 1973 organized labor was engaged in a multipronged

10. As was noted at the time by Giovanni Berlinguer, "Il nodo politico delle pensioni," *Rinascita* 25 (5 July 1968), 3.

11. The text of the accord has been published in Eugenio Guidi et al., eds., *Movimento sindacale e contrattazione collettiva, 1945–1973*, 4th ed. (Milan: F. Angeli, 1974), 533–36.

attempt—the "development contracts" as they were called—to win commitments for southern investment from most of the country's larger firms. These attempts at determining the geographic location of new investments fused with demands to maintain employment levels in existing firms and to obtain information on future capital investments and technological reorganization. Although the latter gradually displaced the former as threats to existing employment deepened in the 1970s, directing new investments to the south had originally been deemed directly within the interests of employed northern workers, in part because of the potential consequences of future labor migration from the south, but principally because of the dramatic increase in the scope of the union's bargaining power that success would ensure.[12] The strategy did not involve sacrificing the immediate aims of the northern industrial work force to protect the long-term interests of the southern unemployed or the working class as a whole, but rather invoked a fusion of long- and short-term goals characteristic of the period.

During the early 1970s, then, political action was seen as contained within, hinging on, and emanating from market activities. The strategy of reforms was, as one national union leader put it, "the prolongation and the extension of the worker-owner confrontation to outside the factory."[13] Even at the height of rank-and-file mobilization, the confederations never relinquished their very traditional notion that they were political actors and that organized labor was necessarily concerned with issues of general social transformation *even in its market dealings*. The political arena was used for contractual ends, as the market was used to obtain general sociopolitical goals. These characteristics made the Italian union movement's strategy the most radical in Western Europe at the time.

The attempt to use direct action to obtain general goals of social change laid the confederations open to the charge of what is referred to as pansyndacalism. The confederations were accused of performing tasks rightfully pertaining to the political parties. Unionists themselves encouraged such interpretations, arguing that the parties' capacity to direct social change was wholly inadequate. "There is no power group today, except the union, that can speak in the name of all workers,"[14] harangued the general

12. See Luigi Mariucci, "Sindacato e lotte operaie nella crisi eonomica: dal''Piano del lavoro' al nuovo modello di sviluppo," *Politica del Diritto*, no. 6 (August 1975), especially 481–85.

13. Sergio Garavini, "Autonomia operaia e nuove oggettività capitalistiche nella crisi economica," *Quaderni di Rassegna Sindacale* 14 (January–February 1976), 49.

14. Bruno Storti, "Relazione del Segretario generale," in CISL, Ufficio Stampa, ed., *Atti del VII Congresso Confederale*, Roma, 18–21 giugno 1973 (Rome: CISL, 1974), 81.

secretary of the CISL in 1973. But the unions were largely unsuccessful in their claim to translate social conflict into policy reform. The few reforms won, including the revision of the pension system and the adoption of the Statuto dei Lavoratori, did not displace the political parties but rather depended on their parliamentary initiatives. And by 1975 the unions' always partial attempts to construct an autonomous political strategy beyond the parliamentary realm had largely been frustrated. Radicalism gradually exhausted itself as a national strategy as the conditions initially favoring it—especially mass collective action—withered.

An important 1975 agreement between the Federazione Unitaria and the peak business association, the Confindustria, altering the system of wage indexation (the scala mobile) provided the last major victory of this dual politicocontractual strategy. The government deliberately refrained from interfering in the negotiations, which resulted in a bipartite accord extending indexation coverage and significantly reducing wage differentials. In the face of Italy's subsequently high inflation rates, workers' wages would be protected at something between 85 and 95 percent. The Italian working class emerged as among the best protected in Western Europe against the inflation of the 1970s.[15] The accord also proved highly inflationary—indeed, it has been labeled the "inflationary pact"[16]—and constituted the most controversial issue of Italian national politics in the first half of the 1980s. It sharply reduced the importance of collective bargaining by rendering an increasingly large share of wage gains automatic: the agreement thus had a centralizing impact on the wage determination process, one probably intended by its signatories.

The responses of the three labor confederations to rank-and-file militancy at the end of the 1960s had been enthusiastic. Along with promoting the various institutional changes already examined in chapter 2, the newly established Federazione Unitaria extended both its contractual and its political activities. Welding these into a forceful, double-pronged, and largely radical attack, it made important gains running the gamut from wages to labor legislation. The intensity of rank-and-file militancy and the suprisingly rapid tempo of victory encouraged organized labor to act as if partisan politics were of only secondary importance, as if direct union action would suffice without the support of other social groups or political

15. On the agreement, see Lauralba Bellardi and Elena Pisani, eds., *Sindacato e contrattazione collettiva in Italia nel 1975* (Milan: F. Angeli, 1978), 82–83, 128–29.

16. Mario Dal Co and Paolo Perulli, "The Trilateral Agreement of 1983: Social Pact or Political Truce?" in *Economic Crisis, Trade Unions and the State*, ed. Otto Jacobi et al. (London: Croom Helm, 1986), 158 ff.

parties. Locked into the opposition, and in the absence of any electoral advance, the PCI at the time had modest political resources. Only with its electoral gains in the mid-1970s would the party begin to be able to reassert a more moderate strategy in its dealings with organized labor.

Austerity and the National Unity Experiment: 1976–79

By the mid-1970s, Italian economic performance had worsened both in relation to earlier periods and relative to that of the OECD as a whole. Italian inflation rates were well above the OECD average, productivity and growth rates were lower, and investment was extremely sluggish. Between 1973 and 1979, for instance, Italy's consumer price index rose by an annual average of more than 16 percent, while that of the two dozen OECD countries rose by only 10 percent.[17] Annual average economic growth between 1974 and 1979 was 2.3 percent in Italy compared with 3 percent in France, 2.8 percent in West Germany, 5 percent in Japan, 3.1 percent in Canada, and 3.3 percent in the United States. Of the major capitalist economies, only the United Kingdom suffered a lower rate of growth, with an annual average increase in GDP of 1.8 percent over the period.[18]

It is difficult to distinguish Italy's economic problems from the ways they were handled, and mishandled, by political authorities. The endemic political weakness and internal fragmentation of the DC was reflected in its inability to respond to what was perceived as a growing domestic economic crisis. Until the early 1980s, the combination of a labor movement too powerful to be summarily dismissed and a political situation that also provided a strong leftward impetus, both electorally and in terms of the DC's coalition options, ruled out severe antilabor policies. On the other hand, because the DC is not only a catchall party but also a business-oriented party, with long-standing albeit weakened ties to Italy's fragmented capitalist class, so neither could it enact policies wholly responsive to labor. Unable to fulfill the demands of either labor or business, the centrist governments of the 1970s simply frustrated both, producing economic policies that, by both omission and commission, managed to aggravate the very real international pressures in play.

In the middle of the decade, labor's gains of the hot autumn finally

17. OECD, *Economic Outlook: Historical Statistics,* table 8.11.

18. Reported in OECD, *Economic Surveys: Italy* (Paris: OECD, 1979), appendix, "Basic Statistics: International Comparisons."

acquired partisan form with the victories of the Left in the 1975 local elections and the PCI's historic victory in the 1976 national balloting. In the June elections the party won a record 34.4 percent of the vote. The overall left-wing vote was a startling 46.7 percent. The electoral results of 1976 reopened the question of the PCI's participation in the national government. It would now be difficult, if not impossible, to govern against the Communists; moreover, the historic compromise strategy had already indicated the party's willingness to collaborate with its longtime political opponent.

The party's enlarged parliamentary position promised organized labor greater indirect leverage over social reform, while the mobilizing capacity of the unions indirectly offered the PCI more extensive social penetration than it would otherwise have possessed. The interests of the two actors did not, however, entirely coincide. Whereas organized labor would have liked the PCI to speak aggressively for labor in Parliament, the party's ambiguous political legitimacy meant it needed to use its union and working-class ties as credibility props. For the DC, a tentative opening toward the Communists had become necessary less because of the latter's new electoral strength per se than because it offered a chance to head off some of the economic consequences of labor's recently acquired market powers. Determined to demonstrate its commitment to moderation to the DC and allied social groups, the party used its expanding political resources in an attempt to gain the cooperation of organized labor.

The PCI between Government and Opposition

Between 1976 and 1979 the Communists gradually approached national political power, although they never obtained cabinet positions. In July of 1977 they signed, along with the Christian Democratic, Socialist, Republican, Social Democratic, and Liberal parties, a programmatic accord. The following year they passed from a position of parliamentary "non-no-confidence" to open support of the Christian Democratic–dominated government. In early 1979, however, the Communists withdrew their support of the government, and a few months later they suffered their first electoral setback in the postwar period. In late 1980, in a major change of policy, the PCI finally renounced the historic compromise in favor of a strategy aimed at eventually transferring executive power to parties to the left of the DC.

A summary this compressed cannot do justice to the intricacies of what is referred to as the phase of national unity, which have been well explored elsewhere.[19] But a major feature of the period was the extent to which the Communist party became identified with the government even while remaining formally outside it. Neither in opposition nor in government, the party was caught between two conflicting exigencies. One was to demonstrate to the DC that the PCI's political collaboration was essential for social peace and economic growth. The other was that of assuring its own core working-class constituency that national political collaboration was a more effective lever for social change than was social unrest. The first problem could be solved if the PCI succeeded both in demonstrating a privileged political relationship with the core industrial working class and in reducing its industrial militancy. The second could be solved if the PCI's involvement in parliamentary compromises for social and economic policy could be said to result in legislation significantly more favorable to the working class than would have been achieved had the party remained in open opposition. In either case, success hinged on relations with the industrial working class.

The PCI's claim to governmental responsibility was thus closely tied to its capacity to offer reductions in Italy's very high levels of industrial conflict by displacing class-specific demands with those that could tie together broader, cross-class interests. The party's problem was that industrial actions were largely directed by the unions, whereas its own factory presence was of limited scope. The PCI's political fortunes thus became critically linked to the possible formulation of a parallel strategy by organized labor. Moderation in the party required moderation of the unions as well, and party pressures on organized labor became directed to this end.

In the early months of 1977 the PCI embraced austerity, thereby demonstrating its commitment to shouldering the burden of economic crisis and dampening popular mobilization. Elaborated within the confines of the historic compromise, austerity became the party's central, perhaps sole, claim to governmental responsibility. Promising working-class sacrifices, particularly with respect to wages, in exchange for political collaboration, the PCI used austerity to reassure the DC and non-Communist social groups that its cabinet participation would engender "responsible"

19. For instance, by Joseph LaPalombara, "Two Steps Forward, One Step Back: The PCI's Struggle for Legitimacy," in *Italy at the Polls, 1979: A Study of the Parliamentary Elections*, ed. Howard. R. Penniman (Washington, D.C.: American Enterprise Institute, 1981). For an ambitious attempt to develop a theoretical interpretation of the period, see Sidney Tarrow, "Historic Compromise or Bourgeois Majority? Eurocommunism in Italy, 1976–1979," in *National Communism in Western Europe: A Third Way for Socialism?* ed. Howard Machin (London: Methuen, 1983).

working-class behavior and prevent a breakdown of democracy. In a variation on the theme of the historic compromise, austerity was presented by general secretary Enrico Berlinguer as "an act of unity" in order to "solicit the other parties to begin . . . a common job." It was not meant to involve "a program of transition to a socialist society: [but,] more modestly, . . . it should . . . delineate economic and social development" with characteristics that could appeal to all strata of society.[20] In short: "A policy of austerity . . . should have as its goal—and it is for this that it can, must be made by the workers' movement—the establishment of justice, efficiency, order, and . . . a new morality. . . . [that] even if it involves (and it necessarily must, by its very nature) certain renunciations and certain sacrifices, simultaneously acquires the significance of renewal and becomes, in reality, a liberating act for the broad masses."[21] But even while playing on fears of reaction and repression, the PCI simultaneously presented austerity as the most convincing evidence of the political and industrial strength of the working class in the mid-1970s. As Berlinguer put it: "The old ruling classes and the old political personnel know that by now they are no longer able to *impose* sacrifices on the working class and Italian workers: today *they must ask, and they do ask,* for sacrifices."[22] The stress on working-class power was crucial to the party's own mediating role: only if the working class was sufficiently threatening that its collaboration had to be sought would the PCI be able to act as the instrument for gaining its cooperation.

Social and industrial conflict was thus increasingly viewed by the PCI as politically destabilizing. The kind of gains that could primarily be won through it—wages and other direct benefits—were seen not merely as less significant than those that would be won through national political collaboration but as contributing to the country's economic and political instability. As one of the party's most important national leaders put it: "We have never accepted and we do not accept unilateral and tendentious analyses that pinpoint the exclusive or primary cause of the crisis of the accumulation process in the cost of labor or even outright in the level reached by collectively bargained wages. But we cannot ignore the weight that the related increase of wages and pensions has assumed, and the effect

20. Enrico Berlinguer, "Conclusioni al convegno degli intellettuali," Roma, 15 gennaio 1977, reprinted in his *Austerità occasione per trasformare l'Italia* (Rome: Editori Riuniti, 1977), 24–25.

21. Ibid., 18–19.

22. Enrico Berlinguer, "Conclusioni all'assemblea degli operai comunisti lombardi," Milano, 30 gennaio 1977, reprinted in ibid., 52. Emphasis in the original.

that a containment of the wage dynamic can have for increasing the margins of investment."[23] Containing wages in order to fuel investments in the country's underdeveloped south was a major and consistent theme in the PCI's public rhetoric during this period. By demonstrating a capacity to control economic factors, the PCI hoped to reveal a capacity to govern.

By the latter part of the decade the Communist party thus found itself in a paradoxical situation. Its claims to political power rested on its links to the industrial working class—a highly mobilized class at that. Yet political power could be won only by demonstrating an ability to restrain the actions of that very constituency. Moreover, given the country's postwar political history and the existing international political constraints, demobilization had to take effect before the PCI's entry into the national government. This made the task infinitely more onerous. If the PCI was offering the working class its capacity to redirect Italy's economic policy in exchange for reductions in industrial militancy and sacrifices of material benefits, results would have to be taken largely on faith.

Union Strategy under National Unity

By 1975 the strategy of reforms had reached an impasse. Direct union consultation with government had proved largely ineffectual for obtaining policy reforms. As one unionist, summarizing a point of view widely diffused in national union circles, admitted:

> The problem has been and still is that of transferring to society the more advanced relations of force which have been conquered in the factory. Using the same method as in factory and contractual negotiations, similar "bargaining rounds" with the government were initiated, on problems first of housing, health reform, transportation, [and] tax reform, and then on investments and employment, prices and public rates, agriculture and the south, the state holding companies, [and] energy. There have been some results, for certain rates (transportation, electricity) and for the reform of the pension system, but for the rest we have won, in the best of cases . . . *promises of commitments* that then have not been maintained.[24]

23. Giorgio Napolitano, "Relazione," in PCI, *VII Conferenza operaia del Partito comunista italiano,* Napoli, 3–5 marzo 1978 (Rome: Editori Riuniti, 1978), 35.

24. Mario Didò, "Questi cinque anni," *Quaderni di Rassegna Sindacale* 12 (November–December 1974), 6. Emphasis in the original.

The strategy of reforms waned. The divarication between market and political strategies that had been temporarily suspended, as it were, during the late 1960s and early 1970s gradually resurfaced. Whereas the hot autumn and the subsequent period had been marked by what CGIL leader Bruno Trentin called "a fusion of immediate objectives and more general objectives of social transformation,"[25] by 1976 the first signs of a resubordination of contractual to political, short- to long-term gains appeared. Pressures for moderation intensified.

In preparing its strategy for the 1976 national industrywide bargaining, for instance, the Federazione Unitaria publicly stated that wage demands could be modified to shift priority to employment.[26] If management would accept the union's right to bargain over private investments, the Federazione Unitaria was prepared to restrain wages.[27] The 1976 "platforms" *(piattaforme)* for the renewals of the industrywide contracts were deliberately designed to emphasize the so-called first part *(prima parte)*, dealing with union rights to information on employment levels and investments. There were, however, important differences between the rights to information that had been won through the "development contracts" signed with the country's largest firms in 1973 and 1974 and the information rights featured in the 1976 CCNLs. In the earlier factory accords the dual issues of investments and information had been viewed—by the unions and, from the little evidence available, also by the rank and file—as significant gains for the workers employed in the firms involved. By 1976, on the other hand, information rights were generally not of immediate interest to the employees whose wage demands were sacrificed. For the first time since the hot autumn, national trade union leaders publicly and officially admitted that they were prepared to sacrifice immediate market gains for the sake of broader and more indirect goals.

Containing immediate demands (particularly wages, both direct and indirect) in order to shift priorities to long-term goals (especially employment) intensified in the following years. In 1977 the confederations signed an important cost-of-labor agreement with the Confindustria in which the

25. Bruno Trentin, "Il sindacato nuovo di fronte alla crisi," excerpt from "Relazione introduttiva al XV Congresso nazionale della FIOM," Roma, 13–18 luglio 1970, reprinted in his *Da sfruttati a produttori: lotte operaie e sviluppo capitalistico dal miracolo economico alla crisi*, 3d ed. (Bari: DeDonato, 1977), 248.

26. Luciano Rufino, "Per una politica dell'occupazione e i rinnovi contrattuali," Federazione Unitaria CGIL-CISL-UIL, Comitato Direttivo, Roma, 1–2 marzo 1976, *Rassegna Sindacale* 22 (11 March 1976), special insert, 13.

27. Federazione Unitaria CGIL-CISL-UIL, "Documento conclusivo," in ibid., 23–24.

unions agreed to a revision of seniority bonuses and severance pay, the eradication of seven paid holidays, factory-level bargaining over the annual calendar, greater flexibility of shift work, more use of overtime, more flexibility of labor within plants and firms, and greater control over absenteeism.[28] All had been considered bulwarks of the union's market power since 1969, and the accord marks the first Italian concession bargaining since then. The confederations, facing a worsening economic situation and intense political pressures, indicated their "willingness to coordinate factory and category bargaining activities, in order to guarantee full coherence with the priority objectives of the fight against inflation and the defense of the *lira,* through the containment of the global cost of labor dynamic and the increase of productivity, the growth of employment and a gradual policy of productive reconversion." And, they added bluntly, "generalized demands for wage increases through articulated bargaining are not proposed."[29]

The agreement appears to have achieved some economic success. According to the OECD, it led to "an appreciable slowdown in wage costs"[30] and contributed to the "remarkable improvements" of the Italian economy in 1978, improvements that included a strong reversal in the balance of payments crisis, a (temporary) halving of the rate of inflation, an expansion of the GDP, and a recovery of investments.[31]

Nonetheless, the accord was far from voluntary: it was perceived by the union movement as, at most, necessary—a second-best solution. The confederations turned to moderation only reluctantly and with considerable suspicion. The offer of "coordination"—code terminology for increased centralized control of collective bargaining—was in great part a reaction to very real government threats to freeze factory bargaining altogether, for instance. This constituted an initial condition, subsequently dropped only thanks to strong union objections, attached to an International Monetary Fund loan then being negotiated.[32] Other concessions in the

28. See Lauralba Bellardi, Giorgio Nardinocchi, and Elena Pisani, eds., *Sindacati e contrattazione collettiva in Italia nel 1976–77* (Milan: F. Angeli, 1979), 112–19, and also 205–12 for the text of the accord.

29. Federazione Unitaria CGIL-CISL-UIL, "Dichiarazione della CGIL-CISL-UIL," reprinted in ibid., 207. For the PCI's enthusiastic reactions, reactions that included exhorting Communist unionists to support the Federazione Unitaria as fully as possible in pursuing this line of conduct, see the comments by Berlinguer, "Conclusioni all'assemblea degli operai comunisti lombardi," 43–45.

30. OECD, *Economic Surveys: Italy* (1979), 21.

31. Ibid., 60. See also Salvati, "Italian Inflation."

32. For details in English, see Flanagan, Soskice, and Ulman, *Unionism, Economic Stabilization, and Incomes Policies*, 551–53.

1977 agreement, particularly those relating to seniority bonuses and severance pay, were defensive maneuvers designed to protect the 1975 agreement on wage indexation, already under extremely heavy attack by both management and the government. Union leaders hesitantly conceded that "directed sacrifices" were now in order to defend wages and working conditions and to show, through the "conscious acceptance of an austerity policy," the union's commitment to expanding employment and reducing inflation.[33]

The factory and firm bargaining that followed during 1977 and 1978 remained relatively contained, in line with confederal policy. Wage demands were moderate.[34] Emphasis was shifted to the first part of the accords, dealing with information and investments. Even the number of accords signed was smaller than it would probably otherwise have been. The subsequent 1979 CCNLs contained wage demands even more visibly. Some expansion of the "first part" of contracts occurred, while bargaining innovations concerned the sensitive issues of labor mobility and a minor and gradual reduction of working hours. The small wage gains demanded were nonegalitarian percentile increases rather than across the board, as had been typical since 1968. Moreover, they were staggered increments rather than immediate and lump sum, again relieving financial pressure on industry and attesting to a containment of wage militancy.[35]

By the time the 1979 national contracts were renewed, however, the Federazione Unitaria had already officially adopted an austerity policy, sanctioning what had become actual practice since 1976. Adoption came in early 1978, in a well-prepared national assembly held at EUR, a Roman suburb. The two day meeting was attended by 1,457 official union delegates, including full-time functionaries as well as rank-and-file representatives and even a small group representing the unemployed.[36] The lengthy document approved at the meeting had initially been presented by the Secretariat of the Federazione Unitaria to the Comitato Direttivo of the CGIL-CISL-UIL at a meeting held on 13–14 January. Between then and 13–14 February, when the EUR assembly took place, the union move-

33. Giorgio Benvenuto, "Posizione e iniziativa del sindacato di fronte alla crisi," Federazione Unitaria CGIL-CISL-UIL, Assemblea nazionale dei quadri, Roma, 7–8 gennaio 1977, *Rassegna Sindacale* 23 (13 January 1977), special insert, 28–29.

34. See OECD, *Economic Surveys: Italy* (1979), 21.

35. On collective bargaining during this period, see Renato Fontana, Giorgio Nardinocchi, and Elena Pisani, eds., *Sindacati e contrattazione collettiva in Italia nel 1978–79* (Milan: F. Angeli, 1981).

36. For a breakdown of the delegates, see *Conquiste del Lavoro* 31 (20 February 1978), 1.

ment sought the official approval of its rank and file, holding some eight thousand factory, provincial, and regional assemblies.[37] The response was frequently fierce, as selected industrial unions in the north strove to amend the Federazione Unitaria's position, pushing it to the left.[38] Internal opposition was channeled by Italy's major industrial union, the Federazione Lavoratori Metalmeccanici, which was especially effective in coordinating and articulating dissent, as the next chapter will detail. Although the bulk of the Federazione's concrete recommendations remained unchanged, the metalworkers achieved the incorporation of key amendments, effectively blocking official union support for an incomes policy. The 12 nays and 103 abstentions in the final EUR vote underestimate the depth of opposition to an official policy of wage containment and increased labor flexibility and mobility.

The importance of the official adoption of austerity lay more with its political implications than with any clear guidelines for collective bargaining behavior, if only because its adoption merely codified changes that were already being implemented. The policy constituted the clearest statement of the bifurcation between the union's market and political activities. With it, the tendency to view market activities as secondary to political action was fully sanctioned. The EUR document read:

> The Federazione CGIL-CISL-UIL holds that, given substantial guarantees concerning the orientations of the government with respect to the growth of public investments, special intervention in the south and a policy of industrial reconversion, it is possible and necessary for the union to assume, autonomously, a line of behavior with respect to the issues of wages and nonmonetary benefits that is coherent with the general objectives of the equality of wages and benefits, the control of inflation and the growth of employment, which are the pivots of its bargaining strategy.
>
> The union, reaffirming what is and has during recent years been its behavior in both industrywide and articulated bargaining, will adopt a policy fully coherent between its own economic and nonmonetary claims and its

37. Number of assemblies estimated by Gianfranco Rastrelli, "Il giudizio del sindacato: conversazione con Enzio Ceremigna e Gianfranco Rastrelli," in *La consultazione: un'esperienza di democrazia sindacale*, ed. Lionello Bignani (Rome: Editrice Sindacale Italiana, 1982), 6.

38. The most extensive reporting of the consultazione was carried by the union's own press agency, the Agenzia Unitaria Sindacale (AUSI), which issued daily press releases covering union activities, as well as the independent left-wing newspaper *Il Manifesto*. The latter was especially attentive in reporting internal dissent. See the coverage devoted by both during January and February 1978. Pertinent documents are available in Stefano Bavacqua and Giuseppe Turani, *La svolta del '78: il sindacato e il Pci dall'intervista di Lama alla conferenza operaia di Napoli* (Milan: Feltrinelli, 1978).

general strategy, which centers on the growth of employment, improving working conditions, the unification of the labor market, [and] continuation of an egalitarian line.[39]

Market activities were now subordinated to political activities, direct action to electoral and state-oriented concerns. The best protection of the long-range interests of the employed work force necessarily involved short-term sacrifices, concluded the Federazione Unitaria. With EUR the confederations reversed the radical strategy they had employed between 1969 and 1975.

Party Proximity to Power and the Adoption of Austerity

By 1978, then, organized labor and the PCI had endorsed parallel austerity policies, both of which called for some unspecified measure of wage restraint and greater flexibility in the use of labor. The policies were more statements of intent and demonstrations of good faith than actual guidelines for collective bargaining. They were imprecise in their standards of implementation, global in their scope, and at least in the case of EUR, in part internally contradictory. Hampered by internal opposition, the confederal EUR policy was at once "softer" and rhetorically more radical than the PCI's austerity policy. It placed greater emphasis on the gains for labor (investments, employment, and industrial planning) that the government could effect in exchange for the union's containment of wage increases and industrial conflict and allowances of greater flexibility in the use of labor.

Although the Federazione Unitaria's collective bargaining policies in the mid-1970s were congruent with the political strategy then being pursued by the Communist party, convergence was not a result of direct party domination of union decision making, which is of limited scope. Nor could it have been mere coincidence. Whereas the Federazione Unitaria's moderation of collective bargaining seems to have principally been the product of changed economic conditions and external political pressures, both domestic and international, the *formal* adoption of an austerity policy in 1978 is best explained by the proximity of the PCI to national power. The PCI needed the unions to guarantee the party's credibility with its

39. Federazione Unitaria CGIL-CSIL-UIL, "Per una svolta di politica economica e di sviluppo civile e democratico," il documento definitivo approvato dall'Assemblea nazionale, Roma, 13–14 febbraio 1978, *Rassegna Sindacale* 24 (23 February 1978), special insert, xxvii.

political quasi-allies. The unions, in turn, hoped for the formation of a friendlier government to rescue their own flagging strategy of policy reform via mass mobilization. Organized labor's political interests largely paralleled those of the PCI in this period. Since both strategies hinged on the PCI's political fortunes, the party gained considerable—though by no means exclusive—sway within the labor movement.

Until the mid-1970s organized labor had retained the informal political recognition it had been granted to represent the working class. It became more and more apparent, however, that this constituted something of a Pyrrhic victory. The central site of policymaking remained Parliament, from which the unions had voluntarily disenfranchised themselves by adopting the incompatibility regulations. Whereas the Federazione Unitaria demonstrated a remarkable capacity to topple governments and to block legislation it considered particularly nasty, it manipulated few instruments capable of directly influencing the formation of public policy. A radical strategy of direct action had proved inadequate in effecting permanent social change. In consequence, as the general secretary of the UIL admitted, "The result is that today the union finds itself in the situation of someone under police surveillance; it can talk about how the country ought to change, but it can do little such that the country does change. It must return to delegating to the parties."[40] Direct bilateral negotiations with the executive branch had failed to achieve much in the way of policy reform, largely because it lacked adequate institutional and partisan support. "We are," the head of the CGIL remarked, acutely summing up the union's dilemma, "a political actor who wants change. But we cannot accomplish change by ourselves. We do not make laws. We do not run banks. We do not administer communes. However," he added, "we can certainly promote change. Thus, we too must work for a different political direction for the country."[41] The same person had inquired rhetorically some five years earlier, "Do we have to continue saying for another ten years that the government should change its policies, or may we begin to say that it is necessary to change governments because we have had the proof that this government doesn't know how to change policies?"[42] Mass

40. Giorgio Benvenuto, *Austerità e democrazia operaia,* interview by Aldo Forbice (Milan: SugarCo, 1977), 65.

41. Luciano Lama, "'Niente patto sociale e la scala mobile guai a chi la tocca,'" interview by Giampaolo Pansa, *La Repubblica*, 26 June 1981, 5.

42. Luciano Lama, quoted in Giorgio Benvenuto et al., "Impegno del sindacato per una svolta politica," round table led by Gino Giugni, *Mondoperaio* 29 (April 1976), 7.

mobilization alone had provided insufficient leverage for obtaining vast and permanent changes in public policy. Not surprisingly, the Federazione Unitaria explicitly recognized that one of the premises for the adoption of EUR lay with the "critical analyses . . . which have been conducted of the inadequate and unsatisfactory results of actions for reform."[43]

In this context, the PCI's possible entry into the national government began to appear the most auspicious—or least infelicitous—solution. Although the Federazione Unitaria continued to claim, somewhat disingenuously, that it could not call openly for the PCI's entry into the government without jeopardizing its own fragile federated arrangements and nonpartisanship,[44] it nonetheless officially hailed each step toward national power taken by the PCI and, through its activities and an encoded rhetoric, emerged as a central actor favoring national unity. As the Secretariat of the Federazione Unitaria put it in its official opening address to the EUR assembly, "We believe that it is in the interests of the union movement to support the positive development of the political dialectic, to avoid lacerating counterpositions and frontal collisions between the political forces or the exclusion of forces [i.e., the PCI] that have rendered a decisive contribution to the construction of the democratic state."[45] With EUR, then, organized labor threw its political weight behind an expansion of national power to include that party most likely to support working-class interests. Overwhelmingly interpreted in just this fashion,[46] EUR

43. Federazione Unitaria CGIL-CISL-UIL (Secretariat), "Relazione della Segreteria presentata da Luigi Macario," Assemblea nazionale dei Consigli Generali e dei delegati, Roma, 13 14 febbraio 1978, *Rassegna Sindacale* 24 (23 February 1978), special insert, ii.

44. In its opening address at the EUR assembly, the Federazione Unitaria stated, in conspicuously ambiguous words: "We are not asking for a new political equilibrium, [or] for a new governmental formula, of which we do not underestimate either the importance or the value"; Federazione Unitaria CGIL-CSIL-UIL (Secretariat), "Relazione della Segreteria presentata da Luigi Macario," viii.

This position was strongly contested within union leadership, especially but not solely by Communists. Two of the CISL's most influential intellectuals also publicly suggested that the Federazione Unitaria renounce its "official agnosticism" with respect to government composition. See Guido Baglioni and Tiziano Treu, "I mutamenti politico-istituzionali e lo spazio dell'azione sindacale" (1976), reprinted in *Il sindacato dell'autonomia: l'evoluzione della Cisl nella e pratica nella cultura*, by Guido Baglioni, 2d ed. (Bari: DeDonato, 1977), 319.

45. Federazione Unitaria CGIL-CISL-UIL (Secretariat), "Relazione della Segreteria presentata da Luigi Macario," iii. The opening address also noted the "favorable position . . . that the Federazione has maintained with respect to the six-party accord and its positive development"; ibid., iii.

46. In part because of an interview given to the press by the general secretary of the CGIL

constituted a tacit offer by organized labor of collaboration with a future government that would include the Communist party. Indeed, the approval of the document was predicated on the assumption that the PCI was about to be given cabinet positions.[47] The union movement as a whole, and non-Communists in particular, knew it was being "manipulated" by the PCI in the latter's efforts to obtain entry to government, but the union's margins for maneuver had become so reduced that no other option appeared feasible.[48] EUR was thus used as political justification for controlling industrial conflict and centralizing wage bargaining in light of the presumably immediate entry of the PCI into the government. Because the political interests of the Federazione Unitaria lay with the formation of a more labor-oriented government, it could not help but cautiously embrace the PCI's own political aims and moderate policy orientation.

Defensive Austerity and Tripartitism under the Center-Left: 1980–85

Following the PCI's withdrawal into the opposition in early 1979, the political context for union moderation altered. In the spring elections that year, the party's share of the popular vote fell for the first time since World War II. The historic compromise and the national unity experiment were discarded, the PSI moved back into coalition with the DC, and the partisan impetus for concerted policymaking shifted from the PCI to the Socialists. Now it was the PSI that intended to foster cooperation with organized labor, both to reinforce the legitimacy of the new center-left coalition and to demonstrate its superiority over national unity in handling economic problems.

By the 1980s, economic problems had begun to exact a heavy toll on labor. The three confederations began losing members for the first time since the 1960s.[49] In the fall of 1980 the FLM lost a major strike at Fiat.

just before the EUR assembly. See Luciano Lama, "I sacrifici che chiediamo agli operai," interview by Eugenio Scalfari, *La Repubblica*, 24 January 1978, 3. The interview is also available as Luciano Lama, "Intervista rilasciata da Luciano Lama al quotidiano 'La Repubblica' il 24 gennaio 1978," reprinted in Bevacqua and Turani, *Svolta del '78*.

47. This came out repeatedly in interviewing national union leaders. For instance, one admitted outright that EUR had been a "miscalculation" because its adoption had been based on this assumption; interview no. 36, national FLM (Secretariat), 24 July 1980.

48. Interview no. 42, national CISL (Secretariat), 21 October 1978.

49. Active membership in the three confederations began to fall in 1981; see the figures reported in Guido Romagnoli, "Sindacalizzazione e rappresentanza," in *Le relazioni sin-*

For various reasons, the strike was profoundly damaging to organized labor as a whole. Industrial restructuring in large industry became intense, throwing union organization into disarray, while labor productivity in manufacturing rose in 1981 and 1982 despite declines in output and a reduction of working hours. These rises in productivity indicate a serious weakening of union power in large industry, as does the growing inability to protect jobs in the same firms.[50] Under national unity, the confederations could argue that their cooperation with the government and the recognition it brought constituted political payoffs for labor's increased market power. Now, however, cooperation became a virtual necessity, a stopgap measure aimed at protecting labor's organizational integrity and minimal credibility with its rank and file. Economic change began severely undercutting labor's autonomy, heightening the claims of moderation.

This second phase of austerity witnessed a major policy achievement: a tripartite cost-of-labor agreement reached on 22 January 1983, generally referred to as the Scotti accord after Vicenzo Scotti, the minister of labor who negotiated its conclusion. However, the first annual attempt to renew the accord resulted in a split among the three confederations, the refusal of the Communist component of the CGIL to underwrite a new agreement, the breakdown of the Federazione Unitaria, and an executive decree again restricting the scala mobile. The 1983 accord had been designed to defend a union movement caught between an economic situation now causing erosion from the bottom up and a political situation that, if not overtly unfriendly, nonetheless no longer offered prospects for the formation of a labor-oriented government. With the PCI back in opposition and veering erratically between moderation and radicalism while labor market conditions increasingly depressed rank-and-file militancy, the union movement found itself strained between an unpromising radicalism and an unhappy moderation.

The PCI in Opposition

If national unity had become ever more uncomfortable for the PCI, the party's new oppositional role was no less so. The decisions to withdraw

---

dacali in Italia: rapporto 1982–83, ed. Guido Baglioni, Marina Camonico, and Ettore Santi, Centro di Studi Sociali e Sindacali (Rome: Edizioni Lavoro, 1984), 213. See also the useful analysis by Nino Magna, "Sindacato: crisi o malattia di crescita?" *Ricerche CeSPE*, supplement to *Politica ed Economia*, nos. 7/8 (July–August 1983), 33–39.

50. OECD, *Economic Surveys, 1983–1984: Italy* (Paris: OECD, 1984), 24–27.

into the opposition and then to renounce the historic compromise stemmed from a growing realization that the party's own militants were simply too bewildered by and suspicious of the way the strategy had been practiced for the organization to retain internal integrity. Complaints gradually percolated up from the party's sections,[51] while increasingly visible opposition to national unity surfaced in the unions, especially the FLM—opposition in which Communists were clearly assuming leading roles. The PCI had failed to convince its own core working-class constituency that the endeavor was worth the price, mainly because the legislation generated by Parliament proved so disappointing. As a national party leader put it some years later, "On the one hand, the DC was no longer able to impose its plans and the interests of its own system of power in Parliament; on the other, the forces of the Left and the workers' movement did not have sufficient force and unity to push through the battle on actual decisions and to initiate a coherent line of structural change."[52] National unity had been a political formula by which the PCI had hoped to gain legitimacy, but to do so the party had watered down many of its more progressive legislative aims.

Opposition allowed the PCI to regain greater internal consensus while weakening relations with the auxiliary social strata that had contributed to its 1976 electoral success. The party returned to emphasizing its class specificity, even to the point of alienating other social groups, yet it simultaneously strove to contain the social tensions its own workerist rhetoric encouraged. The PCI's visible support of the bitter thirty-five-day Fiat strike in late 1980 marked the party's ambivalent return to the core industrial working class. Enrico Berlinguer himself spoke at the factory gates offering the party's complete solidarity with the strikers and its support if Fiat workers were to occupy the factory, even as the PCI was secretly working behind the scenes to negotiate a compromise acceptable to both Fiat's management and the unions.[53] The strike illustrates the paradoxical position of the party in opposition. On the one hand, it sought to demonstrate to its core constituency and the other parties that despite

51. See the results of the research conducted in Bologna by Marzio Barbagli and Piergiorgio Corbetta, "La svolta del Pci," *Il Mulino* 30 (January–February 1981), 95–103, and idem, "Una tattica e due strategie: inchiesta sulla base del Pci," *Il Mulino* 27 (November–December 1978), 957–63.

52. Antonio Montessoro, "Relazione," in PCI, *VIII Conferenza operaia del Partito comunista italiano,* Torino, 2–4 luglio 1982 (Rome: Editori Riuniti, 1983), 19.

53. Reported in Giuseppe Bonazzi, "La lotta dei 35 giorni alla Fiat: un'analisi sociologica," *Ricerche CeSPE*, supplement to *Politica ed Economia*, no. 11 (November 1984), 39.

three years of national unity the PCI could still be trusted to stand by the working class, representing it as no other organization in Italy could. It sought to relegitimate its class specificity and a kind of radical workerism. On the other, the party sought to show its own constituency and the governing parties that it could still represent general national interests and was not about to marginalize itself *à la française*. It sought, therefore, to retain a supraclass reformism. Since success with one meant failure with the other, the party's behavior became erratic and occasionally contradictory, oscillating between moderate propensities and radical desperation.

As economic conditions increasingly placed the unions on the defensive, pushing them into losing strikes, members, and much of their ability to resist government and managerial pressures, the PCI was forced to differentiate itself from organized labor. Precisely because of its marginal capacity to dominate union decision making directly, it began to take positions independent of and even in conflict with the unions. On the one hand, the PCI feared contamination by union failure; on the other, its reduced leverage in the political system as a whole rendered it increasingly reliant on its ties to the working class. If the PCI could not show that it alone represented the industrial working class, regardless of the trade unions, then it had few cards left to play. Without the working class—a mobilized, potentially threatening working class—the PCI was merely an isolated, minority opposition party, politically disfranchised through sheer electoral failure. Starting with a 1979 article by party leader Giorgio Amendola criticizing the unions for their behavior during national unity,[54] the PCI became openly critical of the unions and ever more insistent on its right to articulate independent views on labor and union problems.

Now that the party was at some distance from government, the PCI's interpretation of Italy's economic problems underwent reformulation. Whereas under national unity the party had called repeatedly for working-class sacrifices, suggesting that wages were unnecessarily high, under the new center-left it began to downplay their importance. Reversing earlier positions, an important party leader argued that "the cost of labor and wage indexation are not the principal problems of our economy and industry: the problems of greater concern are productivity, restructuring, reconversion."[55]

54. Giorgio Amendola, "Interrogativi sul 'caso' Fiat," *Rinascita* 36 (9 November 1979), 13–15. See also the various responses carried in subsequent issues through 7 December 1979.

55. Gerardo Chiaromonte, "Intervento conclusivo," in PCI, *VIII Conferenza operaia*, 277.

The PCI never assumed a radically intransigent position, however. Even as it sought to assure the working class of its essentially class-specific orientation—"At Fiat, as in every other factory, when workers and working people engage in struggle, the place for Communists, starting with our own party's general secretary, is at the side of the workers"[56]—it consistently reiterated the need for realism in tackling economic problems, for prudence and compromise in politics. It wanted a mobilized working class in order to demonstrate its own irreplaceable role in negotiating social change and political reform, not because the party favored social conflict for its own sake. The party encouraged direct action only to save electoral ends and substantively moderate policies. So while formally repudiating the historic compromise and national unity, in fact the party never really ruled out the possibility of engaging in such supraclass political alignments in the future.

To the extent that the PCI's political leverage resided with its ties to the working class, deals struck independently between the unions and the state threatened the party's influence. The PCI thus opposed tripartite bargaining among labor, business, and the state, repeatedly attempting to delegitimize the Federazione Unitaria's role in representing the working class in the political arena. It sought to shift the locus of decision making back to Parliament or, when that failed, back to the electorate as a whole. This put the party in direct competition with the union movement for political legitimacy, resulting in unprecedented acrimony between the two.

The Unions: Divided Tripartism

After a year's attempt on the part of the three confederations to construct a joint policy for controlling Italy's worsening inflation rate, organized business launched its first major offensive since the hot autumn. On 1 June 1982, the Confindustria announced that it intended to refuse to renew its 1975 agreement with the Federazione Unitaria regulating the wage indexation system. This would have voided the 1975 agreement as of the end of the year, resulting in a reversion to the prior interconfederal agreement, dating from 1957.[57] The Confindustria's action forced the Federazione Unitaria into prolonged and extensive negotiations with Italy's business associations over all aspects of the cost of labor, including the previously sacred issue of wage indexation. Thanks to the 1975 agreement, combined with a period of high inflation and modest wage de-

56. Ibid., 284.

57. Relevant documents on the Confindustria's cancellation of the 1975 agreement may be found in *Rassegna Sindacale* 28 (10 June 1982), 40–43.

mands, the scala mobile had gained massive weight in wage determination. By 1981, for instance, the CGIL calculated that it accounted for 64 percent of annual wage increases in the industrial sectors, whereas in 1974 the equivalent figure had been only 35 percent.[58] Wage indexation had dramatically reduced the union's control over wage determination. A major concession was beginning to backfire for organized labor.

The Federazione Unitaria entered negotiations late in 1982 on the basis of a nine-point document that had already received rank-and-file approval in a massive round of factory assemblies held in November of that year. The *consultazione* involved almost 34,000 assemblies, attended by more than 2 million of the 4 million employed in the workplaces concerned. Of those attending, 69 percent endorsed the Federazione Unitaria's recommendations,[59] which among other provisions called for eliminating bracket creep, improving family allowances, creating a worker-financed Fondo di Solidarietà (Solidarity Fund) to raise money for investments, defending lower-paid workers' wages, and changing the system of calculating the scala mobile so that its increase would be slowed by some 10 percent. This extravagant display of direct democratic consensus building did little to convince labor's radical dissenting coalition, once again coordinated by the national FLM, which fought for amendments to the confederal document. In this they were encouraged by the PCI, which appealed for changes to the document and, where possible, aided unionists and shop-floor militants in amending the Federazione Unitaria's recommendations.[60] In the end, the PCI supported the tripartite accord only reluctantly and did so at the last possible moment, calling it "limited" and "defensive."[61] However, the accord was signed only after the PCI had been informally approached and had agreed to it.[62]

58. Stefano Patriarca, "Scala mobile e distribuzione del reddito," in *La vertenza sul costo del lavoro e le relazioni industriali*, ed. Giovanna Altieri et al. (Milan: F. Angeli, 1984), 196, table 4.

59. Figures taken from Lorenzo Speranza, "Le consultazioni," in Baglioni, Camonico, and Santi, *Relazioni sindacali in Italia*, 481–82, table 5; slightly different figures are reported in Paola Cerretti, "Le consultazioni di massa del 1982," *Quaderni di Rassegna Sindacale* 21 (September–October 1983), 204, table 5.

60. For the most extreme version of the PCI's position during the assemblies, see Gerardo Chiaromonte, "Una consultazione che può fare davvero chiarezza," *L'Unità*, 3 November 1982, 2.

61. Enrico Berlinguer, "Bilancio e prospettive di una grande lotta," *L'Unità*, 23 January 1983, 1. On the accord in general, see Altieri et al., *Vertenza sul costo del lavoro*, and Tiziano Treu, ed., *Il patto contro l'inflazione: contenuti e documenti delle intese governo-sindacati* (Rome: Edizioni Lavoro, 1984).

62. Reported in Mimmo Carrieri, "Accordi non conclusi, accordi non efficaci, accordi non voluti: la logica negoziale dei governi nelle relazioni industriali," in *Il teorema sin-*

To forestall widespread protest and obtain an agreement between business and labor, the DC-led coalition government acted both as mediator and as a participant during the final round of negotiations. The bargaining itself just escaped formal tripartitism: the confederations and the Confindustria never actually sat at the same table with government authorities but insisted instead on negotiating from separate rooms, with government mediators literally racing back and forth between them. The accord of 22 January, however, was underwritten by all three actors and included commitments by each. For these reasons, it is generally considered Italy's first tripartite incomes policy. The coverage provided by wage indexation was reduced by some 15 percent; collective bargaining for the triennial labor contracts, stalled by the Confindustria since June, was reopened; an eighteen-month ban on plant-level wage bargaining was enforced; and the government agreed to present urgent legislation before Parliament regarding bracket creep and family allowances.[63] The agreement's complex economic trade-offs were designed to protect the real incomes of the employed work force: the subsequent national labor contracts, in conjunction with government measures on bracket creep and family allowances, were meant to compensate for the effects of the reduction of wage indexation coverage. Indeed, the accord contained a clause ensuring government fiscal measures in case of any drop in real incomes.[64] These compensatory measures, which emasculated the potential economic impact of the accord that many confederal leaders would have favored, were largely responses to internal union resistance and opposition to any kind of an incomes policy—an opposition, however, tempered by the fear that, in the absence of any accord at all, business would continue to block the renewal of the national labor contracts. As a result of these various maneuvers, the inflation rate dropped to 15 percent in 1983, compared with nearly 17 percent the previous year.[65] Inflation in 1983 did not, however, stay within the 13 percent maximum foreseen by the accord.

Immediately following 22 January, disagreements broke out between labor and business concerning the interpretation of ambiguous clauses—disagreements that were entirely predictable given that the ambiguities had provided the only basis for the accord in the first place. These con-

---

dacale: flessibilità e competizione nelle relazioni industriali, ed. Mimmo Carrieri and Paolo Perulli (Bologna: Il Mulino, 1985), 144.

63. "Il testo dell'accordo," *Conquiste del Lavoro*, supplement no. 2 to vol. 36 (23 January 1983), special insert, 2–7.

64. See Stefano Patriarca, "Caratteristiche e risultati della politica dei redditi, 1983–1984," in Carrieri and Perulli, *Teorema sindacale*, 66.

65. OECD, *Economic Surveys, 1983–1984*, 47, table 22.

flicts continued for the rest of the year, and the major issue—whether to include fractional remainders in wage indexation coverage on an annual basis—was still unresolved when the first annual verification of the Scotti accord got under way.

This second round of negotiations thus opened inauspiciously.[66] The partisan pressures on the confederations were greater than during the Scotti negotiations, since the new Socialist prime minister, Bettino Craxi, was determined to use a new agreement to marginalize the PCI. The PCI itself was experiencing acute political isolation, and relations between the two parties of Italy's historical Left had deteriorated to their worst point in twenty years. Negotiations proceeded under recurrent threats by all actors and with only tenuous agreement among the three confederations.

On 14 February 1984 the government presented a letter of understanding (*protocollo d'intesa*) in which, among other provisions, the levels of wage indexation provided over the course of the coming year were fixed in advance, regardless of the rate of inflation.[67] The proposal was designed to reduce labor costs and to permanently affect workers' incomes, unlike the 1983 agreement. The scala mobile was to be altered to protect workers' wages only against a maximum of 8 percent annual inflation in 1984, regardless of the real inflation rate.[68] The following day, the Communist component of the CGIL used its majority in the organization's Comitato Direttivo to refuse approval of a new agreement. The CISL and the UIL, along with the Socialists in the CGIL, promised to support a new accord. The government, unable to gain the approval of all three confederations, issued a constitutionally dubious executive decree on 15 February 1984 altering the coverage provided by the wage indexation system in line with the provisions outlined in the protocol. The decree was supported by the CISL, the UIL, Socialists in the CGIL, the business community, and the five parties of the governing coalition. It was opposed on political and constitutional grounds by the PCI, the Communist wing of the CGIL, and minor parties to the left of the PCI. The decree threw the Federazione Unitaria into disarray, virtually severing relations among its three component confederations as well as between Communists and Socialists in the CGIL. Relations subsequently worsened: on 10 June the PCI, supported by the Communist component of the CGIL, lost a national referendum to the five-party Socialist-led government attempting to abrogate the decree, although the vote was narrow (45.7 percent favoring abrogation).

66. Relevant documentation is available in "I documenti del negoziato tra sindacati, governo e imprenditori (novembre '83–febbraio '84)," *Quaderni di Rassegna Sindacale* 21 (November–December 1983), 132–223, and Treu, *Patto contro l'inflazione*.

67. For a copy, see "Documenti del negoziato," 183–203.

68. See Patriarca, "Caratteristiche e risultati della politica dei redditi."

Competition between Union and Party under the Center-Left

The distance of the PCI from the center of executive power after 1979 placed it in increasingly direct competition with organized labor for political resources. Especially after the installation of Italy's first Socialist prime minister, the government's strategy aimed at isolating the Communists by drawing the confederations into the state arena, legitimating them as the major organized representatives of the working class while simultaneously discrediting the party. On the defensive, the party's response could only be to attack the confederations, especially their representativeness, and to repeatedly attempt to mobilize the industrial working class against the union movement. But even this unusually class-specific and potentially radical agenda was not wholly successful, as the failure of the PCI's referendum on the scala mobile demonstrates. The PCI retained enough direct working-class ties to disrupt the workings of the Federazione Unitaria, but not enough to displace it. Acting as a militant agent of radical opposition was for the party a role of limited utility.

As for the unions, decentralized wage bargaining and mass mobilization had become increasingly unrealistic as the bases for national strategy during the course of the 1970s as rank-and-file militancy waned. Economic conditions narrowed the scope of trade-union autonomy: organized labor appeared increasingly unable to control wage determination or otherwise mobilize the rank and file to win. Confronted by the consequences of its own earlier successes—especially an extremely rapid inflation rate blamed increasingly on the union's own wage policy—organized labor was forced to turn to the state for solutions, even when this led to direct confrontations with the Communist party.

Conclusions

This chapter has examined the tensions between the calls for moderation and the claims of mobilization and militancy that shaped relations between the three national labor confederations and the Communist party between 1968 and 1984. The PCI's commitment to a substantially moderate, social democratic strategy remained intact over the period, as we would expect of a supraclass, electorally oriented working-class party. Radical tendencies temporarily surfaced during periods when the party was most removed from national power, however—the hot autumn and the 1980s. Proximity to power, by contrast, helped consolidate moderation.

The policy orientation of organized labor, on the other hand, appears determined only in part by the party's proximity to power. During the hot autumn period (1968–72) the union movement's radical militancy was encouraged both directly by the party and indirectly by the general absence of a reliable labor-affiliated government: by the vacuum created by the long-standing political exclusion of the PCI. The latter in particular made direct action appear to be a strategy more fruitful for social change than parliamentary politics. But even at its height, radicalism was neither entirely self-sustaining nor self-fulfilling: rank-and-file industrial action in the late 1960s elicited a simultaneous initial turn to the state with the strategy of reforms. The strategy of reforms was a state-centric policy orientation that drew on mass mobilization, largely attempting to bypass partisan and parliamentary politics.

As business conditions worsened in the 1970s, labor's ability to sustain policy orientations that depended on mass mobilization and militancy began to decline as well. The PCI's involvement in the national unity experiment and the political resources that came with it induced the union movement to overcommit itself to moderation with the passage of EUR. Although worsening economic conditions account for labor's gradual shift to the practice of wage restraint, the PCI's proximity to power explains why wage restraint was articulated as a formal policy commitment when it was. EUR became necessary because of its partisan implications.

By the 1980s economic conditions had turned against organized labor, forcing even more stringent confederal involvement in incomes policies and commitments to moderation. Previous successes, especially the 1975 agreement on wage indexation, had backfired by dramatically reducing the scope of labor's bargaining autonomy. Backed into a contractual corner, the confederations were forced to renegotiate the scala mobile despite the PCI's halfhearted opposition. With its increased distance from national power, the PCI was unable to gain entrance to the 1982–83 negotiations. Even so, the party acceded to the Scotti accord, whose impact on working-class incomes was negligible. Only when the government proposed measured genuinely damaging to working-class incomes did the PCI finally refuse cooperation and successfully gain the alignment of Communists in the CGIL as well.

The decade between the mid-1970s and the mid-1980s saw the national union confederations reluctantly adopt an ever more moderate orientation in their dealings with the state. Their policies became intensely sensitive to the political arena and increasingly directed at the state itself. Wage moderation and increasingly centralized bargaining were propelled by the PCI between 1976 and 1979 and after that were driven by worsening labor market conditions. The confederations responded to these pressures by relinquishing their earlier commitments to a radical strategy of mass mobilization. Their increasingly moderate policy orientation coincided with their organizational position in the union movement, one that entailed the responsibility for articulating a viable general union strategy.

The emergence of moderation and the increasing centrality of partisan politics did not take place without internal opposition, however. Other components of the union movement proved persistent in their commitment to radical policy orientations. With each step taken toward moderation, the confederations encountered resistance from major industrial unions. The next chapter will begin to examine radical policy orientations at the national level in the metalworkers' unions.

4

The Metalworkers: A Radical Industrial Union Opposes Austerity

Central labor confederations do not make policy alone. Regardless of the political and economic pressures to which they may be subjected, they cannot necessarily count on the automatic support of other parts of organized labor. Strategic priorities and policy orientations may not be identical at all levels of union organization. If in addition subconfederal levels enjoy sufficient independence that their policy orientations may actually matter for organizational behavior generally, national confederations may be forced to attend to their reactions even as they seek to speak for organized labor as a whole.

Among Italy's industrial unions, the Federazione Lavoratori Metalmeccanici was the largest and most powerful. It also acted as the internal mouthpiece for dissent over the adoption of policies of wage restraint. This chapter explores the ways the metalworkers sought to delegitimize moderation and examines their effectiveness in doing so. I argue that the FLM's policy orientation was a product of its own logic of organizational behavior, or the knotting of strategy and structure that defines both how the organization typically behaves and how it understands its distinctive mission and identity. In later chapters, I substantiate more fully claims made here about the relationship between the national FLM's logic of organizational behavior and its provincial organizations. For the moment, I offer some provisional arguments about the importance of patterns of organizational reproduction in fixing the policy orientations of the national FLM. The analysis offered in this chapter also begins to provide the evidence necessary to demonstrate that neither rank-and-file pressure nor the partisanship of union officials accurately accounts for union policy orientations.

Introducing the Metalworkers

In 1982 the three confederations boasted a total of some 6,900,000 active members, with overall unionization at 46 percent and industrial unionization at 48 percent.[1] The metalworkers' federation was the largest single union in each parent confederation, together claiming a total of nearly 1,000,000 members (FIOM-CGIL, 526,850; FIM-CISL, 296,460; UILM-UIL, 141,014),[2] or fully a third of all industrial union members in Italy. Unfortunately, although union membership figures are relatively reliable, government statistics on the size of the work force by industry are not, making it difficult to estimate union density with much accuracy. Unionization in the metalworking industries was probably over 50 percent (see table 15; p. 176).

As the largest, most powerful union federation in the country, the FLM has historically played a significant, often decisive, role in influencing confederal decisions. Although the metalworkers' weakened market position in the 1980s meant the FLM was no longer able to directly challenge the supremacy of the Federazione Unitaria, its continuing resistance to austerity policies severely hampered confederal dealings with the state. The FLM undercut the authority of the Federazione Unitaria. Initially, the metalworkers effectively prevented the emergence of an incomes policy; later, when one had become unavoidable, they ensured that it would be largely ineffective.

The FLM's consistent opposition to policies of wage moderation was argued using classically radical rhetoric. Above all, the federation was concerned to protect a nonelectoral and direct strategy for social change, one driven by shop-floor militancy. Under national unity, the FLM opposed austerity with little external support and against the pressures of the PCI. Under the subsequent center-left government, its dissent was encouraged by the PCI, despite the party's long-standing suspicion of a union it considered irresponsible and unduly radical in orientation. In both contexts, the FLM's opposition was viewed with disfavor by the three con-

1. Reported in Guido Romagnoli, "Sindacalizzazione e rappresentanza," in *Le relazioni sindacali in Italia: rapporto 1982–83*, ed. Guido Baglioni, Marina Camonico, and Ettore Santi, Centro di Studi Sociali e Sindacali (Rome: Edizioni Lavoro, 1984), 213–14, tables 2 and 3.

2. Reported in Claudio Pontacolone, "I sindacati confederali: la Cgil," 222, table 2; Marco Carcano and Corrado Squarzon, "I sindacati confederali: la Cisl," 232, table 3; and Piero Bonifazi, "I sindacati confederali: la Uil," 244, table 1, all in Baglioni, Camonico, and Santi, *Relazioni sindacali in Italia*.

federations, which would have preferred a more domesticated metalworkers' federation.

The FLM's opposition to austerity stemmed from the organization's need to retain internal organizational integrity, coherence, and legitimacy—to protect its logic of organizational behavior and mechanisms of reproduction. The almost unique structure of the union encouraged its historically radical inclinations, which by the mid-1970s had become largely self-perpetuating and autonomous. Above all, the FLM had a strong interest in retaining the politicization and militancy it embodied so strongly during the hot autumn. Without wanting to caricature the federation, I see its ideology as strongly reminiscent of nineteenth century syndicalism, which historian Eric Hobsbawm recently summarized as an attitude that

> included hostility not only to the capitalist boss but to any bureaucracy, public, private or trade unionist, the belief (in G. D. H. Cole's words) that "the producer should have the fullest possible share in the control of the conditions under which he works" and a wish to substitute direct industrial action for politics, unions for parties. The technique relied on preferably spontaneous militancy in direct industrial action, a fight with the gloves off. Any means of effective pressure, i.e. of hurting where it hurt the adversary most, must be used. . . . This was rationalized into the thesis that workers must turn the capitalist's methods against them [*sic*].[3]

Wedded to this radical vision of social change, the FLM represented Italy's most extreme case of a union prepared to act as if orthodox politics and political parties were of only marginal importance. The union tended to behave as a social movement and as if unionism could outdo partisan politics in expressing working-class demands to the political system. And it continued to articulate a radical ideology even as rank-and-file militancy waned and it became increasingly clear that much of the federation's constituency had become more moderate than its leadership. The federation was driven to protect its own logic of organizational behavior not because its officials were ideologues (though to some degree they were), but because ideology had become a critical element in organizational reproduction.

3. Eric Hobsbawm, "The 1970s: Syndicalism without Syndicalists?" (1979), reprinted in his *Worlds of Labour: Further Studies in the History of Labour* (London: Weidenfeld and Nicolson, 1984), 273–74.

The FLM's Response to Austerity

The FLM's opposition to moderation was manifest during the initial adoption of an austerity policy by the Federazione Unitaria in 1978. Resistance was especially effective in the phase before the formal adoption of the EUR policy. This is apparent when we compare the original document written by the Secretariat of the Federazione Unitaria in early January with its subsequent version, approved by the Comitato Direttivo (CD) of the CGIL-CISL-UIL on 13–14 January 1978. The CD is composed of representatives of all affiliated unions as well as union representatives from various geographic areas. The document's critical section was entitled "Cost of Labor." In the Secretariat's original version, this section contained four paragraphs and ran just over a page, or about 260 words.[4] In the revised version that came out of the CD—designed for approval by the rank and file—the same section ran to seven paragraphs. Although the original four were unaltered, an additional three paragraphs had been added as a result of the Secretariat's meeting with other levels of union organization.[5] The section promised that the union movement would exercise wage restraint. But whereas in the original version few conditions were imposed, the revised version had become deliberately ambiguous. The Secretariat's initial recommendations had simply spoken of the need for wage restraint to lower labor costs and to allow the government more complete prior information on wages to aid in policymaking. It had also mentioned that the union wished to safeguard its various bargaining levels (including factory bargaining) and to defend the scala mobile. The amended version, however, added a paragraph in which the union movement reiterated its commitment to a "general strategy, which centers on the growth of employment, improving working conditions, the unification of the labor market, [and] continuation of an egalitarian line," thereby articulating multiple and contradictory goals. It also added a paragraph arguing that "the active participation of workers in the definition of bargaining demands, [and] the full safeguarding of all levels of bargaining are the fundamental instruments for a fully responsible union policy." Finally, a paragraph was inserted in which the union proposed that subnational wage bargaining be extended to public employees.[6] If the Secre-

4. Secretariat CGIL-CISL-UIL, untitled internal document courtesy of UIL, Rome.

5. Federazione CGIL-CISL-UIL, "Proposte per una svolta di politica economica e di sviluppo civile e democratico," Roma, 13–14 gennaio 1978, internal document courtesy of UIL, Rome.

6. Ibid., 22–23.

tariat had hoped to gain control over wage bargaining in order to legitimate both the Communist party and its own role in central negotiations, it had clearly failed. Resistance ensured that the union movement remained committed to wage bargaining at multiple levels, to rank-and-file participation in decision making, and to myriad contradictory general goals. Dissenters effectively prevented central leadership from insulating itself from the claims of the rank and file, thereby undermining confederal authority. Radicals did not threaten rank-and-file rebellion: rather, they simply forced the confederations to admit that they could not necessarily deliver rank-and-file compliance to wage restraint.

Dissenters continued their attempts to alter confederal recommendations, forcing the CGIL-CISL-UIL to repudiate formally any commitment to an incomes policy. Although there were only 12 negative votes and 103 abstentions among the 1,457 delegates who attended the final EUR assembly in 1978,[7] the presentation of over sixty amendments helps indicate the depth of dissent.[8] Before the assembly, the FLM had taken a strong stand against the confederal austerity recommendations with the approval, at its own Comitato Direttivo on 23 and 24 January, of what was generally considered a rival document.[9] The federation formally took issue with the Federazione Unitaria's proposals for the public deficit, taxes and public

7. The debate was summarized in Federazione Unitaria CGIL-CISL-UIL, "Il dibattito," Assemblea nazionale dei Consigli Generale e dei delegati, Roma, 13–14 febbraio 1978, *Rassegna Sindacale* 24 (23 February 1978), special insert, x–xviii. The full minutes of the assembly are available in the archives of the CGIL (Rome) as *Assemblea Nazionale dei Consigli Generali e dei Delegati*, Roma, 13–14 febbraio 1978, unnumbered shelf.

8. There are two ways union meetings in Italy typically handle amendments. One is to take proposals directly from the floor and allow them to be discussed in the full assembly. The second is to require the presentation of amendments in writing to a small group authorized by the chair. Amendments are then reworked by the chair and their proponents until a formulation acceptable to both parties is reached. This version is then presented to the full assembly for final approval. Using this procedure, amendments are only rarely presented to the full assembly that are not recommended for approval by the chair. In the EUR assembly, amendments were handled in this second fashion; by the time they reached the open assembly, they already embodied compromises. For this reason, most of the conflicts generated by the document were hammered out somewhere in the corridors between the Secretariat's office and that of the FLM, out of the public eye. Interviews no. 25, national CISL (Secretariat), 16 June 1980; no. 22, national CGIL-affiliated industrial union (Secretariat), 29 May 1980; and no. 31, national FLM (Secretariat), 26 June 1980.

9. The opening address of the FLM's Secretariat at the Comitato Direttivo of 23–24 January, along with the official concluding document, were originally published as FLM, "Il contributo della FLM alla strategia del movimento sindacale," *FLM Notizie*, no. 136 (2 February 1978), special insert, i–xxxi. The document was reprinted in Stefano Bevacqua and Giuseppe Turani, *La svolta del '78: il sindacato e il Pci dall'intervista di Lama alla Conferenza operaia di Napoli* (Milan: Feltrinelli, 1978).

rates, housing, labor mobility, and collective bargaining, especially some forms of wage containment. The two issues that elicited the most heated responses were labor mobility and wage containment, the cornerstones of the Federazione Unitaria's proposals. Challenging the policy's moderating stand, the FLM called repeatedly for the increased mobilization of the industrial working class in order to guarantee a measure of force behind the union's demands for employment and investments. The pertinent issue that received most attention was just this or, as it was referred to at the time, the issue of a "social contract": local terminology for an incomes policy. The FLM's most insistent criticism of EUR revolved around the policy's implications for the future use of industrial conflict. "In no case," warned the FLM's national Secretariat, "can this platform [EUR] be considered the premise for either an explicit or an implicit social contract."[10] And the document approved by the FLM read:

> In no case can this platform [i.e., EUR] be considered a regulating framework [*accordo quadro*] or a proposal for a social contract; on the contrary, it should be defined as a platform for mass political and social struggle such that the "guarantees" demanded by the union [of the government] will actually be conquered. . . .
>
> This excludes any proposal for the centralization of national contract renewals or for an incomes policy and calls for the consolidation and further development of articulated bargaining in the next few years, without which the general goals of the union's strategy will not be concretely realizable.[11]

On this key issue the FLM won an impressive victory. Whereas neither the document initially presented by the CGIL-CISL-UIL's Secretariat nor that amended at the meeting of the Federazione Unitaria's CD in January had made any mention of a "social contract," the final document adopted in February explicitly rejected one.[12] Thanks to the metalworkers, Italian organized labor found itself in the ambiguous position of promising wage restraint while ruling out an incomes policy.

The FLM's criticisms of the insufficient attention to militancy and industrial action in the EUR strategy continued unabated over the next few months. "EUR," argued the general secretary of the FIOM in June, "is

10. Enzo Mattina, "Relazione," in FLM, "Contributo della FLM alla strategia del movimento sindacale," vi.

11. FLM, "Documento finale," in ibid., xiv–xv.

12. For the final wording adopted in February, see Federazione Unitaria CGIL-CISL-UIL, "Per una svolta di politica economica e di sviluppo civile e democratico," il documento definitivo approvato dall'Assemblea nazionale, Roma, 13–14 febbrario 1978, *Rassegna Sindacale* 24 (23 February 1978), special insert, xx.

the opposite of renunciation and cannot be interpreted by anyone . . . as if it . . . were not a platform of struggle."[13] Another FLM representative warned, in a similar vein, "The vagueness and indeterminacy of present proposals for union initiatives threaten the EUR policy less with not being understood by the workers than with not being translated into concrete, articulated actions of conflict. . . . There is the risk it will be experienced by the workers as a kind of code of union behavior."[14] Finally, a national leader of the FIM polemicized: "The strategy of EUR is a strategy of struggle," adding, "The FLM does not share other 'readings' that are given of the strategy approved at EUR, such as those by management that tend to propose the role of guaranteeing capital accumulation to the union, or those who push for a complete, self-critical rereading of the past ten years of workers' and union struggle."[15] Leaders of all three metalworkers' unions conspicuously and deliberately repudiated those from the confederations who wanted EUR to represent a renunciation of the militant, conflict-oriented strategy had characterized the Italian union movement since 1968. "The improvement of conditions for the employed work force," the general secretary of the CGIL had explained, in a notorious interview given just before the policy's adoption, "must take second place." EUR, he had argued, "is a fundamental shift [in union strategy]. Since 1969, the union has placed its bets on the rigidity of the labor force. . . . [But] we have now realized that an economic system cannot tolerate independent variables. . . . [T]he workers and their union have maintained that wages were an independent variable. . . . [But] this was nonsense, because in an open economy all variables are dependent on each other."[16] A few months later, a Communist leader of the FIOM retorted: "The experience of '68 is at present greatly discussed: . . . '68, '69, and the struggles that were conducted are represented as a parenthesis in the history of our country, as if it were possible to put ten years of national class history between parentheses; a history, therefore, to abandon in some measure and certainly to self-criticize ourselves severely for. . . . [But] without these conquests [of the past ten years], the strategy of EUR would not have been possible."[17] Thus, argued the federation, only by

13. Pio Galli, "Le conclusioni," II Convegno nazionale di organizzazione FLM, Rimini, 15–17 giugno 1978, *FLM Notizie,* no. 146 (12 June 1978), 32.

14. A. Izzo, "Le proposte per una nuova struttura organizzativa," ibid., 28.

15. Rino Caviglioli, "Relazione," ibid., 4–5.

16. Luciano Lama, "I sacrifici che chiediamo agli operai," interview by Eugenio Scalfari, *La Repubblica*, 24 January 1978, 3.

17. Claudio Sabattini, "Intervento," in FIOM-CGIL, *Atti del consiglio nazionale della FIOM-CGIL*, Firenze, 3–4 maggio 1978 (Rome: FIOM, [1978]), 79.

drawing on the strategy of radical militancy for which it had become known during the past two decades could any future gains be won. Rather than passivity and moderation, the FLM insisted that the union movement increase its use of conflict at all levels, above all because "our initiative at the factory level remains the central point from which consensus and support derive."[18] Criticizing the Federazione Unitaria's turn to the increasing moderation of centralized bargaining, the FLM proposed that organized labor retain instead its grass-roots orientation, one aimed at direct social change using mass mobilization.

Over the course of events, the national leadership of the FLM acted to channel and broker the opposition that arose from other industrial unions, especially textiles and chemicals, as well as from union offices in industrialized northern provinces. During the EUR assembly itself, the national Secretariat of the FLM acted as a "clearinghouse" for the discussion of amendments to the confederal document.[19] Before the assembly, the FLM had organized dissent through the document promulgated at its Comitato Direttivo. It intended that these recommendations be presented simultaneously with the confederal document in all factory assemblies in the metalworking industries; as the first national expression of internal union dissent, the FLM's recommendations also served as the model for other industrial unions wary of the confederal proposals.[20]

Despite its attempts to modify the confederal proposals, the FLM did not launch an open attack on wage restraint per se. Its criticisms were tempered by tactical considerations and also by some internal differences of opinion. Within the organization's national Secretariat, reactions to EUR ranged from outright disavowal to lukewarm support, though the range of reactions within the Secretariat was not classifiable by component (FIM-FIOM-UILM), by political affiliation (Communist vs. non-Communist), or by how members actually voted at the national assembly. Owing to the PCI's proximity to national power, it would have been impossible, for instance, for a Communist unionist bitterly opposed to EUR even to

18. Pio Galli, "Relazione introduttiva," in ibid., 19.

19. Interview no. 22, national CGIL-affiliated industrial union (Secretariat), 29 May 1980.

20. For examples of criticisms modeled on those advanced by the national FLM, see, for instance, FLM Bologna, "Ordine del giorno approvato dal Consiglio Generale FLM di Bologna (stralcio)," *AUSI* 8 (8–9 February 1978), 3–4, and the reactions of the national joint textiles federation; FULTA, "Documento conclusivo del Comitato Direttivo nazionale della FULTA (24–25 gennaio 1978)," *AUSI* 8 (25–26 January 1978), 3–6. See also "Due esempi di riforma del documentone sindacale," *Il Manifesto*, 12 February 1978, 2, which covers the reactions of two metalworking factory assemblies. Finally, see CGIL-CISL-UIL Milano, "L'assemblea dei delegati Cgil-Cisl-Uil di Milano: il documento finale," reprinted in Bevacqua and Turani, *Svolta del '78*.

have abstained at the national assembly, let alone to have voted against austerity's adoption. His opposition was necessarily handled "in house."[21] Indeed, the Communist component within the national FLM effectively split in its reactions to EUR: reactions ranged from acute disapproval to moderate skepticism. Partisanship notwithstanding, the national leaderships of the FIM, the FIOM, and the UILM managed to produce a joint document critical of the Federazione Unitaria's proposal. Dissent and resistance in turn set limits on confederal strategy: aside from the alterations already discussed, the FLM prevented the confederations from acquiring a formal role in vetting wage demands in the 1979 national labor contracts, a proposal urged mainly by the CGIL and subsequently dropped.

The FLM's response to the confederal proposals for an austerity policy in early 1978 represents the clearest, most extreme case of dissent by a national union. In 1982 and 1983 as well, the federation played an important role regarding the Federazione Unitaria's proposals for modifying the scala mobile. The nine-point document authored by the Federazione CGIL-CISL-UIL had been drawn up only with considerable difficulty. The three confederations had each elaborated separate recommendations, which they subsequently found difficult to reconcile.[22] Final agreement proved possible only after major industrial unions, the FLM among them, reached compromises that the Federazione Unitaria could then emulate.[23] Even so, the FLM remained critical of the nine-point confederal document, subsequently promulgating an alternative five-point document to be presented simultaneously with the Federazione Unitaria's in the upcoming barrage of factory assemblies.[24] In it, the federation insisted that any reform of the scala mobile take place *simultaneously* with tax reforms, thereby reducing the cost of labor while *automatically* protecting the real incomes of lower-paid workers.

The FLM's goals were twofold. Ideally, the federation would have

21. One Communist in the FLM noted, for instance, that his own reactions to EUR had shifted between January and February 1978 from principled opposition to a slightly more moderate critical stand, presumably both in response to party pressures and in an attempt to reach a compromise with non-Communist but less oppositional members of the FLM's Secretariat.

22. For a summary of the three positions, see Lauralba Bellardi and Elena Pisani, eds., "Rassegna della contrattazione," *Economia e Lavoro* 16 (October–December 1982), 129–40.

23. The FLM's joint proposals are available as FLM, "Comitato direttivo Flm: documento su occupazione, fisco, contratti, riforma di salario," Comitato Direttivo, Roma, 8–9 ottobre 1982, *FLM Notizie*, n.s. 1 (15 October 1982), 5–6.

24. FLM, "Comitato direttivo Flm (Roma, 26 ottobre): documento conclusivo," *FLM Notizie*, n.s. 1 (30 October-15 November 1982), 3–4.

wished to prevent tripartite bargaining altogether. But the Confindustria had blocked negotiations to renew national labor contracts, and the federation's first and principal goal was therefore to accede to whatever was necessary to reopen national contract bargaining. Second, however, the FLM wanted this at the lowest possible cost. It sought to force the Federazione Unitaria to commit itself explicitly and in advance of national negotiations over wage indexation to a full and automatic protection of real working-class incomes: to set boundaries on the concessions the confederations would be able to offer. In fact, the thousands of factory assemblies that followed frequently endorsed amendments along these lines. The three confederations were however at loggerheads over how to reconcile the various amendments raised in the course of the assemblies. The compromise document that emerged following the consultazione incorporated the FLM's proposal regarding the simultaneity of tax reform with modifications of the scala mobile but was still somewhat ambiguous regarding some automatic mechanism for protecting lower-paid workers against changes in the system of wage indexation.[25] Nonetheless, the FLM's position, mirroring that articulated at the time by the PCI, hampered the Federazione Unitaria in dealing with the state and business, forcing it to negotiate from a more rigid position than it would probably otherwise have assumed. The eventual outcome of these negotiations effected simultaneous changes in the tax structure, the scala mobile, and family allowances, effectively protecting workers' real incomes exactly along the lines proposed by the FLM. Finally, negotiations for national labor contracts were eventually reopened thanks to the Scotti accord, although the accord limited both the quantity and the timing of maximum wage increases for industrial sectors. The FLM's dissent was, in short, relatively effective in keeping the confederations more attentive to the impact of wage moderation on workers' incomes than might otherwise have been the case.

Rank-and-File Responses to Austerity

Evidence shows that the FLM consistently opposed austerity policies even in the absence of significant rank-and-file opposition. Although there is little information available on rank-and-file sentiment during the pas-

25. For the final document approved, see Federazione CGIL-CISL-UIL, "Il testo definitivo della piattaforma," Direttivo unitario, Roma, 15–16 novembre 1982, *Conquiste del Lavoro*, supplement 22 to vol. 35 (22 November 1982), 10–13.

sage of EUR, in interviews national officials—including those from the FLM itself—were unanimous in the opinion that the rank and file was favorably inclined to the adoption of austerity, when its views were known at all.[26] Even EUR's fiercest critics did not claim that their opposition had been generated by rank-and-file protest or even that it was particularly representative of rank-and-file opinion. The 7,000 to 8,000 factory assemblies supposedly held to elicit rank-and-file reactions merely served, as one unionist put it, for a "registration of agreement with or dissent over something that had already been decided."[27] And a good number of those interviewed reported that the confederal estimates of the number of factory assemblies conducted were extremely inflated and that far fewer had actually been held.[28] Where factory assemblies were conducted, the confederal document was invariably approved, usually with near unanimity. Where they were not, no loud cries were forthcoming demanding meetings with national labor leaders to hear out the rank and file.

In the case of the modification of the scala mobile, a good deal of evidence exists regarding rank-and-file responses, but it is not easily interpreted. The CGIL, CISL, and UIL together organized nearly 34,000 factory assemblies across firms that together employed more than 4 million workers, or nearly a third of Italy's entire labor force.[29] Of the potential 4 million participants, however, only about half attended the assemblies, and of these, about 15 percent either abstained or did not vote, often leaving the assembly before the vote took place. As a result, only 12 percent of Italy's labor force actually voted on the Federazione Unitaria's recommendations, and only 44 percent voted even in plants where assemblies were held. Even if we take as representative the results only from firms where assemblies were held, assuming that it was logistically impossible to hold assemblies elsewhere, the outcome is difficult to assess owing to the low level of participation in the voting and because it is difficult to know how to interpret nonparticipation.

Still, of those attending the assemblies, some 69 percent voted in favor

26. Interview no. 21, ex-national FLM (Secretariat), 29 May 1980. This finding was repeatedly confirmed, both explicitly and by omission.

27. Interview no. 36, national FLM (Secretariat), 24 July 1980.

28. Interviews no. 25, national CISL (Secretariat), 16 June 1980; no. 23, national FLM (Secretariat), 30 May 1980; no. 22, national CGIL-affiliated industrial union (Secretariat), 29 May 1980; and no. 21, ex-national FLM (Secretariat), 29 May 1980.

29. Data used in this section on the assemblies are reported by Lorenzo Speranza, "Le consultazioni," in Baglioni, Camonico, and Santi, *Relazioni sindacali in Italia*. Where these are considered in relation to the size of the labor force, I have used ISTAT, *Annuario statistico italiano 1983*, 295, table 297, which gives figures on employees (*occupati dipendenti*) for 1982.

of the nine-point confederal document, while 32 percent voted against, abstained, or did not vote. The figure for those who endorsed the confederations' recommendations climbs to 77 percent considered in relation to the number of persons who actually voted. Of those who did vote on the Federazione Unitaria's nine-point document, over a third (37 percent) also voted in favor of amendments calling for the automatic defense of the incomes of lower-paid workers and in favor of the simultaneity of various political economic maneuvers (34 percent). Put another way, of those who voted, only about 40 percent actually approved the nine-point document as it stood.[30] Although no single amendment obtained a majority among voters, the pressure for amending the recommendations in line with the FLM's proposals was therefore significant: the federation successfully generated divisions in rank-and-file reactions.

Dissent was especially pronounced in the metalworking sector, where 44 percent of those who voted endorsed the FLM's alternative five-point document. In this sector, only a quarter of voters approved the Federazione Unitaria's recommendations (compared with the three-quarters approval rate generated across the economy as a whole) and fully one-third voted openly against them.[31] In other words, over half (53 percent) of those Italian workers who voted against the Federazione Unitaria's recommendations were concentrated in the metalworking industries; fully 73 percent of all industrial workers voting against the recommendations were metalworkers.[32] Given that only about a third of industrial employees are engaged in the metalworking industries, the results reveal the success of the FLM in eliciting a disproportionate measure of rank-and-file dissent.

Although the FLM successfully generated far more mass opposition to austerity in 1982 than was visible in other sectors, the consultazione results should not be overinterpreted. They cannot be taken to mean, for instance, that metalworkers are inherently more radical than employees in other Italian industries.[33] Rather, the FLM deliberately offered its constit-

30. That is, of those who voted, about 77 percent approved the document. However, if we subtract the 37 percent of votes also approving amendments on the automatic defense of incomes of lower paid workers, we find that only 40 percent approved the document as it stood. Repeating the same procedure for the 34 percent who endorsed amendments on simultaneity produces a similar result. This procedure was suggested by Speranza, "Consultazioni," 474.

31. Data reported in Sandro Bianchi, "I risultati della consultazione," *FLM Notizie*, n.s. 1 (30 November 1982), 14, table 1.

32. Votes by sector—agriculture, industry, tertiary—were reported in Paola Cerretti, "Le consultazioni di massa del 1982," *Quaderni di Rassegna Sindacale* 21 (September–October 1983), 204, table 4.

33. Corroborating evidence is provided by Renato Mannheimer, Mario Rodriguez, and

uency an opportunity to express a greater diversity of opinion by presenting alternative recommendations seeking to modify those of the Federazione Unitaria. However, the FLM could legitimately claim that the results of its assemblies were more representative than those held in other sectors, thanks to the fact that the federation reached a larger share of its potential constituency than other industrial unions. Overall, workplace assemblies potentially involved just over 4 million workers, or 28 percent of Italy's employees; this is the proportion of the work force employed in plants where assemblies were conducted. In industry, the potential constituency was 36 percent of the work force. But fully 76 percent of all metalworkers was concentrated in plants where assemblies were held. Thirty-five percent of all Italian metalworkers voted in the assemblies, whereas only 12 percent of the entire work force voted. The FLM's remarkable capillary penetration of its sector lent the organization considerable credibility in expressing dissent over the Federazione Unitaria's recommendations. It mobilized its organization against austerity, reaching out to its mass base and channeling opposition.

Nonetheless, there is evidence that the FLM's position was more radical than that of its rank and file. The organization's Comitato Direttivo approved its own five-point document by a majority of 89 percent, compared with the 44 percent of metalworkers who voted in favor of it during factory assemblies.[34] These figures are not truly comparable, of course, since the dynamics of decision making differ considerably between a relatively small, elite group striving for consensus and the mass of the working population. But they indicate that the FLM's radical, dissenting leadership coalition was more compact in its reactions to austerity than its rank and file. The FLM's alternative proposals were not endorsed by a majority even in its own industries. As later chapters will show in detail, however, the FLM was successful in generating substantial opposition in large industry, where "the position [of the confederations] was not approved"[35] and in using the dissent evident there to convince the confederations that modifications of their proposals were vital. The FLM

Chiara Sebastiani, *Gli operai comunisti* (Rome: Riuniti, 1979), 133–34. In an analysis of the political attitudes of Communist working-class activists, based on a survey conducted in early 1978, they find no significant differences according to industrial sector (e.g., textiles vs. metals).

34. The FLM's document received seven negative votes and seven abstentions at the meeting of the CD on 26 October 1982, although the total number of persons attending is not reported. The votes are reported in FLM, "Comitato direttivo Flm (Roma, 26 ottobre): documento conclusivo," 4. The full CD is officially composed of 125 members.

35. Interview no. 128, ex-national FLM (Secretariat), 7 January 1984.

encouraged greater democratic participation in assessing austerity than other unions, but—again, as later chapters will show in more detail—mass participatory democracy does not necessarily entail a more accurate representation of rank-and-file opinion; indeed, the FLM's democratic council structure may have had the effect of systematically distorting constituency opinion even, if not especially, in large industry. Even so, the relative success of the federation in orchestrating mass dissent over austerity served to impress upon the whole of organized labor the existence of deep divisions within the industrial working class over austerity recommendations and thus to limit the Federazione Unitaria's freedom of action in negotiating austerity. And as one confederal source remarked, this is just what the FLM had intended, since amendments "weren't amendments but rather a political challenge [*un discorso politico*]," largely intended to delegitimize austerity policies as a general strategy.[36] Another confederal leader confessed that when workers voted to allow the scala mobile to be modified only on certain conditions—conditions imposed by the FLM—"This was a 'yes' more similar to a 'no.' "[37]

Explaining the Federation's Opposition to Moderation

Why is the FLM as radical as it is? What drove it time and again to contest incomes policies and the increasingly moderate policy orientation of the Federazione Unitaria? I argue below that the federation's organizational logic of behavior—those structures of organizational reproduction that knot strategy and structure into a coherent whole—was one that could not sanction the centralization of wage bargaining, the depression of industrial militancy, and the constriction of union goals to those demanded by external political and economic conditions. The FLM sought to protect its own autonomy and legitimacy, and it was strong enough to disrupt the central confederations in doing so.

Size and Leadership

Traditionally, the three metalworkers' unions have played the role of pilot for the whole of Italian organized labor, spearheading agreements on

36. Interview no. 125, national CISL (Secretariat), 4 January 1984.

37. Interview no. 129, ex-national UIL (Secretariat), 10 January 1984. Both these remarks came from non-Communist union leaders and are thus doubly reliable, given that in 1982 non-Communists had the least interest in admitting the existence of internal dissent to incomes policies.

wages and other issues. Their importance has derived in part from their sheer size. In 1982, for instance, 24 percent of Italy's industrial work force was concentrated in the metalworking industries, and this represents over 10 percent of the country's entire work force.[38] Since they account for such a large proportion of Italian industrial employment, it is not surprising that the metalworking industries have exercised a large influence within organized labor.

But size alone cannot account for the disproportionate influence traditionally exercised by the FIM, the FIOM, and the UILM. These unions have, for instance, been central to union career patterns generally. As of 1984, all three confederal general secretaries—Luciano Lama of the CGIL, Pierre Carniti of the CISL, and Giorgio Benvenuto of the UIL—had come out of their respective metalworkers' federations, where each had first risen to prominence. While no study of union career patterns is available, it is reasonable to surmise that the metalworkers have consistently provided a disproportionate share of local as well as national leadership both for other category unions and for the three confederations.

A second indicator of the disproportionate influence exercised by the three metalworkers' unions resides in their ability to recruit intellectuals onto their staffs, either as full-time functionaries or as external consultants. Adequate data on this have not been released by the confederations, but one measure is the importance outside intellectuals played in leadership training for the FIM-CISL during the 1950s and early 1960s at the CISL's educational institute, the Centro Studi di Firenze.[39] The attraction—indeed, fascination—the metalworkers' federations have exercised on intellectuals has allowed them to deploy leadership groups of exceptional capability and stature, thereby reinforcing their already important position in union leadership recruitment.

Factory Councils

If the metalworkers' unions have tended to exercise a disproportionate influence in Italian organized labor, this has come about through their

38. Calculated from ISTAT, *Annuario statistico italiano, 1983*, 295, table 297.

39. On the Centro Studi and its significance in shaping leadership attitudes in the FIM-CISL, see Silvio Costantini, "La formazione del gruppo dirigente della Cisl (1950–1968)," in *Analisi della CISL: fatti e giudizi di un'esperienza sindacale*, ed. Guido Baglioni, Centro Studi Nazionale Cisl and Centro di Studi Sociali e Sindacali, *Trent'anni di storia sindacale*, 2 vols. (Rome: Edizioni Lavoro, 1980), vol. 1; Benedetto De Cesaris, "La scuola CISL di Firenze negli anni '50," *Quaderni di Rassegna Sindacale* 10 (July–August 1971), 80–94; and Ettore Santi, "Formazione e organizzazione: il caso del Centro Studi della Cisl," in

constant pursuit of strategic innovation. Although a full history of the Italian metalworkers' unions, and especially of the joint FLM, has yet to be written,[40] these organizations have long played the role of strategic avant-garde within Italian organized labor. Most important for present purposes has been the stress laid on decentralized shop-floor representation, namely the consiglio di fabbrica. Established principally during and after the hot autumn, the CdF are a comparatively unusual form of union organization. The strong identification of the FLM with CdFs throughout the 1970s and into the 1980s is a cardinal feature of the federation, crucial to understanding the organization's proclivity to conflict, autonomy from the confederations, and reluctance to embrace austerity recommendations. As I shall document more thoroughly in a moment, factory councils are particularly prone to engage in conflict over issues linked to working conditions and the organization of work. They are the organizational linchpins of the radically democratic use of mass industrial conflict for a highly politicized and decentralized union strategy; they provide the concrete institutional mechanisms for the FLM's strategy of direct action aimed at general social change.

The first collection of factory accords regulating delegates, dating from late 1969, clearly indicates their original strength in the metalworking industries. Just one-half of then existing, pertinent, and known accords had been signed in metalworking plants, and over 80 percent of the more than 260,000 employees represented by delegates worked in the metalworking industries.[41] It would be no exaggeration to say that the delegates and council structures that emerged during the hot autumn were typically

---

Sindacato e organizzazione, ed. Giovanni Gasparini (Milan: F. Angeli, 1978). The Centro is generally credited with providing a new generation of conflict-oriented, noncollaborationist leaders to the FIM as well as other industrial unions affiliated with the CISL.

40. To the best of my knowledge, only one empirical study of the FLM has been conducted since its foundation in 1972. It deals with internal decision making during the drawing up of the bargaining platform for the union's 1972 CCNL renewal. See Tatiana Pipan and Dario Salerni, *Il sindacato come soggetto di equilibrio: ricerca sulla politica contrattuale della FLM* (Milan: Feltrinelli, 1975). A history of the FIM-CISL in the 1960s is Gian Primo Cella, Bruno Manghi, and Paola Piva, *Un sindacato italiano negli anni sessanta: la FIM-CISL dall'associazione alla classe* (Bari: DeDonato, 1972).

41. See Eugenio Guidi, ed., "Analisi e valutazione degli accordi sui delegati," *Quaderni di Rassegna Sindacale* 7 (December 1969), 61. Accords regulating delegates had been signed in the metalworking, textile, chemical, and food industries. A large majority of the seventy-eight plants involved were in the north and center of Italy. Similar findings concerning the preponderance of delegates in the metalworking sector were found by a union inquiry conducted in the early 1970s, reported in Gianni Salvarani and Alberto Bonifazi, *Le nuove strutture del sindacato: origini, esperienze e prospettive del movimento dei delegati*

found in the metalworking industries and that the image of the delegate has since remained that of the archetypal assembly-line worker, in his blue work suit and on strike.

Although initially concentrated in northern metalworking plants, factory councils and delegates became extremely widespread after receiving the endorsement of the Federazione Unitaria. Between 1968 and 1970 they were successfully established in hundreds of Italian firms, especially large northern metalworking plants. With both organizational and juridical recognition forthcoming, the CdFs quickly became relatively stable and legitimate stuctures. In 1972 there were close to 1,000 factory councils in Italy, with just under 10,100 delegates, according to confederal sources. By 1977 there were over 32,000 councils and more than 200,000 delegates elected.[42]

The factory council and delegate structure is unique, both with respect to Italian history and internationally.[43] "Fusing union participation and bargaining power in a joint evolution from below, modeled on the organization of work, delegates and Councils overcome . . . the dualism between representation and bargaining,"[44] as Accornero describes it. The council is simultaneously the recognized union bargaining agent on the shop floor and the most decentralized level of rank-and-file representation, an organ for which all workers, whether union members or not, are invited to vote. Classically, its electoral system maps the productive process: one delegate is elected to represent each "homogeneous work group" or technological segment of the productive cycle.[45] The adoption of the CdFs entailed the displacement of other shop-floor structures and decentralized the focus of industrial and political working-class action in Italy.

---

in Italia (Milan: F. Angeli, 1973), 74–75. More than half of all known delegates across seventy-eight provinces in the manufacturing industries were in metalworking industries.

42. Federazione Unitaria CGIL-CISL-UIL (uffici organizzazione), "Duecentomila delegati la forza dell'unità e della democrazia sindacale," *Rassegna Sindacale* 23 (2 June 1977), 60.

43. Alessandro Pizzorno, "Fra azione di classe e sistemi corporativi: osservazioni comparate sulle rappresentanze del lavoro nei paesi capitalistici avanzati," in *Problemi del movimento sindacale in Italia, 1943–1973*, vol. 16 of *Annali Fondazione G. Feltrinelli, 1974–1975*, ed. Aris Accornero (Milan: Feltrinelli, 1976).

44. Aris Accornero, "Le strutture di base negli anni '50," *Quaderni di Rassegna Sindacale* 12 (July–August 1974), 121.

45. See Sergio Garavini, "Strutture dell'autonomia operaia sul luogo di lavoro," *Quaderni di Rassegna Sindacale* 7 (December 1969), 19–27. The metalworkers' unions had jointly adopted the electoral system based on homogeneous work groups in 1970, when they officially agreed to make the CdF "the joint union structure" at the plant level; FLM, "La mozione unitaria dei metallurgici sui nuovi organismi sindacali: il documento finale," *Rassegna Sindacale* 16 (29 March 1970), 27.

The metalworkers' justification for establishing CdFs was classically radical in its intentions.

> The worker is organized in a section by the boss [*padrone*] in order to produce, but these elements of unity and of organization, which the boss establishes for the goals of production and profit, can also be used by the worker as an element of unity and organization, which serve for his own struggle; and the relationship that the organization of work establishes among workers in a section can also be used by these same workers in a plan of solidarity and unity, for the ends of the class struggle, in such a way that elements of unity and discipline, indispensable for production and profit . . . , can become—section by section—elements of *conscious* unity and discipline among workers for the ends of the class struggle.[46]

In short: "The delegate is such to the extent that he is the expression of a homogeneous work group; that is, he corresponds to the boss's organization of work—*inverted.*"[47] This notion of shop-floor union representation proposes that the organization of work in industry can be turned directly against the capitalist and used for general goals of social change.

For the FLM, the emergence of the CdF signaled an opportunity to build grass-roots antibureaucratic structures particularly adept at bargaining over working conditions while coordinating largely spontaneous industrial militancy aimed at refocusing Italy's political attention on the factory rather than on Parliament. No union has benefited more from the emergence and legitimation of factory councils than the FLM, so strongly identified with their establishment and so resilient in its defense of them. Even into the 1980s, the FLM was known as *il sindacato dei consigli.*

Some evidence exists confirming that delegates, too, tend to understand their own commitments in this way—that their self-definitions as union militants are deeply political—and that they constitute a self-conscious, largely self-selected radically inclined strata of workers. The survey of industrial delegates conducted in Piedmont in the mid-1980s, referred to in chapter 2, found, for instance, that nearly half (46 percent) conceived of their roles in explicitly political terms, as aimed at general social transformation.[48] (The various possible responses are listed on p. 41.) Particularly interesting are the breakdowns according to length of service as a delegate. Delegates first elected before 1970—the hot autumn's dele-

46. Garavini, "Strutture dell'autonomia operaia," 19.

47. Ibid., 21. Emphasis in the original.

48. IRES-CGIL Piemonte, ed., *Delegati in Piemonte: una ricerca in cento fabbriche*, Formazione e cultura FIOM-CGIL Piemonte (Milan: F. Angeli, 1986), 82, table 39.

gates, in other words—indicated political functions as their major task by a margin of two to one (66 percent), whereas fewer than a third (29 percent) of those elected between 1980 and 1983 responded in this way.[49] If we take these answers (the major task of the union delegate is "to contribute to the workers' development in order to change society" or "to contribute to the development of the workers' consciousness of their own conditions of exploitation") as indicative of radical propensities, the data suggest that radical orientations are more pronounced among delegates first elected during the wave of mass mobilization of the hot autumn. And it is just these delegates who tend to be concentrated in executive positions in factory councils and thus to hold particularly powerful positions within shop-floor union bodies.[50] As later chapters will argue in greater detail, the radicalism of the national FLM is partially sustained by the radicalism of its CdFs in major firms.

The Importance of Factory Councils in Articulated Bargaining

The few data available on the workings of consigli di fabbrica eloquently attest to their importance, at least through the mid-1980s. As one observer has noted, "the *delegati*—and through them the rank and file—retain substantial autonomy."[51] Table 4 presents data on bargaining agents for factory accords in the metalworking sector between 1976 and 1978. The findings are based on a limited survey conducted by the peak business association in the sector, the Federazione delle Industrie Meccaniche (Federmeccanica) of its own affiliated firms, and the generalizability of the data is certainly open to question. The results are nonetheless extremely impressive.[52]

49. Intermediate figures were 60 percent for those elected between 1970 and 1974 and 48 percent for those elected between 1975 and 1979. Reported in ibid., 84, table 40.

50. Ibid., 84.

51. Charles Sabel, "The Internal Politics of Trade Unions," in *Organizing Interests in Western Europe: Corporatism, Pluralism, and the Transformation of Politics*, ed. Suzanne D. Berger (Cambridge: Cambridge University Press, 1981), 241.

52. The survey involved an extremely slim proportion of Federmeccanica adherents: from 1 percent to 9 percent per geographic area per year. Excluded entirely are firms not affiliated with the Federmeccanica and, presumably, firms in which no factory bargaining took place. The survey breaks the country into three geographic areas: the northeast, the northwest, and the rest of Italy. See table 4 for details. Because the findings were presented as percentages, it was impossible to reaggregate them nationally. The survey also broke down firms by size: 1–100 employees; 101–200 employees; 201–500 employees; and over 500 employees.

Table 4. Who Bargains: Agents in Metalworking Factory Bargaining, 1976–78 (Percentages)

Agent	Northwest		Northeast		Rest of Italy	
	All[a]	500+[a]	All	500+	All	500+
1976						
National	0	0	0	0	0	0
Provincial or zonal	35	45	40	47	46	67
RSA/CdF	61	45	55	47	54	33
Other	4	10	5	6	0	0
1977						
National	1	3	0	5	4	14
Provincial or zonal	43	50	43	43	45	43
RSA/CdF	54	41	52	38	48	36
Other	2	6	5	14	3	7
1978						
National	0	0	0	0	0	0
Provincial or zonal	42	41	44	43	49	66
RSA/CdF	57	59	52	57	40	33
Other	1	0	4	0	11	0

Source: Courtesy of Federmeccanica, Rome.
Note: Northwest: Piedmont, Valle d'Aosta, Lombardy, and Liguria. Northeast: Trentino Alto-Adige, Veneto, Friuli-Venezia Giulia, and Emilia-Romagna. Rest of Italy: Tuscany, Umbria, Marches, Lazio, Campania, Puglia, Calabria, Sicily, and Sardinia.
[a]All, all plants; 500+, plants with at least 500 employees.

Between 40 percent and 60 percent of agents involved in factory bargaining are either RSAs or consigli di fabbrica. (The Statuto dei Lavoratori recognized RSAs as bargaining agents; usually elected delegates are also named RSAs by the union in order to obtain such formal recognition by management. In some firms, accords recognizing delegates as such also exist.) The bulk of other actors involved are provincial or other full-time local officials; national officials are almost never involved directly in bargaining at this level. The proportion of shop-floor representatives directly involved in the bargaining process falls as we move south and is strongest in the northwest of the country, reflecting the still stronger role CdFs play in the areas of the country where they first arose in the late 1960s.

Table 4 also presents equivalent data for firms with at least five hundred employees. In larger firms, provincial and even national union officials are more likely to have a hand in articulated bargaining. Even so, the continued autonomy of the shop-floor representatives is striking.[53] They constitute between a third and a half of all union bargaining agents even in large industry.

Shop-floor representatives not only participate extensively in the bargaining process, frequently they do so autonomously—without, that is, the immediate supervision of full-time union functionaries. One available indicator of this is the proportion of factory accords signed by shop-floor representatives. A Federmeccanica analysis of one hundred factory accords signed between July 1979 and May 1980 revealed that 62 percent were signed by either provincial or full-time zonal union functionaries, whereas 37 percent were signed by either RSAs or CdFs.[54] Over a third of articulated bargaining was carried out with the active involvement of shop-floor representatives, and very possibly without the direct supervision of full-time officials, attesting to the relative autonomy of CdFs in collective bargaining.

Over 90 percent of these accords contained wage clauses of one type or another. Indeed, Italy's national statistical office estimated that in 1975 and 1978, for instance, actual earnings for metalworkers were 40 to 60 percent above nationally bargained wages.[55] But wages were far from constituting the only claims advanced in articulated bargaining. Two-thirds of the accords examined also contained clauses regarding work and safety conditions (*ambiente di lavoro*); nearly half won rights to information on future production and investments, and 44 percent contained clauses on employment, mainly managerial promises that existing employment would be maintained given present market conditions. Forty-four percent of the accords also dealt with job classification issues. A variety of other topics (eating facilities, work organization, production, etc.) were taken up in smaller numbers of accords. And although most accords specified an expiration date of less than a year and a half, only 10 percent contained peace clauses, or commitments to refrain from present-

53. Similar findings are reported by Ida Regalia, *Eletti e abbandonati: modelli e stili di rappresentanza in fabbrica* (Bologna: Il Mulino, 1984), 268.

54. Federmeccanica, "Contrattazione articolata: contenuto degli accordi integrativi aziendali successivi al CCNL 16.7.1979 per l'industria metalmeccanica-Situazione al 9.5.1980," 2, internal document dated 9 May 1980, courteously prepared for the author. One percent of accords were signed by workers without any recognized representative status.

55. L. Settanni, ed., "Come includere i contratti aziendali nel campo di studio della rilevazione delle retribuzioni contrattuali," Istituto Centrale di Statistica, Servizio delle statistiche del lavoro e dei bilanci di famiglia, paper presented at a seminar on "Sistema Comunitario di Statistiche sui Salari," document no. 1, Luxembourg, 17–19 September 1980, 2–4.

ing additional demands before the accord had expired. CdFs not only bargain, but bargain continually; there are no formal restrictions on their right to strike or the scope of issues they may consider. Articulated bargaining in Italy thus both raises the wage floor set in industrywide contracts and improves plant-specific working conditions.

Who bargains is not, of course, the same as who decides. Most articulated bargaining occurs under the guidance and supervision of provincial officials and within a policy framework provided by national directives. But the data above make clear the important contribution made to this process by shop-floor union representatives. Given that CdFs are concentrated disproportionately in the metalworking industries, as well as the importance of these agents to articulated bargaining, the FLM's attachment to decentralized collective bargaining comes as no surprise. To retain legitimacy with its own CdFs, the national federation found it difficult to endorse the highly centralized political bargaining increasingly promoted by the confederations as of the mid-1970s. To the degree that the Federazione Unitaria's growing policy moderation entailed stripping CdFs of some of their independence, the FLM's opposition was predictable.

Strike Activity in the Metalworking Industries

For much of the postwar period the metalworking industries have continued the leading role in strike activity they obtained early in the century, coinciding with the initial expansion of the automobile industry. Since World War I, "the contribution of this sector has become increasingly elevated and decisive in all principal conflictual explosions," as a study of Italian strikes in the twentieth century has noted.[56] The FLM is the most conflict-prone Italian industrial union.

The metalworking industries have played a clear role in leading industrial conflict during peak years. As Lorenzo Bordogna and Giancarlo Provasi noted in their historical analysis of Italian strikes, "every wave [of conflict] coincides with the renewal of the industrywide contract for the metalworkers' category."[57] Table 5 shows that years in which the metalworking industries renewed their national contracts (1959, 1962, 1966, 1969, 1973, 1976, and 1979) were marked by especially pronounced

56. Lorenzo Bordogna and Giancarlo Provasi, "Il movimento degli scioperi in Italia (1881–1973)," in *Il movimento degli scioperi nel XX secolo*, ed. Gian Primo Cella (Bologna: Il Mulino, 1979), 228.

57. Ibid., 233.

Table 5. Volume of Conflict for Years of Industrywide Bargaining: Metalworking and Other Industries, 1959–79

Year	Metalworking Industries	Other Industries	Ratio (metals/other)
1959	39.45	8.46	4.7
1962	104.90	12.49	8.4
1966	65.38	13.45	4.9
1969	140.70	34.75	4.0
1973	63.03	19.20	3.2
1976	34.88	18.16	1.9
1979	52.39	21.03	2.5
Average	71.53	18.22	3.9

Sources: See appendix B.

differences between the volume of conflict in that sector and in other industrial sectors. On average, the volume of conflict in metals was four times that in other industries. The metalworking sector was typically used for pattern bargaining: its markedly high levels of conflict tended to be linked to innovative contract demands, which the metalworking industries won first, allowing other sectors to imitate their settlement. Particularly in the early and mid-1960s, the metalworking sector constituted the leading edge of contract bargaining, opening the way for a renewal of labor militancy in Italy after the subdued 1950s. The period culminated with the hot autumn of 1969, by which time other industrial sectors had begun to catch up with the metalworking industries in using industrial conflict. By the late 1970s, the metalworking sector still led the way in contract bargaining, but its role had suffered compression.

Examinations of strike frequency, size, duration, and volume show the strength of the metalworking sector in conditioning overall strike activity as well. Table 6 compares the metalworking industries with other Italian industries for these four measures of conflict.[58] The results show that since 1950 strikes in the metalworking industries have on average been longer, larger, and more frequent than in other industrial sectors. The overall volume of conflict has, on average, been just about double for the former. By the 1970s this difference was due principally to the differences in relative strike size. As of the hot autumn, strikes in the metalworking industries were 60–70 percent larger than in other industrial sectors. This testifies to the FLM's capillary organization and to the federation's capacity to mobilize its rank and file well beyond other industrial unions.

58. For details on the construction of indicators, see appendix B.

Table 6. Periodized Annual Means of Strike Indicators: Metalworking and Other Industries, 1950–80

Sector	1950–58	1959–68	1969–74	1975–80	1950–80
Duration					
Metals	11.04	44.03	31.89	14.45	26.38
Other	21.08	30.35	28.76	10.67	23.54
Size					
Metals	1,628	886	1,806	3,887	1,860
Other	1,089	710	1,112	2,901	1,322
Frequency[a]					
Metals	0.66	0.75	0.86	0.54	0.71
Other	0.40	0.67	0.85	0.53	0.60
Volume[a]					
Metals	9.90	28.77	51.25	27.31	27.36
Other	7.53	13.92	23.90	16.97	14.51

Sources: See appendix B.
[a]Frequency and volume not available for 1950.

The metalworking sector is not merely larger than other industrial sectors: its working class is more highly mobilized, more visible, and a more significant public actor. The greater mobilizational ability of the FLM lends it significant weight in dealing with the confederations.

The Autonomy of the FLM from the Confederations

Factory councils occupy a peculiar status in contemporary Italian labor: they are the single official and operational body that does not suffer vertical fragmentation. All other organizational bodies are either affiliated with one of the three confederations or, in the case of those bodies that are the product of triorganizational agreements, subject to numerous if variable restrictions on their composition. The widespread presence of fused bodies at the bottom of the organization tends to encourage unity at the top as well. The FLM's especially strong association with the CdFs reinforces its autonomy from both partisan and confederal pressures.

Equally important in this regard is the composition of the federation's membership. In 1972 the newborn organization formally instituted joint membership unaffiliated with any of the three confederations. The agreement specified that the membership levels of each component organization (the FIOM, the FIM, and the UILM) would be frozen *(congelato)* at their existing levels and that new members would be permitted to take out only unaffiliated, independent FLM membership (the *senza scelte confederali* [SSCs], which would translate literally as "those without confederal choices"). By 1974 almost 86,000 of the more than 1,000,000 members of the three unions were SSC,[59] and in 1980 the FLM (unofficially) estimated that some 60 percent of its members were not affiliated with any of the three parent confederations.[60] Similarly, the organization proposed the transfer of organizational headquarters at all levels into joint offices, the establishment of joint books and financing, and the joint regulation of the composition of all leadership organs, to the extent of encouraging the recruitment of confederally unaffiliated functionaries. In 1974, forty of the organization's ninety-four provincial offices were already rented or owned jointly, or such a process was under way. Fully seventy-seven had enacted agreements concerning joint funding or bookkeeping, or both, while twenty-two provinces had agreements for the joint regulation of full-time functionaries.[61]

In pushing for new forms of organizational unity, the three unions were simultaneously calling for greater autonomy from the confederations and from the political parties. Historically, the three metalworkers' unions had long been the most aggressive proponents of unity of action and, later, organic unity.[62] In 1958 the FIM and the FIOM of Brescia conducted a joint strike at the OM-Fiat, paving the way for a long battle against separate factory accords, common in the 1950s, that discriminated against the FIOM.[63] By 1959 the three organizations were calling a limited number of joint strikes and, despite setbacks (especially at Fiat in Turin), triorganizational bargaining gradually became the norm. Encountering strong resistance from their respective parent confederations, the three metalworkers' unions nonetheless continued their uphill battle for in-

59. FLM, Commissione nazionale d'organizzazione, ed., *Esperienze FLM/3*, III Conferenza nazionale delegati FLM, Bologna, 10–13 luglio 1975 (Rome: FLM, [1975]), 99.

60. Interview no. 39, national FLM, 27 July 1980. The CGIL's own estimates are the same; see Eligio Biagioni, Stefania Palmieri, and Tatiana Pipan, *Indagine sul sindacato: profilo organizzativo della Cgil* (Rome: Editrice Sindacale Italiana, 1980), chap. 6.

61. FLM, *Esperienze FLM*, I Convegno nazionale di organizzazione FLM (Rome: FLM, [1974]), 76–78.

62. Unity of action refers to commonly agreed-upon mechanisms for triorganizational decision making and joint actions. Organic unity was the proposal for a complete merger of the three organizations. With the federated agreement of 1972 among the CGIL-CISL-UIL, the likelihood of attaining organic unity sharply declined.

63. See Paola Piva, "La Fim dal 1959 al 1968: cronologia," in Cella, Manghi, and Piva, *Sindacato italiano negli anni sessanta*, 112–14, and Sergio Turone, *Storia del sindacato in Italia, 1943–1980* (Bari: Laterza, 1981), 243–46. Even during the 1950s, joint bargaining among the three organizations was not unknown. Triorganizational accords were reached with Olivetti in 1956 and with ENI in 1957, for instance. Reported in Fausto Sabbatucci, "La contrattazione dal dopoguerra a oggi: il livello aziendale," *Quaderni di Rassegna Sindacale* 10 (March–April 1971), 42.

creased organizational unity, finally establishing the Federazione Lavoratori Metalmeccanici in 1972.[64] The FLM emerged as the closest thing to a truly unified union organization in the country.

Thanks to its 60 percent joint membership, solid triorganizational bodies at the bottom, and complicated agreements for the joint supervision of activities such as financing and personnel, the FLM gained a strong interest in asserting its independence from the three confederations. "The FLM's leadership has more interest in sticking together than in responding to their appropriate confederations," complained a national confederal official, echoing the disgruntled sentiments of the confederations as a whole.[65] While each component of the FLM necessarily interacts with its parent confederation, the three have evolved a mutual protection system for decision making. Each can shift responsibility onto the other two for decisions not wholly approved of by the confederation with which it is affiliated; the confederations, in turn, find the FLM's decision-making process opaque and difficult to control.[66] Moving too near any one confederation could antagonize FLM leaders affiliated with the other two. All three thus have strong interests in pursuing organizational autonomy and innovation: once in place, particular union structures carry with them persistent consequences for organizational behavior and policy orientations.

The confederations were thus well aware that the FLM's structure encouraged its policy autonomy. With the weakening of the FLM in the 1980s due to restructuring in large industry, the confederations moved to alter the FLM's membership composition. Aware that policy orientations in the FLM were now being driven mainly by the structure of the federation itself and had become organizationally self-perpetuating, the confederations pressured the national FLM into altering its regulations regarding factory councils and membership late in 1983. "Homogeneous work groups" were replaced by "electoral colleges" (known as "homogeneous areas") as the electoral units for factory delegates. Each area would elect

64. Documents relating to the formation of the FLM may be found in the section entitled "Le decisioni della categoria dal 1970 a oggi-Documenti," in *Esperienze e orientamenti*, ed. FIOM-CGIL, Conferenza nazionale quadri Fiom, Bologna, 24–26 giugno, 1973 (numero unico) [1973]. See also the draft of the never-adopted joint statute; FIM-FIOM-UILM, "Proposta di statuto sulle strutture: proposte di regolamento congressuale," prepared for the Congresso Costitutivo del sindacato unitario dei metalmeccanici, presented at the Consiglio Generale Unitario FIM-FIOM-UILM, Modena, 21–23 marzo 1972, supplement to *Unità Operaia*, no. 2 ([1972]).

65. Interview no. 47, national UIL, 31 October 1980.

66. Interview no. 47, national UIL, 31 October 1980.

multiple representatives rather than one, as had been the case under the previous regulations. Although elections would still nominally proceed using blank slates (on which workers would write in the name of one colleague they wanted elected), candidates would be introduced by an electoral commission (which included representatives of the FLM from outside the factory) at a factory assembly before the election itself. It was understood that the election of multiple delegates from a single area would allow the three components of the FLM to strike deals regarding the number of delegates affiliated with each of three organizations; the attachment to homogeneous work groups had been a fundamental bulwark of union unity in the FLM. Some factories and some provinces had always used areas rather than homogeneous work groups for electing delegates, for instance, and this had always been taken as evidence of a low degree of internal unity. In addition to this alteration of the structure of the CdFs, the national FLM moved to abolish joint membership (the senza scelte confederali), ordering regional offices to begin soliciting confederal adhesion for all FLM members and to dissolve the administrative quotas established some ten years earlier.[67] These changes reveal an FLM unable to resist confederal pressures and a union movement sensitive to the importance of organizational features in perpetuating policy orientations.

Ideological Innovation in the FLM

The FLM has consistently exhibited a radically democratic and uniquely politicized ideology in Italy, one that fuses the federation's focus on councils and conflict. This ideology, which in many ways resembles the classic European socialist syndicalism of the previous century, is apparent too in the way the organization explains the numerous innovations in collective bargaining it has furthered. The FLM has been a self-consciously radical innovator in the Italian labor movement, a union that has consistently understood its organizational mission as one directed at general social change.

An extensive history of metalworkers' innovations could be drawn up with respect to virtually every aspect of their organizational and contractual behavior. Typically, they have led to battles with the confederations

67. Preliminary new regulations on these matters were reported in FLM Piemonte, "La partecipazione dei lavoratori alle scelte del sindacato," documento approvato dal Comitato Direttivo FLM nazionale del 4/5 ottobre 1983 sul regolamento per l'elezione dei consigli di fabbrica, tesseramento e gestione delle risorse, scelte confederali, assemblee, *Nota Per I Delegati*, no. 18 (October 1983).

for both practical and ideological reasons. The metalworkers' unions were the first to approve incompatibility regulations (as early as 1966, in the case of the FIOM);[68] the first and strongest proponents of factory councils, workshop assemblies, and other forms of rank-and-file democracy; the strongest supporters of egalitarian wage demands; the first to experiment with a new, more egalitarian system of job classification; the first to fight for workers' educational benefits; the major force in winning new health and safety regulations; the most aggressive proponents of changes in work organization and particularly assembly line work; the staunchest defenders of restrictions on overtime, internal mobility, and other forms of shop-floor rigidity; the strongest supporters of radical kinds of social conflict such as "autoreductions" of public transportation fares; the first to battle for the "first part" of labor accords and contracts on information rights and investments for the south. Not coincidentally, they have also been the most likely to strike and to orchestrate large strikes, as I have shown above; organizational and strategic innovation has gone hand in hand with a radical and occasionally violent use of social and industrial conflict.

The FLM has been the most strenuous and consistent advocate for what I earlier called the politicization of market relations (see chap. 3). It has argued that politics begins with industrial and social conflict, and even that politics—or at least the best politics—are those conducted by social movements, not those negotiated by parties in parliaments. An FLM document from 1975 makes this point clearly: "We can force the government not to exclude the union from the formulation of economic policy . . . only with an informed direction on the part of the workers, only by further propelling articulated initiatives." And, added the federation, "The only basis for, and the fundamental premise of, the construction of a new social organization, which will be capable of eradicating the logic of clientelistic power and returning real capabilities of intervention, to the institutions, along with a real representative capacity, are the potential for struggle expressed by the workers."[69] Social and industrial conflict itself can directly condition political change: the FLM's goal has been to use working

68. A copy of the regulations is FIOM, "Modifiche allo Statuto della FIOM: votate dal Comitato Centrale riunito a Roma il 2 ottobre 1966," in FIOM, "Metalmeccanici e sindacato," Tavola rotonda, Desenzano sul Garda, 5–6–7 ottobre 1966, *Esperienze e Orientamenti*, Bollettino dell'ufficio organizzazione della FIOM, no. 10 (October 1966), 102–3.

69. FLM, "Documento preparatorio della III Conferenza nazionale delegati FLM," Bologna, 10–13 luglio 1975, in FLM, Commissione nazionale d'organizzazione, ed., *Esperienze FLM/3*, 141.

class militancy to effect a social revolution.[70] Never particularly sensitive to the intricacies and exigencies of partisan politics, the FLM developed a notion of social and political change informed by a radically democratic and profoundly conflictual vision of working-class behavior. Only increased democratic participation by the rank and file in industrial conflict ("articulated initiatives") can compel the government to adopt social and economic policies favorable to working class interests ("force the government"). And only a compulsive repetition of direct conflict will produce irreversible, fundamental social and political change ("a new social organization, which will be capable of eradicating the logic of clientelistic power") based on working-class interests. "The strike," proclaimed the general secretary of the FIM in 1970, "is the only way the class struggle will really develop."[71]

This radical notion of direct links between social conflict and political change had significant consequences for the FLM's policy orientation during the 1970s and 1980s. It became intimately bound up with the organization's suspicion of incomes policies in particular and of partisan politics and policy moderation in general. Two examples may serve as illustrations. First, the FLM was a constant critic of the strategy of reforms in the first half of the 1970s, arguing that the strategy was insufficiently democratic in its methods, inadequately aggressive in its demands, and unnecessarily cautious in its use of direct conflict. The FIOM made the point this way: "Important criticisms should also be expressed of the strategy of reforms conducted in recent months, both with respect to the way goals were defined and how the platform [of demands] was constructed and with respect to the way the means of struggle were chosen and the way conflict itself was consequently guided. Objectives and the means of conflict were not defined in such a way so as to stimulate the participation of the workers, and thus an extensive and conscious mobilization."[72] The vehicle for this "conscious mobilization" was, ideally, the factory council. The FLM's criticism was tied to the fear that the newly

70. See Aris Accornero, "Sindacato e rivoluzione sociale: il caso italiano degli anni '70," *Laboratorio Politico* 1 (July–August 1981), 5–34.

71. [Pierre Carniti], *Assemblea organizzativa della FIM-CISL*, Brescia, 3–5 luglio 1970 (Rome: FIM, [1970]), 93.

72. FIOM-CGIL, "La risoluzione finale del XV Congresso," Roma, 13–18 luglio 1970, reprinted in FIOM-CGIL, *Esperienze e orientamenti* (1973), 27. See also the comments by Bruno Trentin, "Relazione introduttiva al XV Congresso nazionale della FIOM," Roma, 13–18 luglio 1970, partially reprinted as "Il sindacato nuovo di fronte alla crisi," in his *Da sfruttati a produttori: lotte operaie e sviluppo capitalistico dal miracolo economico alla crisi*, 3d ed. (Bari: DeDonato, 1977), 247.

emerged factory councils and the strongest industrial unions that encouraged them would suffer as the confederations assumed new and centralizing powers with the strategy of reforms. In response, the federation argued that the political significance of union action was not confined to the strategy of reforms but was also evident in union strategies for bargaining over the use—and not just the price—of the labor force. The industrial arena constituted not merely the site for improving wages and benefits, but also the privileged locus of public life and political conflict. Its special political status was, in turn, guaranteed by its decentralized, democratic, and participatory nature.

Second, the notion that industrial activity is inherently political in both its causes and its consequences encouraged the FLM to propel conflict well beyond the bounds of what one might define as "normal" industrial relations. Not only were strikes used as political weapons, as with the FLM's 1977 demonstration in Rome that catalyzed the fall of the Italian government, but industrial conflicts were themselves waged on political grounds.

A good illustration is job classification, an ostensibly somewhat technical issue that unions everywhere deal with. In its most radical form, the proposal for a new system of job classification, eventually won nationally for the entire industry in 1972 in the form of the *inquadramento unico* (IU) (single classification system), was meant to attack the capitalist organization of work. The potential political implications were described by one of its early proponents as follows: "An action of contestation of these factors [i.e., work organization] leads to a radical critique of the relations of capitalist power. The organization of the modern firm reproduces within itself, under the mystifying guise of objectivity and technical necessity, the relations of power that the system needs for its conservation."[73] The FIM made the same point in an official document: "There is a tight connection between the conditions of the workers in the factory and their conditions in society; the subordination and exploitation that characterize the former are manifested as social and political marginalization in the latter."[74]

The battle against the system of job classification that had been widely diffused in Italian industry in the 1960s was in essence a fight for two

73. Gian Primo Cella, "Rapporti fra organizzazione, tecnologia produttiva e alienazione del lavoro" (1970), reprinted in his *Divisione del lavoro e iniziative operaie* (Bari: DeDonato, 1972), 52.

74. FIM-CISL, "Mozioni conclusive delle commissioni," in FIM-CISL, *3 assemblea organizzativa della FIM-CISL*, 76.

things. First, the new system entailed a drastic reduction in the number of levels. It featured only eight, including both blue- and white-collar workers, whereas previously there had been upward of two dozen wage levels, varying by firm. Second, the IU formally overlapped blue- and white-collar classificatory scales, potentially permitting enlarged internal mobility. These apparently technical issues were seen as central to a battle aimed at demonstrating "the reversibility of the division of labor," which in turn "acquires its full significance to the extent that it is transferred into a contestation of general social strategy."[75] Conflicts over social conditions, in turn, would then involve "an element of political consciousness and orientation."[76] The attention to job classification was thus justified on the grounds of its potential political consequences. In battling an anachronistic system of job classification, semiskilled workers, argued the FLM, would draw a more general lesson concerning the importance of unity and solidarity and, eventually, would extend that lesson from the shop floor to political battles against equally anachronistic and oppressive conditions in society at large. The fight for a simplified system of classification would thus become a fight against capitalist social relations. As the FIM remarked:

> Recent contractual struggles have risen above the limits of technical and monetary demand making, in order increasingly to aim at a change in the reality of exploitation and subordination of the workers in the factory. The results thus far have not been absolutely satisfactory; there still exists a split

75. Gian Primo Cella and Bruno Manghi, "Analisi critica del sistema di qualifiche" (1970), reprinted in Cella, *Divisione del lavoro,* 93–94. See Pipan and Salerni, *Sindacato come soggetto di equilibrio,* for a history of the internal debates that eventually led to the formulation of the 1972 CCNL demand for the IU. For an analysis of the same debates in the 1960s, emphasizing the roles of the metalworkers' unions in Milan and Turin, see Marino Regini and Emilio Reyneri, *Lotte operaie e organizzazione del lavoro*, 8th ed. (Venice: Marsilio, 1977), especially part 2. See also Antonio Lettieri, "Note su qualifiche scuola e orari di lavoro," *Problemi del Socialismo,* n.s. 12 (November–December 1970), 802–16, for an evaluation of the first successful experiment with the new form of job classification, at Italsider in 1970, by one of the unionists most closely associated with it.

76. Sergio Garavini, "Qualifiche e organizzazione del lavoro" (1973), partially reprinted as "Crisi del talorismo e sistema delle qualifiche," in *Professionalità e salario: dall'inquadramento unico all'appiattimento retributivo*, ed. Renato Fontana (Rome: Editrice Sindacale Italiana, 1979), 45. Interest in the inquadramento unico was often part of a conscious attempt to represent semiskilled workers—the so-called *operaio-massa*—who had previously been largely neglected in demand formulation. See the two Cella essays referred to above, as well as Cella, "Organizzazione del lavoro: lotte operaie e risposta padronale" (1971), reprinted in his *Divisione del lavoro;* also Regini and Reyneri, *Lotte operaie e organizzazione del lavoro,* especially the sections on flat wage increases and the demands for automatic skill upgrading during 1967–68 (73–91).

> between the diffused consciousness of the workers that the factory . . . must be changed, that science and technique are not neutral at all, but strictly functional to the interests of the system that uses them, and the capacity to transform this . . . knowledge into objectives of struggle.[77]

The ideological interpretations the inquadramento unico occasioned were not exceptions but typical examples of the FLM's radical politicization of industrial conflict, strictly linked to the democratic ideology that informed the FLM's structure of representation. For industrial activities to acquire their full significance, they must not simply be highly militant. Conflict must also be "informed": rank-and-file political consciousness acquires primary importance. As the analysis of the FLM's criticisms of the strategy of reforms suggested earlier, mass participation and political change became indissolubly linked for the federation. Under such conditions, militancy became a good in itself, valued because it fueled a strategy of general social transformation.

The Organizational Logic of Radicalism

This sophisticated radical ideology affected all spheres of the FLM. Ideology became so bound up with strategy and structure that it constituted an internal, relatively autonomous, and self-perpetuating organizational logic. Principles of organizational behavior and legitimacy became self-referencing and mutually reinforcing: to reproduce itself over time—to continue attracting militants, members, and officials—the organization required that its logic of organizational behavior remain intact.

The FLM's own analysis of the principles of collective action sustaining the organization made the point clearly. The FIOM's national secretary for organization explained:

> Why do workers join the union? For many reasons . . . which could be substantially reduced to three fundamental factors: for the protection of individual rights and the services the union provides; for the improvement of working conditions and factory life that result from collective bargaining; and because of more idealistic and political motivations, strongly present in

77. FIM-CISL, "Mozioni conclusive delle commissioni," 76. The theoretical bases for the argument against the "neutrality" of technological processes under capitalism must be traced to the rereading of Marx by Raniero Panzieri, "Sull'uso capitalistico delle macchine nel neocapitalismo" (1961) *Quaderni Rossi,* no. 1 (reprinted; Milan: Sapere Edizioni, 1970), 53–72.

> the industrial categories, particularly in the metalworking categories, that have to do with the general desire for a change in the relations of force in function of new arrangements of power in society.[78]

The organization is not blind to the importance of selective incentives ("individual rights and . . . services"). But the FLM's national leadership also believes that members join the organization because they trust it to fight for general sociopolitical change, transcending industrial relations as such. Indeed, the secretary's remarks reveal an organization deeply sensitive to the limits of instrumental rationality and individual self-interest in mobilizing the rank and file; an organization that has consciously used alternative ideological means to induce mass support. The ideologization of the FLM had shifted the bases of its organizational appeal. In the past, ideologically motivated union membership in Italy was a secondary reflex, a function primarily of partisan political affiliation.[79] After 1969, however, the FLM made strong political claims independent of partisan determinants. The union itself had become a site of mass politicization, a form of politicization based mainly on collective and expressive rationality. Dispensing with ideology would have required reconstructing its organizational mission along alternative lines and transforming the organization's mechanisms of attraction of militants and officials. Radicalism thus became autonomous and self-perpetuating for the national FLM, detached from the conditions that originally produced it.

Cast in the 1960s and consolidated in the 1970s, organizational purpose subsequently generated a stable logic of organizational behavior, in which goals, means, and principles of action became frozen. The parameters of the FLM's organizational integrity were for nearly twenty years defined by factory councils, articulated bargaining, industrial conflict and mass mobilization, triorganizational unity, and a radical ideology of social revolution beyond the bounds of partisan politics. Proposals for incomes policies threatened this internal circuit from all directions. They would have reduced the bargaining roles of shop-floor delegates, inhibited decentralized bargaining, dampened mass mobilization, reintroduced partisan differences into union decision making, and shifted the locus of

78. Ermanno Borghesi, "La questione della democrazia," *Quaderni di Rassegna Sindacale* 19 (May–August 1981), 96.

79. See Guido Romagnoli and Maurizio Rossi, "La sindacalizzazione in Italia fra ciclo economico, conflitto e facilitazioni istituzionali," in *La sindacalizzazione tra ideologia e pratica: il caso italiano 1950/1970*, ed. Guido Romagnoli, Centro Studi Nazionale CISL Firenze (Rome: Edizioni Lavoro, 1980), I:95–124.

social change from the industrial arena to an elite, state-centered policy sphere. National federations could be assured only that their influence within organized labor would be severely diminished by the implementation of austerity policies, and no industrial union could have had any strong intrinsic organizational attraction to austerity for this very reason. But it was the FLM that opposed austerity most strenuously: its structure of representation, linkages to its own CdFs and rank and file, and its ideology all guaranteed that the federation's dissent would be overdetermined.

Dissent was thus entirely predictable and not in the least unexpected. In pursuing policy moderation, the confederations knew they would encounter resistance from the FLM: the only question was how public the resistance would become and whether dissidents would succeed in mobilizing the rank and file behind them and in constructing broad alliances with other components of organized labor. The predictability of dissent stemmed from the fact that the FLM's responses to the new political and economic pressures of the late 1970s and early 1980s reflected organizationally encoded and self-perpetuating "givens" rather than rationally calculated reactions to external stimuli. As the next section will demonstrate empirically, the FLM was not opposed to wage moderation per se, however. It was not promoting the immediate wage claims of workers in its opposition to incomes policies. Rather, the federation spoke for an alternative set of collective, organizational interests that, for historical and structural reasons, were incompatible with incomes policies as they were understood by the central confederations.

Wage Moderation and the FLM

Despite the FLM's consistent policy opposition to austerity, evidence shows that the federation did not undermine it through collective bargaining. During the first phase of austerity, strike activity in the metalworking sector was atypically compressed. The industrywide bargaining rounds that took place in 1976 and 1979, during the phase of national unity, were relatively tame affairs (see table 5). The volume of conflict in the metalworking industries was still larger than in other industrial sectors, but by a considerably smaller margin than in all other contract renewals since 1959. Detailed quantitative evidence is still unavailable for the phase from 1980 to 1985, but an analysis of the platforms for the contract renewals that should have taken place in 1982 (but were delayed by the Confindustria's threat to void the 1975 agreement on the scala mobile) shows that the FLM's demands were within confederal guidelines.[80]

There is, moreover, little evidence that the federation deliberately defied confederal directives. Rather, it sought to "reinterpret" them in ways the confederations found objectionable.[81] More important, thanks to the FLM, confederal wage guidelines were always imprecise enough to allow a variety of quite legitimate "interpretations." In anticipation of the resistance they knew they would encounter, the confederations were forced to propose incomes policies with a wide margin of interpretative flexibility. Fearful of its inability to control internal consensus, the Federazione Unitaria simply could not afford to commit itself to precise standards of implementation. And whenever it tried to achieve precision it was forced to alter its recommendations to encompass ambiguity.

The Federazione Unitaria's internal strategy was thus an attempt to isolate known centers of militancy from mass support and to prevent the construction of broad antiausterity alliances within organized labor. Had the confederations articulated clear and precise wage guidelines, dissidents would have had a greater opportunity to mobilize rank-and-file support against the center. Signs of real rank-and-file rebellion would in turn have empowered dissidents and allowed them to construct broader alliances with other groups within the labor movement. The confederations, in short, could not have elaborated more precise and stringent recommendations without running the risk of open internal rebellion. By setting the agenda in such a way as to induce resistance solely on organizational grounds, they maintained relatively effective control and marginalized dissidents politically. The best strategy for the confederations, given their knowledge that dissent was inevitable, consisted in articulating ambiguous and weak austerity recommendations.

The best response by dissidents, on the other hand, was precisely the one they chose: to attempt to confuse the confederations about the potential for rank-and-file rebellion and to reinterpret austerity in ways that would gain them internal allies. Knowing they were in no position to force the confederations to repudiate wage restraint altogether—and aware that this was simply not a viable option, for strictly economic reasons—opponents sought to render austerity economically irrelevant and politically illegitimate. The FLM's strategy of resistance thus bespoke a language of

80. See Tiziano Treu, ed., *Il patto contro l'inflazione: contenuti e documenti delle intese governo-sindacati* (Rome: Edizioni Lavoro, 1984), 89–90.

81. Interview no. 37, national FLM (Secretariat), 24 July 1980.

opposition: "Factionalism does not only endanger the leaders by revealing the possibility of independent thinking. Far more threatening to their security is the permanent possibility that the underdog faction will try to muster support for its position among the subaltern functionaries and, through them, the members. . . . [W]hether or not the underdogs are successful is immaterial: What counts is simply that orthodoxy and political control are contested. . . . [T]he autonomy of the leaders is diminished."[82] The next chapter will begin to examine how the federation attempted "to muster support for its position among the subaltern functionaries" in the provinces.

82. Sabel, "Internal Politics of Trade Unions," 229.

5

Policy on the Periphery: Provincial Responses to Austerity

In responding to central calls for incomes policies, opponents deliberately sought to construct broad internal alliances. The national FLM called on its provincial offices to oppose incomes policies and to take the message of opposition to the rank and file. But at the local level, only some offices of the FLM followed the lead of the national federation. This chapter will describe how provincial representatives are selectively incorporated into the FLM's national decision-making bodies and then analyze the responses to austerity by the labor movement in the four provinces selected for detailed investigation. In two of the provinces, the labor movement exhibited a moderate orientation similar to the Federazione Unitaria's. In the other two, by contrast, the labor movement's policy orientation was even more radical than that of the national FLM.

Linking Center to Periphery: The Roles of Provincial Unionists

Three factors—leeway in representation, discretion in implementation, and a context of bureaucratic informality—provide the institutional parameters for the influence of provincial officials in their dealings with their national offices.

Provincial officials are key mediators between national union decision making and the needs, interests, and volition of factory councils and the rank and file. They are the lowest level of full-time union officials; below them one finds the CdFs, which, though some of their members may be engaged in full-time union work, are nonetheless composed of activists and militants, not paid functionaries. Provincial officials are included in national decision-making bodies, where they are expected to speak for their constituencies. A great deal of leeway is provided for the act of "speaking for": the business of reaching common decisions involves interpretation, compromise, and bargaining. Because of the strength of factory councils and the importance of maintaining the consensus of the rank and file when union membership is not mandatory, provincial officials participate actively in most stages of national decision making.

Although elite recruitment occurs principally through co-optation, provincial functionaries, particularly those from larger provinces, wield their own power resources and are not expected merely to ratify decisions made by the federation's national Secretariat. Provincial officials constitute an important independent body in the union's organization, if only because of the absence of formal restrictions on wage bargaining and strikes by CdFs. Provincial functionaries comprise the bulk of full-time union officials, and their activities maintain the organization on a daily basis. In 1976, for instance, there were just under 8,000 full-time political functionaries across the three confederations who worked at the provincial level and another 1,500 provincial technical staff.[1] Provincial category unionists are responsible for the bulk of collective bargaining that occurs in Italy, and virtually everything but negotiation for national labor contract renewals falls under their direct supervision. They regularly respond to the claims of a variety of other actors, from the disgruntled worker who rips up his union card in provincial headquarters, to the telephone call from a bankrupt factory owner looking for someone to buy him out, to the protests of irate citizens complaining that striking workers are blocking traffic on a main thoroughfare. They sit on a large number of quasi-public and public commissions and bodies; they consult and bargain with local government; they organize cultural events, restaurants, strikes, demonstrations, and sample surveys; and they supervise, when they do not actually attend, factory assemblies, meetings of factory councils, public debates, meetings with political parties and other social organizations, workers' educational courses, and an inordinate number of internal meetings. They are very busy people, typically working a ten-hour day six days of the week, and their status is not commensurate with their responsibilities. Their roles are multiform, the skills demanded of them are many, and the pay is relatively low. Job burnout is high, turnover is often rapid, and job satisfaction is uneven at best. Since most officials in industrial unions are on paid temporary leave from their regular jobs—leaves authorized by a provision in the

1. Reported in Salvatore Coi, "Sindacati in Italia: iscritti, apparato, finanziamento," *Il Mulino* 28 (March–April 1976), 222.

1970 Statuto dei Lavoratori—they normally reenter production after leaving the union.

Because they fall between the union's national offices and the rank and file, provincial officials are largely entrusted with implementing national policy. Implementation, like the task of speaking for their constituencies, permits considerable discretion and reinforces the independent powers of provincial officials. An illustration of how discretion may verge on failure to implement makes the point. The various decisions involved in establishing the joint FLM in place of the FIOM, FIM, and UILM were made with the involvement of provincial officials. Each province was left considerable latitude in working out its own arrangements for issuing FLM membership cards, establishing joint bookkeeping and financing, and so forth. Even in the early 1980s the national offices of the FLM did not retain accurate and current information on the extent of FLM versus FIM-FIOM-UILM membership at the provincial level. The Roman office had no instruments for systematically collecting these data and no way to compel provincial officials to hand them over. The latter often had little interest in revealing their own weaknesses and hence could refuse their own national offices full membership data.[2] Even worse, a series of southern and central provinces never instituted joint membership, financing, or bookkeeping at all, and the national FLM had no means of enforcing compliance.[3]

Thanks to their importance in expressing constituency interests and their roles in implementation, provincial officials are vital in constructing internal organizational consensus. Because these processes occur in a context of bureaucratic informality, the actual rules of the game are flexible and subject to considerable interpretation by the officials themselves. The informality of rule making in Italian unions is extreme and typically produces considerable disjunction between actual organizational behavior and the few formal rules that exist.[4] This problem is exacerbated in the case of the FLM, which is officially both the sum of its three component organizations (the FIM-CISL, the FIOM-CGIL, and the UILM-UIL) and a neostatutory, independent organization.[5] Confusing overlapping regula-

2. Interview no. 38, national FLM, 27 July 1980.

3. Interview no. 27, national FLM (Secretariat), 17 June 1980.

4. See Giuseppe Della Rocca, "Introduzione," in *Potere e democrazia nel sindacato*, ed. Giuseppe Della Rocca (Rome: Edizioni Lavoro, 1979).

5. A look at the statute of the FIOM indicates this curious status of the FLM. The FLM has "established its own decision-making structures" that are nonetheless "formed from the decision-making organisms of the FIOM, the FIM, and the UILM." Similarly, each component is "part of the distinct Confederations," yet "the decisions made with respect to

tions allow even wider margins of discretion in the FLM than in other Italian unions.

Provincial Variations in Responses to Austerity

Not all provincial FLM offices followed the national federation in resisting incomes policies in the 1970s and 1980s. Responses to confederal moderation were not homogeneous on the periphery, and decentralization alone did not necessarily generate antiausterity opposition. Few in the Italian labor movement actually embraced austerity with enthusiasm; it was in the best of cases a policy to be endured, not celebrated. Yet the FLM in Turin and Pordenone, like the national federation, consistently assumed positions critical of moderation, whereas the FLM in Modena and Cuneo exhibited orientations closer to those of the national confederations. Despite this manifest diversity of organizational responses, the union movement's rank and file largely acquiesced to moderation, even when their union representatives may not have done so. Dissent was not a direct function of the opinions expressed by the union movement's mass base. Rather, responses to austerity reflected persistent and relatively autonomous logics of organizational behavior that shaped the interactions of provincial union offices in dealing with national union leadership. To begin to substantiate this argument, the rest of this chapter will examine responses to austerity policies in four provinces at two points in time. I again describe reactions in 1978 and 1982, as I already did for national actors, and show that both opposition and reconciliation were patterned, predictable, and organizationally autonomous responses to austerity.

Introducing the Provinces

Cuneo is a small, relatively agricultural province of some 546,000 residents just to the south of Turin, also in the region of Piedmont. More

joint policies by the joint decision-making organisms of the FLM are binding on the FIOM." The statute is also exceedingly vague in its discussions of the composition and formation of certain decision-making bodies. The FIOM's Comitato Esecutivo, which becomes the organization's component in the FLM's Comitato Direttivo, is nominated by the Comitato Centrale according to unspecified criteria and with an unspecified number of members, for instance. See FIOM-CGIL, *Statuto, approvato all'unanimità al XVI Congresso (1977) della FIOM* ([Rome]: FIOM, [ca. 1977]), 1.

than a quarter of its labor force is still involved in agriculture, historically the domain of its numerous peasant landowners. Although it is an isolated, semirural province, myriad small factories and artisanal workshops dot its contemporary landscape, and a third of its labor force is at present engaged in industry. The ties between agriculture and industry have never been wholly severed, and most industrial workers still have relatives cultivating the land; seasonal absenteeism occurs regularly as these workers continue to participate in their families' agricultural production. Cuneo is in many respects outside the mainstream of modern Italian life, and educational levels remain low and traditions strong. Though the province is a historical reservoir of seasonal out-migration, typically for harvesting in France, the comings and goings of its male work force have not succeeded in altering the area's basic conservatism. Only a tiny fraction of its marriages are civil ceremonies;[6] the strength of Catholicism, along with that of the Christian Democratic party, remains uncontested.

With a population of 597,000, Modena (in the region of Emilia-Romagna) is only slightly larger than Cuneo, but its economic and cultural dynamism sets it worlds apart. The 16 percent of its labor force still in agriculture maintains a highly productive and well-integrated system of capitalist agricultural production.[7] Nearly half of its labor force is employed across the thousands of often highly profitable and internationally competitive small firms and artisanal workshops in the province. The success of both these sectors has made Modena the wealthiest province in the country. The city of Modena is the site of one of Italy's finest universities, and educational levels are generally high in the province. Secularization is about the national average, and the church plays only a minor role in the organization of social life. A center of agricultural militancy and anarchosocialism at the turn of the century, Modena is still one of the "reddest" areas in the country. The Communist party has exercised uncontested political and cultural dominance there since the war, favoring the development of modern social services and the growth of small industry while fostering such a highly integrated associational network that local party functionaries today boast that each Modenese has "at least five membership cards in his pocket."[8] Observers across the political spectrum are apt to remark that the province resembles a Northern European social democracy more than it does southern Italy.

6. For provincial data on this measure of secularization, see Fabrizio Carmignani, ed., "Immagine socio-economica delle province italiane," *Congiuntura Sociale*, no. 2 (February 1979), 6, table 3.

7. Sebastiano Brusco, *Agricoltura ricca e classi sociali* (Milan: Feltrinelli, 1979).

8. Interview no. 72, PCI Modena (Secretariat), 12 February 1981.

Pordenone, in the region of Friuli-Venezia Giulia, the smallest of the four provinces, with a population of 274,000, mirrors Modena in the distribution of its labor force, but its industrial structure is far newer and more concentrated. Industrialization penetrated the area only in the 1960s, finally reversing the historical use of the province as a reservoir of extensive labor out-migration. Even now its industrial work force remains largely intact territorially, commuting to work in the provincial cities from family residences in small, semirural villages.[9] Older industries are now largely defunct or relatively marginal. Postwar industrialization has been bipolar, involving the expansion of both a great number of very small firms and the dramatic growth of Zanussi, Europe's largest manufacturer of household appliances. This spurt of industrialization did much to spur secularization and modernization in the area. The Christian Democratic party no longer monopolizes local government, as the Communist party gained increasing electoral appeal during the 1970s. Still a highly proletarian party in Pordenone, the PCI is linked to Italy's most conflictual industrial work force: Pordenone ranked first among all Italian provinces in industrial conflict during the 1970s.[10]

The largest province studied is Turin, home to over 2 million persons and to Fiat, Italy's largest private employer. The center of growth of the automobile industry since before World War I, Turin now has only 4 percent of its labor force employed in agriculture; over half work in industry, making it one of Italy's most industrialized provinces. The city is dominated both economically and culturally by Fiat, much as Zanussi dominates Pordenone. As in Pordenone, Turin's major employer runs the capital city's newspaper, its banks, numerous services and tertiary activities, and for a long time ran its government as well. But the thousands upon thousands of southern immigrants who moved to Turin in the 1950s and 1960s to find work, and who have settled there permanently, have changed the face of the city. Once an enlightened if somewhat insular francophile, bourgeois cultural and political center, and the country's first capital after Italian unification, Turin became both culturally hybrid and politically left-wing. The Communists held local power between 1975 and 1985, attempting simultaneously to retain their hold on their traditional Piedmontese blue-collar base, to represent the southern migrants who had brought them to power but largely remained culturally extraneous to the party, and to appease, if not actually to woo, Fiat's management. Much

9. Pierluigi Grandinetti and Roberto Grandinetti, *Il caso Friuli: arretratezza o sviluppo?* (Udine: Cooperativa "Il Campo," 1979), chap. 4.

10. Carmignani, "Immagine socio-economica delle province italiane," 18, table 9.

like Pordenone writ large, Turin underwent rapid, even traumatic, socioeconomic change in the 1950s and 1960s and experienced equally radical political changes in consequence.

The Consultazioni of 1978 and 1982

The mechanisms of building national consent were similar in 1978, when organized labor adopted the EUR policy, and in 1982, when it agreed to a revision of Italy's wage indexation system. Both were accompanied by what came to be known as consultazioni, the procedure of consulting the rank and file for its reaction to policy recommendations before their formal adoption. Consultazioni are infrequent in Italy, being conducted only for the most important national issues. Between 1975 and 1985, only three were orchestrated economywide, all concentrated on austerity issues.[11] They involve massive numbers of factory, and occasionally multifactory, worker assemblies, held on company premises, during working hours, and generally lasting two hours. Local union officials, typically flanked by members of factory councils, explain the relevant policy recommendations. National category union officials help conduct assemblies for their unions, usually in provinces where local organizational resources are strained; confederal officials attend only especially important or potentially difficult assemblies. The policy recommendations are considered by distributing written copies of the pertinent confederal document—either at the assembly itself or earlier, through the factory council—and reviewing the salient points. Alternative recommendations made by national federations or local union offices may also be reviewed, usually on the basis of written documents. Open comments from the floor (*interventi*) are then taken, giving both delegates and workers a chance to express opinions and perhaps offer amendments. A union functionary will then offer concluding remarks and, as in the 1982 assemblies, a ratification vote, usually through an open show of hands, may be taken and recorded. Workers may be asked to vote on the confederal document itself, on an amended document recommended by other union offices, on multiple documents, or on amendments proposed from the floor. Since open worker assemblies almost always approve whatever recommenda-

11. The third, which will not be examined here, was held in early 1982 on the basis of a ten-point confederal document aimed at restraining inflation. The national recommendations became moot with the Confindustria's withdrawal from the 1975 scala mobile agreement in June of that year, eventually resulting in the consultazione of October–November.

tions the union presents, at issue is not the vote itself but rather the choice—made by union functionaries in conjunction with factory delegates—of which set of recommendations to present and vote on. Leadership groups rarely encourage overt rank-and-file rebellion by presenting recommendations on which they do not ask for approval. Rather, they generate internal dissent by presenting alternative or amended recommendations, in the form of amendments or formal motions (*ordini del giorno*).

Shop-floor assemblies are surrounded by a barrage of meetings of various union offices. In the case of EUR, the assemblies were preceded by meetings of national federations and usually followed by meetings of local category unions and then provincewide meetings of all CGIL-CISL-UIL components. The whole process culminated with a national assembly, where the EUR recommendations were formally approved following the battle of the amendments. In 1982, on the other hand, the confederations officially required that meetings of national federations and regional CGIL-CISL-UIL offices (which would include representatives from regional category unions) take place before the factory assemblies and that regional union offices coordinate the assemblies, maintain written records of the votes, and communicate the results directly to national headquarters.[12] Procedural visibility, they hoped, would make it more difficult for dissenting leadership groups to mobilize the rank and file while also rendering the outcome of the consultazione easier to interpret. The Federazione Unitaria's Secretariat itself undertook the job of interpreting and aggregating the amendments that had arisen during the course of the consultazione and then revising its policy recommendations. The consultazione terminated with a meeting of the Direttivo Unitario CGIL-CISL-UIL rather than a national assembly; since the former, unlike the latter, is composed exclusively of full-time union functionaries, the Secretariat retained greater control over decision making.

Considerable caution is in order in interpreting the data generated by the 1982 consultazione. At the insistence of the national confederations, regional union offices were required to forward complete figures on the voting that took place in the factory assemblies. In some assemblies workers voted only on confederal recommendations. In others they voted exclusively on a locally amended version of the recommendations. In some they voted twice, once on each. In still others they voted on some other set

12. For the requirements instituted, see Federazione CGIL-CISL-UIL, "Modalità della consultazione," reprinted in Lorenzo Speranza, "Le consultazioni," in *Le relazioni sindacali in Italia: rapporto 1982–83*, ed. Guido Baglioni, Marina Camonico, and Ettore Santi, Centro di Studi Sociali e Sindacali (Rome: Edizioni Lavoro, 1984), 499–500.

of recommendations entirely. And in some, finally, they voted on the national recommendations or a locally amended version, or both, plus separate amendments or formal motions. Interpreting the data is therefore extremely difficult; depending on the deflator used (number of employees, number of voters, number of participants at the assemblies, number of votes cast in relation to one or more set of recommendations), we can generate radically different percentages of workers favoring one set of recommendations or another. I have thus constructed multiple sets of figures, but my major argument is that the critical point is not how workers actually voted but rather what they were asked to vote on and whether they bothered to vote at all.

Reconciliation to Moderation in Modena and Cuneo

Union officials in both Modena and Cuneo reported that their offices largely favored adopting austerity policies in 1978 and 1982. In 1978 factory assemblies were held in both provinces to present the confederal document to the rank and file,[13] followed by meetings of category unions and then CGIL-CISL-UIL provincial asemblies to discuss the confederal recommendations. "EUR was approved [*è passata*]," unionists in both provinces reported,[14] even when they openly criticized the policy during the interview.[15] No Modenese or Cuneese who attended the national assembly in February, whether representing the FLM or any other provincial

13. In Modena, at least two hundred assemblies were held across industrial sectors, not a particularly impressive score given the enormous number of plants in the province. (According to the 1981 industrial census, there were over 21,000 plants in the province.) Assemblies were probably limited to larger plants, which in Modena would include those with more than two hundred employees. Estimates on the number of assemblies reported in Saverio Caruso, "Immagini della classe operaia modenese: la recente consultazione sindacale," *Quaderni Modenesi,* n.s. 4 (March 1978), 28–30.

14. Interviews no. 59, CGIL Cuneo (Secretariat), 13 January 1981; no. 60, FLM Cuneo (Secretariat), 13 January 1981; no. 61, FLM Cuneo (Secretariat), 14 January 1981; no. 62, FLM Cuneo (Secretariat), 14 January 1981; no. 64, CISL Cuneo (Secretariat), 14 January 1981; no. 70, FLM Modena (Secretariat), 18 February 1981; no. 71, CGIL Modena (Secretariat), 9 February 1981; no. 74, FLM Modena (Secretariat), 18 February 1981; no. 75, FLM Modena (Secretariat), 18 February 1981; and no. 78, FLM Modena, 21 February 1981.

15. Even when unionists change their views on important issues, they are not likely to misrepresent their earlier positions, despite the minor embarrassment involved. By 1980 and 1981 it was common for Italian unionists to criticize EUR, and when interviewed, they did so in all four provinces. But only in Turin and Pordenone did they systematically report having expressed equally critical views at the time of EUR's adoption.

union organization, voted against or abstained on the final policy recommendations.

The character of acceptance differed between the two provinces, however. In Cuneo, part of the local FLM's leadership—including members of the Communist party—made attempts at launching resistance *à la torinese*.[16] But dissidents within the FLM proved unable to challenge provincial consensus. All other relevant actors—the CGIL, CISL, UIL, the PCI, and shop-floor union activists—endorsed EUR. The CGIL and the FIOM's factory cadres constituted major hindrances, refusing to support opposition as they did in Turin and Pordenone. Completely isolated, the FLM's provincial officials relinquished any thought of dissent, and the consensus that emerged in Cuneo's union movement strongly favored the policy's adoption.

In Modena, by contrast, what little opposition there was appeared "nearly individual," originating with a few extraparliamentary leftists in the FIM and the CISL.[17] Internally divided and extemely small compared with the CGIL, the Modenese CISL was unable to translate potential opposition into official recommendations. Among members of the CGIL's largely Communist rank and file the response was passive acceptance,[18] similar to the passive acquiescence to the PCI's strategy during the national unity period.[19] Assured of the rank and file's continued, albeit unenthusiastic, loyalty, the provincial CGIL ensured the compact endorsement of austerity, and there was no open dissent.

The situation in 1982 regarding proposed cutbacks in wage indexation did not differ significantly from that four years earlier. Thanks to the reorganization of the union that had occurred in the meantime, potential dissidents in the Cuneese FLM found themselves in a stronger position in the province. The Federazione CGIL-CISL-UIL had officially abolished

16. Interview no. 60, FLM Cuneo (Secretariat), 13 January 1981. Also discussed in interview no. 63, UIL Cuneo (Secretariat), 14 January 1981. Although Cuneo is only about forty miles from Turin, traditionally it does not fall within the political orbit of the latter. Unionists in Cuneo systematically reported extremely few contacts with their colleagues in Turin and said that, of the few contacts they did have with unionists outside Cuneo, most were with the national offices of the federation. With the establishment of the region in the union's structure in 1980, the situation altered slightly, and unionists in Cuneo became more likely to go to Turin to attend meetings, though usually with minor effect. Interview no. 106, FIOM Cuneo (Secretariat), 15 December 1983.

17. Interview no. 78, FLM Modena, 21 February 1981. Also mentioned in interview no. 74, FLM Modena (Secretariat), 18 February 1981.

18. See Caruso, "Immagini della classe operaia modenese," 28–30.

19. See Marzio Barbagli and Piergiorgio Corbetta, "La svolta del Pci," *Il Mulino* 30 (January–February 1981), 95–130.

its provincial offices, establishing instead regional ones and comprensori, geographic areas generally smaller than the provinces had been. Major policy decisions were now largely entrusted to the regions, and within the region of Piedmont, the Turinese dominated. The new structure allowed some of the Cuneese FLM to ride Turinese coattails and present the regional FLM's proposed amendments to factory assemblies, as Table 7 shows.[20] The amendments largely resembled those endorsed by the national FLM, and their thrust was the full and automatic protection of real working-class incomes. The Cuneese FLM nonetheless remained as isolated in the province as it had been during adoption of the EUR policy: the local CGIL-CISL-UIL refused to recommend amendments to the Federazione Unitaria's document. Nor did any other category union in Cuneo, and of the three comprensori that now made up the province, in only two did FLM officials actually propagate the regional modifications.[21] "Amendments," the local CISL noted dryly, "exist practically only among the metalworkers' unions."[22]

The opportunity to vote on an amended document allowed the FLM a greater measure of rank-and-file consensus than other category unions could muster. In the comprensorio of Cuneo-Mondovì, for instance, 96 percent of metalworkers voting on the amended recommendations favored them, whereas the approval rate in other industries—on the Federazione Unitaria's unmodified document—was only 72 percent.[23] Such an outcome did not convince other local union offices that the rank and file in the metalworking sector differed significantly from its counterpart in other industries, however—only that it would generally approve whatever its union asked.[24]

In Modena, the FLM took what it considered a "realistic" position

20. Abstentions or, in the case of secret ballots, blank returns are not reported. Analysis shows no significant differences by province in the percentages of voters who abstained or handed in blank ballots, which was generally between 5 and 10 percent.

21. Interviews no. 107, CISL Saluzzo-Savigliano-Fossano (Secretariat), 15 December 1983, and no. 109, CGIL Saluzzo-Savigliano-Fossano, 15 December 1983. The three comprensori of Cuneo are Saluzzo-Savigliano-Fossano, Alba-Bra, and Cuneo-Mondovì. In Alba-Bra the FLM was divided. The amended regional document was presented in some factories, whereas in others the Federazione CGIL-CISL-UIL's original document was presented.

22. "La consultazione da noi," *Cronache Sindacali*, periodico CISL del comprensorio Saluzzo-Savigliano-Fossano, 1 (November 1982), 2.

23. Reported in ibid., 1. Participation rates at the assemblies were similar across sectors.

24. Interview no. 107, CISL Saluzzo-Savigliano-Fossano (Secretariat), 15 December 1983.

Table 7. Consultazione Results, Metalworking Sector: October–November 1982 (Percentages)

	Participants/ Employees	Voters/ Participants	Voters/ Employees	Votes on CGIL-CISL-UIL/ Voters	Votes on locally amended/Voters	CGIL-CISL-UIL Recommendations						Locally Amended Recommendations					
						Approved			Rejected			Approved			Rejected		
						E	P	Votes	E	P	Votes	E	P	Votes	E	P	Votes
Turin	42	81	43	18	82	1	3	21	4	11	73	18	43	64	8	18	27
Cuneo	59	94	55	5	95	1	1	10	2	4	81	47	80	90	3	5	6
Pordenone[a]	48	88	47	100	100	n.a.						35	73	83	4	9	11
Modena	63	92	58	100	92	53	84	91	3	5	5	50	76	93	2	3	4
Bologna	58	91	53	100	38	18	31	34	32	55	60	7	13	37	10	18	51
Piedmont	46	84	38	19	83	2	4	22	5	11	70	22	48	68	8	16	24
Emilia-Romagna	61	91	56	100	72	38	62	68	15	25	27	33	53	81	5	9	14
Friuli-Venezia Giulia[a]	42	88	37	n.a.[b]	n.a.	n.a.											
Turin																	
Mirafiori	31	58	18	27	55	1	1	1	5	15	97	7	23	72	2	6	19
Rivalta	39	71	27	13	87	1	1	1	3	9	97	23	59	96	1	1	2
plants > 1,000[c]	32	70	23	18	81	1	1	7	4	11	89	11	33	59	7	20	35
plants ≤ 1,000	62	72	44	19	80	2	3	18	6	10	75	27	44	76	6	10	18
Pordenone[a]																	
Zanussi	35	79	28	100	100	n.a.						23	64	82	3	10	12
Other	63	94	60	100	100	n.a.						50	78	83	6	9	9
Italy	n.a.	n.a.	n.a.	n.a.	n.a.	11	n.a.	24[d]	14	n.a.	30	21	n.a.	44	n.a.		

Sources: Italy, Turin, Cuneo, Modena, Piedmont, Emilia-Romagna, Friuli-Venezia Giulia, and Italy calculated from Sandro Bianchi, Fernando Liuzzi, and Irene Spezzano, "I risultati della consultazione," *FLM Notizie*, n.s. 1 (30 November 1982), 14, table 1; 18–19, tables 3 and 3 bis; and 23, table 5. All figures for Pordenone courtesy of FLM Pordenone. Disaggregated Turinese calculations based on figures courtesy of FLM Piedmont.

Note: Employees (E) = number of employees in plants where assemblies were held. Participants (P) = number of such employees who attended assemblies. Voters = number of such employees who voted on any set of recommendations, amendments, or formal motions. Number of voters may be higher than number of participants where secret ballots were used. Number of voters may be higher than number of votes on CGIL-CISL-UIL national recommendations plus locally amended recommendations where some assemblies voted on some different set of items altogether. Votes = number of votes counted (for, against, abstentions) on a particular set of recommendations. Number of votes may be higher than number of voters where workers voted twice (on both CGIL-CISL-UIL national recommendations and on locally amended recommendations).

[a]In Pordenone, employees voted simultaneously on CGIL-CISL-UIL recommendations and locally amended recommendations. For the region of Friuli-Venezia Giulia, it is impossible to distinguish votes according to which set of recommendations was presented.

[b]N.a. = not available.

[c]Excludes Olivetti and Honeywell (Ivrea), where figures were not comparable.

[d]Calculated in relation to number of voters, not votes. National figures do not distinguish rejections of CGIL-CISL-UIL recommendations from those of locally amended recommendations.

during the consultazione of November 1982,[25] steering a middle course between the far more radical union offices in neighboring Bologna, the regional CGIL-CISL-UIL in Emilia, the national FLM, and the national confederations. Typically, workers were asked to approve the Federazione CGIL-CISL-UIL's document as well as a bundle of items endorsed by the regional CGIL-CISL-UIL.[26] The regional proposals, like those elaborated by the national FLM, focused on the issues of simultaneity and the "sure" protection of the incomes of lower-paid workers through tax reform, aimed at protecting real incomes. The local "law of organization" ensured that the Modenese FLM would follow the guidelines laid out by its national offices, despite the fact that amendments aimed at protecting the incomes of lower-paid workers were incongruent with local conditions where wages were relatively high.[27] The local FLM judged it inadvisable to insist that amendments be considered binding on the national confederations, however, and generally assumed a softer, less aggressive position than the national federation.[28]

The relative moderation of the Modenese FLM is particularly evident when we compare its assemblies with those held in metalworking firms in Bologna and across the region of Emilia-Romagna, where the provinces of Modena and Bologna are situated. In the comprensorio of Bologna, the national CGIL-CISL-UIL recommendations received only 34 percent of the vote in assemblies and were rejected outright by 60 percent, as table 7 shows. In Emilia as a whole, confederal recommendations were approved by 68 percent of metalworkers voting in assemblies. But in the combined comprensori of Modena and Sassuolo, which together constitute the province of Modena, the national document was approved by a resounding 91 percent of those who voted during the assemblies. Compared with their counterparts in the rest of the region, the Modenese FLM exercised greater vigor in eliciting the rank and file's support for austerity in 1982.

In Bologna, even the regional CGIL-CISL-UIL amendments were not considered sufficiently radical and were approved by only 37 percent of the metalworkers who voted on them. But only 38 percent of those who voted on the national confederal recommendations were also given the

25. Interview no. 122, FLM Modena (Secretariat), 27 December 1983.

26. The latter is contained in a leaflet distributed to the rank and file that also included the Federazione CGIL-CISL-UIL's original proposals; Federazione Territoriale CGIL-CISL-UIL Modena, "Proposte della Federazione CGIL CISL UIL per una piattaforma unitaria sulla difesa dell'occupazione, i rinnovi contrattuali e la riforma del costo del lavoro" ([Modena], [1982]).

27. Interview no. 123, FLM Modena (Secretariat), 27 December 1983.

28. Interview no. 122, FLM Modena (Secretariat), 27 December 1983.

opportunity to vote on the amended regional proposals; by refusing to endorse the regional CGIL-CISL-UIL proposals to modify the national document, the FLM in Bologna conspicuously and deliberately enhanced opposition.[29] Overall, the Bolognese FLM was largely successful in inducing its rank and file to reject all proposals for austerity, even those the national confederations considered far from stringent. In Modena, by contrast, 92 percent of those who voted on the national CGIL-CISL-UIL proposals also voted on the regional CGIL-CISL-UIL recommendations, which received 93 percent support from those who voted on them. Compared with their Bolognese colleagues—whose position was deviant in relation to the region as a whole—the Modenese look like paragons of restraint.[30]

In both Cuneo and Modena, the union movement offered considerable support for austerity proposals. This moderate policy orientation in turn received considerable rank-and-file support: the participation rate at assemblies in both provinces was about 60 percent, compared with approximately 45 percent in Turin and Pordenone. Moreover, of those attending factory assemblies, more stayed to vote in Cuneo and Modena than in Turin and Pordenone: over 90 percent in both cases. Finally, in both Cuneo and Modena, locally amended recommendations were supported in greater proportions than in Turin and Pordenone. Union actors in both provinces repeatedly sanctioned austerity, taking positions decidedly more moderate than their counterparts in other union offices in their respective regions, and both received widespread rank-and-file support for doing so. Both FLMs have acted in ways significantly less oppositional than their national federation and more in line with confederal injunctions. Finally,

29. The same was true in the compresorio of Alba-Bra in the province of Cuneo. About a third of workers who voted in the factory assemblies there were allowed to vote only on the confederal recommendations, which they predictably rejected by 81 percent. The rejection rate for those who voted on the FLM's amended version in the comprensorio was only 21 percent.

30. For reasons that are largely unknown, the Bolognese union movement has been one of Italy's most radical for many years. Since the composition of the labor force is similar to that in Modena, the differences between the two organizations are more likely to reside with their functionaries than the rank and file. Although it is true that the union movement in Bologna has for more than fifteen years been under the control of an extremely talented, well-educated, and bright group of Communist radicals—who seem to derive a certain pleasure from defying party reformism—and that they are sufficiently self-conscious and internally unified to constitute a virtual faction, it is not clear why such a group was able to obtain and then maintain power there. Indeed, even members of the group are unable to explain why Bologna should differ from neighboring provinces in this regard. That it does renders union leadership in Bologna highly atypical for the red zone.

the FLM's policy orientations in these provinces were largely representative of those assumed by the whole of organized labor in each.

Resistance to Moderation in Turin and Pordenone

The FLM in both Turin and Pordenone manifested explicit and public dissent over the adoption of austerity recommendations in 1978 and 1982. FLM representatives from Turin and Pordenone who attended the national assembly voted against or abstained on EUR in 1978, and in 1982 the union movement in the two provinces successfully promulgated amended policy documents.

The FLM in Turin took a strong stand against the Federazione Unitaria's austerity recommendations in 1978. The first public signs of dissent appeared on 19 January 1978 at a meeting of what is called the Consiglione, Mirafiori's umbrella consiglio di fabbrica. As Italy's largest Fiat plant, Mirafiori is highly visible, and dissent there could not help but receive public notice. The assembly's opening address, presented under the eyes of three important representatives of the national confederations, stated:

> In a situation such as that at Fiat, where real wages have been contained for years, we hold that the proposed availability [of the confederations to contain wages] in exchange for guarantees [for changes in national economic policymaking] is not representative of the facts of the situation, insofar as they already conform. . . .
>
> It is not sufficient to affirm something so obvious as the need for the coordination of bargaining strategy by the confederations with respect to the cost of labor, but . . . to confront the problem . . . with the workers. . . .
>
> On the problem of the gradual implementation of wage gains [in the upcoming industrywide bargaining] over the next three years: it is one thing to guide this in relation to a debate with the workers . . . and quite another to make it become a question of principle and a norm, in that this would tend to eradicate articulated bargaining.

The introductory address concluded: "The discussion of the Federazione Unitaria's document should be modified on the questions of wages and mobility, for the reasons already given."[31]

31. Consiglio di fabbrica, Mirafiori (Fiat-Turin), "Relazione introduttiva al Consiglione di Mirafiori," Torino, 19 gennaio 1978, partially reprinted in FLM Torino, ed., "Dal consiglione di Mirafiori all'Assemblea dell'Eur," *Il Consiglione,* bollettino dei Delegati della Mirafiori, no. 11 (May 1978), 4–6.

Commenting on the assembly, Sergio Garavini, who attended as the official representative of the national offices of the CGIL, admitted frankly that its participants had displayed a "relatively clear intolerance with respect to the confederal document," since "on critical points, the orientation of the Federazione [Unitaria], more than contested on it own merits, is experienced as a political maneuver substantially separate from the reality of class conflict occurring in the factories [and as] producing discontent and demoralization among the workers."[32]

After the meeting, widely covered in the national press, the Turinese FLM launched a complete round of shop-floor assemblies in order to mount an effective campaign against the confederal recommendations. As a wall poster explaining what had taken place at the meeting on the nineteenth announced: "we have substantive critical reactions to certain points contained in the platform, . . . especially to the cost of labor, [and] labor mobility."[33] Notes drawn up by the FLM's provincial offices outlined how the two-hour strike/assemblies should be conducted, indicating that the following points should receive special emphasis: "No to SOCIAL CONTRACT, but [instead] proposals for conflict, for the development of conflict and bargaining (the social contract is treaty, renunciation of bargaining, freezing of our demands). . . . No wage cap, neither national (incomes policy) nor bargained, nor at the firm level . . . but availability to contain and implement wage gains over time if autonomously decided in light of guarantees on: investments and employment, [and the] containment of inflation."[34] Thus the FLM substantially criticized the confederal document before its rank and file. Nonetheless, as one local unionist remarked: "It was the ugliest point in our relationship with the rank and file [*la gente*]."[35] The union did not dare reject the confederal proposals outright. Opposition in such a delicate political context was bound to be seen as "antisouthern" and "corporatist," as one unionist put it.[36] The

32. Sergio Garavini, "Le nuove condizioni di lotta nella crisi economica," *Rinascita* 35 (10 February 1978), 5.

33. FLM, Commissione informazione della 5ª Lega, ed., "Giornale Murale del Consiglio di fabbrica di Mirafiori," reprinted in *Il Consiglione*, no. 11 (May 1978), 5.

34. FLM Torino, "Traccia per riunioni e assemblee," 3–4, internal document dated 26 January 1978, courtesy of FLM Turin. Emphasis in the original.

35. Interview no. 33, FLM Turin (Secretariat), 7 July 1980.

36. Interview no. 17, ex-FLM Turin (Secretariat), 23 May 1980. "Antisouthern" was a derogatory term used with reference to the employed northern industrial work force when it appeared less than enthusiastic in making "sacrifices" on behalf of unemployed southerners. "Corporatist" in Italian political terminology refers to particularistic behavior. The term generally carries a strong morally pejorative connotation; corporatist actions are by definition "selfish." For brief comments on the relation between this meaning of "corpora-

success of the confederations and of the PCI in delegitimizing dissent put the local unions in the awkward position of trying to present austerity to the rank and file as crucial in its statement of goals and yet inadequate in its concrete program of action.[37] As one local unionist coyly noted, the Turinese FLM had not actually been "against" EUR: it had just advanced its own "interpretation" of austerity, an interpretation, he argued, more "conflictual" than that of the confederations.[38] When dissent cannot be openly articulated, its expression assumes a sly evasiveness. But it may be equally effective.

The FLM's attempts to stir up the rank and file's opposition to the EUR recommendations contrast with what was almost uniformly perceived by local unionists as widespread constituency *acceptance* of austerity. Even unionists who abstained on the policy at the national assembly admitted that the general reaction of the rank and file was conditional support, a sort of "we'll give it a try" attitude.[39] The result seems to have been what one unionist referred to as "submission": neither rebellion nor full-fledged, active, and informed consent.[40] As in Modena and Cuneo, the Turinese rank and file appeared passively reconciled to austerity in 1978.

Despite the lack of active resistance on the part of the rank and file, the Turinese FLM persevered in its criticisms. A meeting of the CGIL-CISL-UIL's provincial offices was held on 3 and 4 February in order to assess the reactions of the various provincial unions to the confederal recommendations. The introductory address reiterated the FLM's firm opposition to either a social contract or an incomes policy and indicated a provincial CGIL-CISL-UIL prepared to fight for substantial modifications of the confederal document at the forthcoming national assembly: "When we

---

tist" and its sense when used in such expressions as "neocorporatist," see Leo Panitch, "Recent Theorizations of Corporatism: Reflections on a Growth Industry," *British Journal of Sociology* 31 (June 1980), 177–78.

37. Various unionists explicitly mentioned the partisan political isolation of opposition to EUR as a crucial factor explaining their weakness in obtaining any substantial modifications of confederal austerity proposals. Aside from the interview just mentioned, interview no. 35, ex-FLM Turin (Secretariat), 15 July 1980.

38. Interview no. 1, FLM Turin (Secretariat), 23 June 1980.

39. Interview no. 17, ex-FLM Turin (Secretriat), 23 May 1980. Rank and file acceptance of austerity was also mentioned in interviews no. 33, FLM Turin (Secretariat), 7 July 1980, and no. 35, ex-FLM Turin (Secretariat), 15 July 1980. Similar impressions were found by Vittorio Sivo, "La mappa del dissenso sindacale dopo il direttivo Cgil-Cisl-Uil," *La Repubblica*, 17 January 1978, 15. Sivo notes that the unexpected feature of working-class responses to austerity was that "it is the intermediary cadres, the leaders on the periphery, far more than the so-called 'base,' who resist" (17).

40. Interview no. 33, FLM Turin (Secretariat), 7 July 1980.

talk about wages, about wage policy, and the gains we hope to win on this front, . . . it is also necessary to point out our rigidity, in the sense of defending the levels of bargaining we have already conquered, thanks to the experience of articulated bargaining."[41] The address went on to point out that while it had once been possible to "link" wage demands with those for employment and investments in the south of Italy, this had proved possible only "with the direct participation of the workers,"[42] emphasizing the dissidents' preoccupation with rank-and-file democracy and participation. Reference was made to the need to reject outright any kind of incomes policy, in which wages would be considered dependent on profits,[43] in direct repudiation of the comments made just a few days earlier by the general secretary of the CGIL. The address went on to call for a vast and continuous unleashing of articulated conflict and mass mobilization. Although the Turinese never formally objected in principle to austerity but rather appeared only to propose tactical amendments, cumulatively their recommendations verged on altering its spirit.

The Turinese FLM sent only five representatives to the EUR assembly in February.[44] Joined by some of the representatives of the Turinese CGIL-CISL-UIL, three abstained on the final document. Replicating those differences found in the national FLM, no Communists were among the abstainers. Nonetheless, leading Communist unionists from Turin, both in the FIOM and in the provincial CGIL, were instrumental in helping obtain the few amendments won. The reluctance of Communist unionists to publicize their disapproval through abstention should be understood within the context of an ingrained habit of formal unanimity, one non-Communist colleague explained, not as an indication of actual substantive agreement.[45]

The Turinese FLM's response to national austerity recommendations in 1982 paralleled its reactions nearly five years earlier. The organization assumed a position even more intransigent than that of its national federation, recommending alternative proposals to those enunciated by the Federazione CGIL-CISL-UIL and arguing that the results of the factory assemblies should be strictly binding on the confederations. With the full

41. CGIL-CISL-UIL, Federazione di Torino, "Relazione presentata a nome della Segreteria Unitaria CGIL-CISL-UIL da Silvio Canapè," assemblea provinciale dei delegati e quadri sindacali, Torino, 3–4 febbraio 1978, 14, internal document courtesy of FLM Turin.

42. Ibid., 14.

43. Ibid., 15.

44. Interview no. 10, FLM Turin, 21 March 1980. Also reported in *Il Manifesto* (4 February 1978).

45. Interview no. 17, ex-FLM Turin (Secretariat), 23 May 1980.

support of the local CGIL-CISL-UIL, the Turinese fought for rank-and-file support of amendments on the usual issues of simultaneity and lower-paid workers, with the aim of ensuring the automatic protection of workers' real incomes.

The national FLM had responded to the Federazione CGIL-CISL-UIL's austerity recommendations in a meeting of its own Comitato Direttivo on 26 October. The regional Piedmontese CGIL-CISL-UIL's Comitato Direttivo met the same day to evaluate the confederal proposals, issuing a final statement along lines similar to those articulated by the national FLM.[46] The following day, the Consiglio Generale of the Piedmontese FLM met to draw up similar recommendations, arguing that "within the recommendations of the national CGIL-CISL-UIL, the principal objective to pursue remains the defense of real wages, to pursue with tax changes so as to assure a simultaneity between a reduction of taxes and wage reform which, along with the renewal of the industrywide labor contracts, will obtain the objective of safeguarding purchasing power."[47] In other words, the FLM recommended "a contemporaneous solution between the new wage indexation mechanism and tax reform" and maintained that such proposals should be considered "fundamental elements to insert in the recommendations of the Federazione CGIL-CISL-UIL."[48] Indeed, such amendments should be formally binding on the confederations: the FLM held that only once such "specifications" had been adopted could it ask workers to approve the confederal austerity proposals.[49] The organization of factory assemblies thus proceeded on the supposition that the FLM would formally request approval of the Federazione Unitaria's recommendations only with binding amendments attached.[50]

The three comprensori (Ivrea, Pinerolo, and Torino) that now made up the province of Turin saw 615 assemblies in metalworking plants, potentially involving over 150,000 employees, although the participation rate was only 42 percent.[51] A mere 7,000 employees were asked to vote solely

46. CGIL-CISL-UIL Piemonte, "Documento conclusivo del Comitato Direttivo regionale CGIL-CISL-UIL—26-10-82," internal document courtesy of FLM Piedmont.

47. FLM Piemonte, "Ordine del Giorno conclusivo del Consiglio Generale FLM, 27.10.1982," *Nota per i Delegati,* occasional leaflet publication issued by the FLM Piemonte, no. 16 (October 1982).

48. Ibid.

49. FLM Piemonte, "Scaletta per assemblee su 'consultazione,'" internal document dated 29 October 1982, courtesy of FLM Piedmont.

50. FLM Piedmont, "Disposizione per l'effettuazione delle consultazioni," internal document dated 28 October 1982, courtesy of FLM Piedmont.

51. Data reported in this analysis not included in table 7 are drawn from Bianchi, Liuzzi, and Spezzano, "Risultati della consultazione," 18–19, tables 3 and 3 bis, or from data courtesy of FLM Piedmont.

on the confederal recommendations and those who were asked rejected them by an overwhelming margin of 83 percent.[52] Two-thirds of workers voting (some 36,000) were presented only the FLM Piedmont's amended version of austerity, which 70 percent of them approved. This version incorporated a long amendment to the national proposals, an amendment also endorsed by the Piedmontese CGIL-CISL-UIL, thereby effectively making it official policy for the region.[53] Another 13,000 votes were counted among employees who voted twice: once on the confederal recommendations and again on the regionally amended version. In these assemblies, the latter received the approval of only 42 percent of the voters, tying with the number of voters who rejected even the amended version outright. Presenting both sets of recommendations encouraged rejections: in assemblies where only the amended recommendations were presented, rejections came to some 27 percent; assemblies with double voting rejected even the FLM's recommendations by 41 percent. Finally, some assemblies were presented both a locally amended version of the confederal recommendations and a separate FLM amendment reiterating the local union's position, on which nearly 24,000 workers voted. Of those who voted on this amendment, 49 percent approved it. Overall, as table 7 shows, the FLM's amended version of austerity was approved by 64 percent of those Turinese given the opportunity to vote on it, whereas the confederal version was approved by a mere 21 percent of voters to whom it was submitted.

The assemblies proved especially trying in some of the largest metalworking plants in the province. At Mirafiori, Italy's largest single factory, then employing a work force of nearly 38,000, the participation rate at the assemblies was only 31 percent, and of those who bothered to attend the assemblies, only 58 percent voted. Put another way, of the whole of Mirafiori's work force, only 18 percent voted on austerity recommendations. About a quarter of the votes were counted on the national confederal recommendations, which were overwhelmingly rejected by 97 percent of those who voted on them. More than half of Mirafiori's voters were asked to approve the FLM's amended version, and they did so by nearly three-quarters. (The remainder voted on alternative recommendations or mo-

52. This procedure was not the FLM's policy. It occurred in cases where factory councils insisted, with the aim of soliciting outright rejection, when the attempt to pass even an amended version of austerity was perceived as a "trick" aimed at artificially generating rank-and-file consensus. Interviews no. 120, FLM Piedmont (Secretariat), 22 December 1983 and no. 121, ex-FLM Turin (Secretariat), 22 December 1983.

53. "Emendamento od ordine del giorno vincolante riferito al punto 7–capoverso II-della proposta CGIL-CISL-UIL," internal document courtesy of FLM Piedmont.

tions.) At Fiat Rivalta, which then employed some 11,500 persons, the outcome was better for the FLM: although the participation rate was not much higher, a larger proportion of participants stayed to vote, and the FLM's locally amended recommendations were approved by 96 percent of the workers who voted on them. The differences between Mirafiori and Rivalta seem best explained by what workers were asked to vote on. At Rivalta, the FLM took a compact stand in presenting locally amended recommendations, which were approved with virtual unanimity (96 percent of votes on them were favorable). At Mirafiori, the FLM presented a variety of policy recommendations in different assemblies. This had the effect of substantially lowering the proportion of favorable votes even on the locally amended recommendations (72 percent). A critical distinction thus appears between plants where the union sought rank-and-file consensus on a single set of recommendations and those where it instead generated rank-and-file divisions as a result of its own internal divisions.

The FLM's difficulties in drawing Fiat employees to the assemblies attracted public notice[54] and contributed to the union movement's strong sense that austerity recommendations were experiencing particular difficulties in large plants. Comparing Turinese plants with more than 1,000 employees with smaller plants shows that the participation rate in large plants was only about half that in small plants. Once workers were at the assemblies, they stayed to vote: getting them there in the first place proved more difficult in large plants. And in large plants the rejection rates of both the original confederal proposals and the locally amended recommendations were considerably higher than in small ones: nearly 90 and 35 percent, respectively, compared with 75 and under 20 in small plants.

The CGIL-CISL-UIL offices in Piedmont stressed the support amendments had received in reporting on their assemblies to the central confederations: "The overwhelming majority of favorable votes refer to the [confederal] recommendations modified by binding amendments or motions. Consequently, in Piedmont a 'yes' has clearly prevailed in the consultazione, conditional to the inclusion of clear positions to be considered binding regarding the simultaneity of the tax question, the automatic protection of low and medium incomes, the 10 percent reduction of the scala mobile."[55] In summarizing the results of the consultazione, the

54. See, for instance, "Costo-lavoro: le assemblee approvano con emendamenti," *L'Unità*, Turinese edition, 5 November 1982, 12, which compares preliminary assembly results of Fiat and non-Fiat plants in the area, as well as Maurizio Ricci, "Scala mobile, gli operai bocciano i piani sindacali," *La Repubblica*, 3 November 1982, 1.

55. Federazione CGIL-CISL-UIL Piemonte, "Ordine del giorno del Comitato Direttivo regionale della Federazione CGIL CISL UIL piemontese del 11/11/82," 1, telex sent to the

FLM, too, noted that "the amendment presented by the FLM of Piedmont in practically the whole of the debate within organs internal to the union and in the worker assemblies obtained sufficient verification," despite the "nonnegligible problems regarding the participation of workers in the assemblies and the voting."[56]

Responses of the Pordenonese FLM to austerity proposals paralleled those in Turin. In 1978 the provincial FLM held two meetings with its largest CdF, at the Zanussi plant in Porcia. At the first, the union distributed copies of the Federazione Unitaria's proposals, which had not yet been seen in full by the delegates. A "desultory [*scarsissimo*]" debate ensued, and the document was approved nearly unanimously. At a second meeting the FLM presented its national office's criticisms of the confederal recommendations and a small debate again followed.[57]

According to provincial unionists and factory delegates, no factory assemblies were held in Pordenone in 1978 to discuss the Federazione Unitaria's austerity recommendations.[58] The net result was that the confederal proposals for austerity were almost entirely ignored by the rank and file. After a provincial CGIL-CISL-UIL assembly held before the national meeting,[59] what little debate there had been dissipated, and EUR "quietly passed over the heads of the workers," as typically occurs in Pordenone on debates coordinated nationally on general issues.[60]

Federazione CGIL-CISL-UIL, copy courtesy of Archivio CGIL (ufficio organizzativo), Rome.

56. FLM Piemonte, "Comunicato della Segreteria F.L.M. Piemonte sull'esito della consultazione," 1, Torino, internal document dated 24 November 1982, courtesy of FLM Piedmont.

57. Interview no. 90, two members of the executive of the consiglio di fabbrica, Zanussi (Porcia), 1 March 1980.

58. Interviews no. 84, FLM Pordenone (Secretariat), 26 February 1981; no. 86, FLM Pordenone (Secretariat), 27 February 1981; no. 91, FLM Pordenone (Secretariat), 2 March 1981; and no. 94, CISL Pordenone (Secretariat), 3 March 1981. One unionist hinted that this decision had been occasioned by fear of widespread rank-and-file disapproval of austerity. Given the reactions of the CdF at Zanussi, this seems a dubious proposition. More likely, the FLM's decision to dispense with the factory assemblies was due to a mixture of impatience, internal disagreements about how to communicate the issues, and logistic problems. In early 1978 a bargaining round (*vertenza*) was under way at Zanussi (Porcia) over the issue of the night shift in the plastic workshop. The logistics of trying simultaneously to keep the work force mobilized and informed on a bargaining issue and to hold two-hour assemblies over remote and complex national issues are very tricky.

59. Interview no. 86, FLM Pordenone (Secretariat), 27 February 1981. A national leader of the UIL attended from Rome.

60. Interview no. 90, two members of the executive of the consiglio di fabbrica, Zanussi (Porcia), 1 March 1981. General rank-and-file apathy and low assembly participation regarding issues of general strategic import were also mentioned in interview no. 91, FLM Pordenone (Secretariat), 2 March 1981.

Nonetheless, some of the Pordenone FIM and UILM delegates attending the EUR assembly on 13 and 14 February 1978 voted against or abstained on the final recommendations. Contrary votes came from members and supporters of Democrazia Proletaria (DP), a small extraparliamentary left-wing organization whose adherents were instructed to vote against the document.[61] The votes of DP delegates were coordinated nationally and stemmed from general political considerations. They were designed, like some of the abstaining votes, to delegitimize trade union support for a government of national unity. The abstainers from Pordenone, on the other hand, closely resembled those from Turin. Although general political considerations were not entirely absent, the major impetus seems to have come from exquisitely trade union considerations: "resistance to any kind of limitation on collective bargaining"[62] and a desire to protect rank-and-file democracy and mobilizational capacity. Resistance to austerity was, in other words, bound up with issues of strategic priorities and orientations.

The reaction of Communist unionists in Pordenone also resembled that in Turin. Even Communist trade unionists experienced EUR "as a renunciation" and as purely "manipulative" for the political needs of the PCI.[63] The CGIL reported that, as for asking the rank and file for "sacrifices"—the PCI's key austerity slogan—"we never used that term," substituting instead the less offensive call for "coherent choices."[64]

Although Communist unionists in Pordenone did not play the same nationally important role as did their colleagues from Turin in fighting for amendments at the EUR assembly, if only because they were far fewer and carried less political weight, neither did their responses parallel those of the Cuneese or Modenese. Unlike the latter, Pordenonese Communist unionists did not attempt either to carry the message of austerity to the rank and file or to pressure non-Communist dissidents into renouncing

61. Interview no. 22, national CGIL-affiliated industrial union (Secretariat), 29 May 1980. Most DP delegates attended from Milan, the organization's major base. The leadership of the abstaining faction tried to get them to compromise their position and abstain, in order to make dissent as effective as possible in obtaining key amendments, but the DP was intransigent.

62. Interview no. 22, national CGIL-affiliated industrial union (Secretariat), 29 May 1980. The respondent, one of the national coordinators of dissent, categorized opposition into two partially overlapping components: "resistance to any kind of limitation of collective bargaining," and opposition, whether from the Left or the Right, to the formation of a national unity government.

63. Interview no. 86, FLM Pordenone (Secretariat), 27 February 1981, confirmed in interview no. 91, FLM Pordenone (Secretariat), 2 March 1981.

64. Interview no. 95, CGIL Pordenone (Secretariat), 3 March 1981.

public opposition. Unlike the former, where potentially dissident Communists in the FIOM were held in check by the CGIL, there do not seem to have been any significant divergences between the responses of these two actors. Pordenonese Communists in both the FIOM and the CGIL attempted to dissociate themselves from the policy as much as possible, colluding with the CISL and the UIL to avoid direct encounters over it with the rank and file.

The reactions of the Pordenonese union movement to austerity recommendations in 1982 again resembled those in Turin. The provincial CGIL-CISL-UIL issued an amendment, similar to that proposed by the national FLM, that was used for the factory assemblies.[65] So, too, did the regional offices of the CGIL-CISL-UIL, such that "in the overwhelming majority of the assemblies the recommendations were approved explicitly or implicitly along with a motion proposed by the regional Federazione CGIL-CISL-UIL and the comprensori of Trieste and Pordenone that reconsiders the problems of the full protection of purchasing power of the lowest-paid through bargaining, tax changes and an improvement of family allowances."[66] The amendments were supported by the Pordenonese FLM,[67] and the consultazione was conducted on the basis of a locally amended version of the confederal austerity recommendations, a version the local union movement argued should be considered binding on the confederations.

The results, though better than those in Turin, were still doubtful in the province's largest plants. In the metalworking industries overall, 123 assemblies were held, potentially involving nearly 12,000 workers, although the participation rate was under 50 percent. Of those who attended the assemblies, 88 percent stayed to vote on the regionally amended recommendations, and of those who voted, 83 percent approved the proposals. However, this generally positive outcome did not hold at Zanussi, Pordenone's largest firm, with six plants located in the province, including the largest in Porcia. In the Zanussi plants, though the tallies of the actual votes were similar to those for the province as a whole, the par-

65. Federazione Provinciale CGIL-CISL-UIL, Comitato Direttivo, "Documento del Comitato Direttivo Federazione provinciale CGIL-CISL-UIL," Pordenone, 28 ottobre 1982, internal document dated 29 October 1982, courtesy of FLM Pordenone.

66. CGIL-CISL-UIL Regionale Friuli-Venezia Giulia (Segreteria), untitled telex to the Dipartimento organizzazione CGIL, Rome, dated 12 November 1982, 2, Archivio CGIL (ufficio organizzazione), Rome, courtesy of CGIL, Rome.

67. Interviews no. 114, FLM Pordenone (Secretariat), 20 December 1983; no. 115, FLM Pordenone (Secretariat), 20 December 1983; and no. 119, FLM Pordenone (Secretariat), 21 December 1983.

ticipation rate fell to a mere 35 percent, compared with 63 percent in the rest of the sector. Those who did vote overwhelmingly approved the amended proposals (82 percent), however. As in Turin, the Pordenonese union movement experienced considerable difficulty in eliciting the cooperation of employees in large industry.

In both Turin and Pordenone, the FLM assumed aggressive anti-austerity positions in 1978 and 1982. In both cases, dissent was even more pronounced than that of the national offices of the federation. In 1978 these FLMs sent representatives to the national assembly, representatives who voted against or abstained on the central recommendations, something no one from Cuneo or Modena did. In 1982 these FLMs not only endosed particularly stringent amendments but argued that they should be binding on the confederations, an argument not advanced by either Cuneese or Modenese. And in both Turin and Pordenone, too, the FLM's position was supported by the provincial and regional CGIL-CISL-UIL offices, making the metalworkers representative of union reactions to austerity in the province as a whole.

The Role of the Communist Party

In 1978 the PCI supported austerity measures; in 1982 it opposed them. National policy was not, however, replicated by the party's provincial Federations in the four cases under consideration. Rather, each Federation acted to reinforce local union reactions when these corresponded to the party's national policy but did virtually nothing against the union when it did not.

In 1978, when the union movements in Turin and Pordenone exhibited antagonism to EUR, they did so in direct opposition to the national policy of the Communist party. Despite this, the local Federations never publicly contested union resistance to austerity. In Pordenone the party simply ignored the whole debate, never even printing up one leaflet asking workers to support EUR.[68] In Turin, the party's monthly newspaper aimed at Fiat Mirafiori workers de-emphasized austerity, presenting the policy as one that would not jeopardize workers' incomes and downplaying the "sacrifices" aspect. An editorial written just as the Federazione Unitaria was in the process of seeking rank-and-file approval for EUR read, for instance: "When one talks about a policy of sacrifices . . . we should understand this properly, and above all we should make sure this is under-

68. Interview no. 116, ex-PCI Pordenone (Secretariat), 20 December 1983. This was verified by a thorough check of the Federation's archives.

stood by the population. There are some rich and ultrarich Italians, whose income levels should be lowered and by a good deal; . . . Then there are sacrifices that, in greater or lesser measure, specific intermediate strata should make. Then there are other strata, including some workers, of whom in essence one asks that they not advance, at least for a certain period, demands that go beyond the defense of their present income in real terms."[69] Even as the union movements in Turin and Pordenone contested national party policy, the local Federations refrained from overt and public conflict with them, presenting the party's austerity policy in extremely muted tones.

In 1982, when the party's national policy had altered, its Turinese and Pordenone offices helped their union movements to mobilize the rank and file against the national union confederations. Throughout the course of the consultazione, the Turinese PCI actively aided the union, resulting in a "tactical convergence"[70] between the two wings of the labor movement. The local party Federation reported: "Our battle in this consultazione is above all to obtain ameliorating amendments to the recommendations of the Federazione Unitaria,"[71] amendments that replicated those endorsed by the Turinese union movement.[72] It alerted the public that the Turinese Federation felt the national austerity recommendations contained "some ambiguous points" that should be "corrected."[73] In Pordenone, too, the PCI played an active role in the consultazione, issuing a number of leaflets sharply critical of the Federazione CGIL-CISL-UIL's proposals and calling for amendments.

In Cuneo and Modena, by contrast, the party took an active role in supporting austerity in 1978 but refrained from mobilizing the rank and file against it in 1982. As in Turin and Pordenone, its positions largely paralleled those assumed by the local unions. In Modena there was "no

69. Unsigned editorial, *Mirafiori*, mensile a cura delle sezioni del PCI della Fiat Mirafiori, XXI, supplement to no. 2 (February 1978), 8.

70. Interview no. 102, FLM Piedmont (Secretariat), 13 December 1983; also reported in interview no. 121, ex-FLM Piedmont (Secretariat), 22 December 1983.

71. Piero Fassino, interview by Guido Compagna, "Torino: il Pci conferma la battaglia a favore degli emendamenti," *Il Sole-24 Ore*, 5 November 1982, 10.

72. PCI Torino, "Ipotesi di emendamento da proporre nelle riunioni dei consigli di fabbrica e nelle assemblee sulla proposta CGIL-CISL-UIL," internal document, Archivio Federazione PCI Torino (box "Salario-scala mobile-costo lavoro"), courtesy of PCI Turin. Copies of the amendment were given to Communist factory militants to present in the assemblies.

73. Federazione Torinese del PCI, "Costo del lavoro: la proposta CGIL-CISL-UIL e la posizione del P.C.I.," leaflet ([1982]), Archivio Federazione PCI Torino (box "Salario-scala mobile-costo lavoro"), courtesy of PCI Turin.

difference" between the party's and the union's positions in 1978; the party considered austerity "a major engagement [*impegno*]."[74] In Cuneo, although under national unity "in the factory it was difficult to be a Communist [*fare il comunista*]" the party helped enforce "compatibilities" in order to legitimate itself nationally.[75]

In 1982, however, even as the national party's position was critical of the union movement's proposals to alter the scala mobile, the Cuneese Federation was not actively involved in the consultazione,[76] while in Modena, though the Federation may have supported the FLM's amendments,[77] it refrained from "exacerbating" the situation by taking an independent public position, distributing leaflets, or otherwise trying to mobilize factory militants.[78] Nor did the local PCI pressure the union into taking a more radical position,[79] since the Modenese Federation considered the attempts by national party figures to turn the working class against the Federazione Unitaria's austerity recommendations "tactically in error."[80] Rather than aligning with those national leaders of the PCI most intent on preventing a tripartite agreement, the PCI in Modena supported the national union confederations.[81] Where the union movement exhibited most opposition to austerity in 1982, it received the active support of the PCI, in line with the party's national policy at the time. But the party spurred dissent only in localities where the union movement's own position was already markedly hostile to austerity and remained passive where it was not. And the major mechanism employed was largely indirect, consisting in mobilizing shop-floor militants to help organized labor get amendments attached to confederal recommendations.

Organizational Autonomy from the Rank and File

Provincial union responses to austerity did not necessarily reflect the rank and file's opinions about confederal recommendations for wage containment. In 1978 union officials from all four provinces agreed that the

74. Interview no. 79, ex-PCI Modena (Secretariat), 20 February 1981.
75. Interview no. 65, PCI Cuneo (Secretariat), 15 June 1980.
76. Interview no. 108, PCI Cuneo (Secretariat), 15 December 1983.
77. Interview no. 122, FLM Modena (Secretariat), 27 December 1983.
78. Interview no. 124, PCI Modena (Secretariat), 28 December 1983.
79. Interview no. 122, FLM Modena (Secretariat), 27 December 1983.
80. Interview no. 124, PCI Modena (Secretariat), 28 December 1983.
81. Interviews no. 123, FLM Modena (Secretariat), 27 December 1983 and no. 122, FLM Modena (Secretariat), 27 December 1983.

rank and file, while generally not enthusiastic, acquiesced in the EUR policy. Formal mechanisms for the expression of rank-and-file opinion were not well developed at the time; but even in the absence of ratification procedures, dissidents never claimed they were accurately transmitting rank-and-file responses to the policy recommendations.

The introduction of formal ratification mechanisms in 1982—instituted at the insistence of the three confederations, in large part in an effort to contain local discretion in "interpreting" rank-and-file opinion—did little to depress internal union conflict. The overall results were sufficiently ambiguous and uneven—deliberately so—to justify both supporters and opponents of the national recommendations to alter the wage indexation system. Nevertheless, the empirical evidence suggests that, once again, dissidents were not simply reacting to rank-and-file rebellion but rather attempting to catalyze it in ways they could control so as to use it for their own purposes. As one national union leader wrote, consultazioni work mainly as "a survey . . . to 'measure' the degree of influence of various elites,"[82] not as mechanisms that accurately transmit rank-and-file opinion.

The most conspicuous indicator of this is the widespread presentation of union-sponsored amendments, obviously drawn up before the factory assemblies even took place. Using the amended recommendations, union officials attempted to anticipate what they argued could have been widespread and decisive rank-and-file opposition in the absence of alternative recommendations. Their fears apparently proved justified: where metalworkers were asked to vote solely on the confederal recommendations, they tended to reject them. This is true for the case of Bologna, the compresorio of Alba-Bra in Cuneo, and the factory assemblies in Turin in which only the confederal recommendations were presented. The FLM's amended version, alternatively, received widespread support; approval rates ranged from two-thirds to over 90 percent of those who voted on it. This is not surprising: if asked to choose between a proposal that does not explictly rule out a reduction in one's standard of living and one that repeatedly promises its protection, one would naturally prefer the latter. And rebellion may seem a legitimate and reasonable response under conditions in which one is deliberately denied this particular choice. We have no idea how workers would have voted had the option of amended recommendations not existed, and there are no grounds for extrapolating from

82. Bruno Manghi, "Minoranze convocate in fretta e furia: quel che il vertice sindacale chiama 'consultazione,'" *Il Manifesto* (30 January 1982), 1.

the Bolognese, Alba-Bra, or Turinese examples to conclude that they would have rejected the Federazione CGIL-CISL-UIL's proposals had there been no alternative. At the very least, the evidence shows that workers had no principled objections to tampering with the system of wage indexation or keeping real incomes from rising for some relatively short period.

More to the point, there is little evidence of a significant correlation between variations in rank-and-file responses and variations in union responses in 1982. The union movement in Turin and Pordenone took a hard line on protecting workers' incomes in 1982; those in Cuneo and Modena did not. In the latter two provinces, workers who voted on the locally amended recommendations approved them by 90 and 93 percent, respectively, as table 7 shows. But in Pordenone, 83 percent of voters approved similar proposals, hardly a sign of widespread rank-and-file discontent. The equivalent figure for Turin is considerably lower: only 64 percent of workers who voted on the FLM's recommendations approved them. This disguises the difference between assemblies that voted only on the FLM's recommendations and those that voted twice, once on the FLM's version and once on the national document. In assemblies where the FLM's proposal was the only one submitted for approval, support rose to 70 percent; in assemblies in which both sets of recommendations were voted on, only 41 percent of voters approved the FLM's proposals. Rank-and-file responses were strongly influenced by which particular set of recommendations was presented, and this decision was made by full-time union officials in conjunction with the relevant factory delegates. Much of the difference in rank-and-file reactions across the four provinces was artificially created by the union movement itself and resulted from the choice of what recommendations to present at the assemblies.

Of particular importance are the apparent differences in rank-and-file reactions in large industry. We have seen that in both Turin and Pordenone, the FLM notified national officials of special difficulties in conducting the assemblies in Fiat and at Zanussi. But these difficulties were not necessarily the result of outright rank-and-file rejection of austerity recommendations. As table 7 shows, there was no difference between the percentage of Zanussi workers who endorsed the FLM's amended proposals and the percentage obtained in the province's other metalworking plants: in both cases, more than 80 percent of the votes were positive. In Turin, by contrast, significant differences seem to obtain between large and small plants. But there appears to be no necessary cross-provincial relation between rank-and-file opposition and plant size, and there is little evidence of any intrinsic difference in rank-and-file reactions according to plant size. The Bolognese managed to generate widespread opposition, as we have seen, even in small industry simply by refusing to allow amended recommendations to be presented at the factory assemblies. And across the country as a whole, only 13 percent of plants with more than 500 employees rejected austerity recommendations in 1982.[83] The only empirical analysis conducted of the consultazione argues that the findings "do not confirm the opinion that sees the recommendations 'rejected' in most of large industry"; in fact, adds the study, "controlling for plant size, geographic location is the decisive variable accounting for differences in participation and voting rates."[84]

It was the reactions in large industry, however, that eventually led to the incorporation of amendments into the final national proposals, even though the confederations were aware that "none of them alone received a majority consensus" across Italy.[85] On the basis of rank-and-file responses such as occurred at Mirafiori, the national FLM successfully convinced the confederations that in large industry "the position [of the Federazione CGIL-CISL-UIL] had not been approved."[86] Although the Federazione Unitaria argued that such cases, "far from being representative of a tendency, should be analyzed to understand what historical and organizational factors provoked such a displacement and distance from the overall situation," it also admitted that "in more than a few important cases of large firms, the recommendations were rejected."[87] The FLM's efforts to generate opposition in large industry legitimated the federation's efforts to see the confederal recommendations altered. As the national FLM argued, in its review of the consultazione: "In the [metalworking] categories, the assemblies for the consultazione were full of disputes [*un andamento assai contrastato*]. 'Nays' reached 30 percent and were mainly concentrated in firms with more than 500 employees; that is, in the heart of the working class that has characterized the FLM during the past fifteen years of battles and conquests."[88] By concentrating dissent in large

83. Spaventa, "Consultazioni," 484, table 9.

84. Ibid., 471.

85. Mario Colombo, "La consultazione: una tappa del cambiamento sindacale orientata al cambiamento sociale," relazione introduttiva, in Federazione CGIL-CISL-UIL, "I lavori del Direttivo unitario," Roma, 15–16 novembre 1982, *Conquiste del Lavoro*, supplement no. 22 to vol. 35 (22 November 1982), 3.

86. Interview no. 128, ex-national FLM (Secretariat), 7 January 1983. Also discussed in interview no. 130, national CGIL (Secretariat), 10 January 1983.

87. Colombo, "Consultazione," 3.

88. Paolo Franco, relazione to the FLM Comitato Direttivo, Roma, 16–17 dicembre 1982, 1, version mailed from "FLM, Ufficio Stampa" to "tutte le FLM regionali e comprensoriali non collegate tx [telex]," dated 17 December 1982.

industry, the federation made it publicly visible and politically salient. Even without majority endorsement, the FLM had strong grounds for driving home to the confederations the necessity of incorporating amendments: the federation could show definitively that unamended proposals were rejected outright in some—though not all—large firms. "The data," argued a national official of the FLM, "cannot be evaluated merely numerically." If austerity proposals are not approved in large factories, these results should be carefully "interpreted," because even if a majority of Italian employees endorse austerity recommendations, Italian labor cannot elaborate a strategy that is explicitly repudiated by workers in strategically central locations.[89] Numerically the differences may have been relatively marginal; politically they were crucial.

Large Industry's Influence over National Policy

We have seen thus far that provinces characterized by large industry appear especially apt to house radical union movements, movements that repeatedly have exhibited policy orientations hostile to incomes policies. Although we do not yet know why this is the case, radicalism is strongest where industry is concentrated, and the national FLM is overwhelmingly sensitive to the needs and opinions expressed by officials from provinces marked by large industry. The federation's national CD tends toward a representation of provinces characterized by industrial concentration, excluding those with more fragmentary industrial structures.

The Comitato Direttivo, the FLM's highest decision making body, is simultaneously geographically and organizationally based. In 1980 it was composed of 104 geographically selected representatives plus the entire national Secretariat, itself consisting of twenty-one members.[90] These 104 representatives were divided more or less equally among the three component organizations, the FIM, the FIOM and the UILM, as was the national Secretariat.[91]

89. Interview no. 128, ex-national FLM (Secretariat), 7 January 1984.

90. It is unclear to me whether the rest of the full-time national apparatus is also included. If so, this would extend membership to another 33 persons. Even if not formally part of the CD, members of the national political apparatus may attend their meetings.

91. According to one official, the equal division of membership among the three components was an accidental product of the transition the CD was then undergoing from a provincial to a regional basis. In 1977 the three components had agreed that membership in the CD would be 43 percent FIOM, 34 percent FIM, and 23 percent UILM. Interview no. 20, national FLM (Secretariat), 17 June 1980.

Thirty-four of Italy's ninty-four provinces were directly represented to the CD, as were seven of its twenty regions.[92] Smaller provinces with relatively few employees in the metalworking industries had no CD representation. Regional representation, moreover, overlapped with that already held by strong provinces rather than providing for the independent representation of those otherwise neglected. In at least four of the seven regions included in the CD, regional representatives were all from provinces that already had their own members.[93]

Other national bodies do include representatives from smaller, more marginal provinces. The Consiglio Generale Unitario (CGU) includes representatives from all ninety-four Italian provinces as well as shop-floor cadres, typically long-standing members of factory council executives, who account for about a third of its total members. However, the CGU meets only biannually and is not entrusted with decision-making powers. The CD is the FLM's highest decision-making body and is structured so as to incorporate disproportionately local centers of radicalism and militancy directly into the decision-making processes of the national FLM, thereby propelling the federation's radical vocation from below.

Two consequences of these arrangements merit consideration. First, the composition of the CD increases the legitimacy of the FLM's radical unionism, particularly as regards differences of opinion with the three confederations. The federation's national leadership can justifiably claim that decisions viewed unfavorably by the confederations were nonetheless representative of the opinions expressed by officials from the most important areas of the country. Second, the legitimacy of radical local offices is increased, thanks both to their direct involvement in national decision making and to the related likelihood that the policies that emerge will

92. The provinces with direct representation were: Alessandria, Novara, Turin, Genoa, Bergamo, Brescia, Lecco, Mantova, Milan, Varese, Pordenone, Trieste, Venice, Vicenza, Padova, Bologna, Forlì, Modena, Ravenna, Florence, Piombino, Ancona, Massa Carrara, Terni, Frosinone, Latina, Rome, Aquila, Caserta, Naples, Bari, Taranto, Palermo, and Syracuse. The regions represented were: Piedmont, Liguria, Lombardy, Friuli, the Veneto, Emilia-Romagna, and Tuscany. Eighty-one of the 104 were provincial representatives, and the remainder were regional. In 1978, when EUR was approved, the CD was entirely provincially based, since the creation of the regions in union organization had not yet taken place. All data on the composition of the FLM's CD were provided by the national offices of the FLM, Rome.

93. Piedmont, Lombardy, Friuli, and Emilia-Romagna were the only regions I was sufficiently familiar with to draw this conclusion after examining the data provided. In interview no. 20, national FLM (Secretariat), 17 June 1980, one official explained that the CD traditionally represented only the most important and largest provinces; there is no reason to expect that the shift to the regions was meant to change this.

more or less coincide with their recommendations. The exclusion of certain kinds of provinces from the CD is thus an arrangement mutually satisfactory both to the national FLM and to the more radical provincial union organizations. By disproportionately representing local leadership groups tied to large industry, it enhances the national FLM's ability to pursue its radical vocation.

Does this mark the national FLM as genuinely unrepresentative? It is impossible to answer this question in purely formal, organizational terms. There is no one correct technical solution to the problem of designing a national body to reflect accurately the interests and sentiments of an extremely heterogeneous work force spread across ninety-four provinces, and it is unclear whether "accurate" representation—however constructed—would serve the organization (and its constituents) well in any case. But substantively the answer is clear and speaks directly to the main concerns of this book. During the wave of mass mobilization that occurred between 1968 and 1972, it was politically both feasible and desirable for the national FLM to establish especially close links to large industry, since it was there that mobilization was most publicly visible and could be most effectively used to construct a successful national strategy. Large industry was used to spearhead collective bargaining; for this reason, workers even in smaller plants could later benefit from the gains won by their counterparts in the country's largest firms. And whether true or not, a radical national strategy certainly appeared to capture effectively much of rank-and-file discontent. The strategy, in short, *worked*, both organizationally and politically. But by the late 1970s and early 1980s, not only was the place of large industry in the Italian economy shifting—average firm size was falling (see table 9 [p. 162] and the discussion there)—but rank-and-file militancy had waned. By then the disproportionate represention of large industry to the federation's national body, rather than successfully playing off the enthusiasm of the most active and most militant segments of the working class, had the effect of systematically distorting constituency opinion. In 1982, for instance, participation rates at factory assemblies were higher in those provinces where the FLM's position on austerity was more moderate. By then the FLM's national structure had the effect of autonomously propelling a radical policy orientation increasingly out of touch with actual rank-and-file behavior and opinion. Strategy had become embedded in structure, and structure was now independently generating strategy in a way that was increasingly problematic. Once in place, organizational structures acquire something of a life of their own.

But why are provinces with radical union movements dominated by large industry? Why did antiausterity opposition repeatedly surface in areas of the country marked by large factories? To begin to answer these questions, the next chapter will sort through a series of plausible environmental explanations for unions' strategic orientations.

6

Cherished Hypotheses: Provincial Unions in their Environments

Why do union policy orientations vary? Why do some union groups accept moderation when others oppose it? Moving down to the local level to answer these questions accomplishes two things. First, I show that the different national policy orientations already examined drew strength from and corresponded to similar variations at all levels of union organization. Different policy orientations, in short, are not mere fictions of power-seeking national leaders but are rooted in complex organizational articulations. Neither superficial nor accidental, policy orientations reflect persistent logics of organizational behavior. Second, the local level provides an ideal site to test some hypotheses commonly used to explan variations in union policy. We gain considerable economic, political, and organizational variation without sacrificing a stable national context. The local level offers a more controlled set of environments for analysis than that permitted by cross-national comparisons.

This chapter follows the Webbs' instructions to the investigator to "cherish all the hypotheses he can lay his hands on."[1] I examine seven plausible economic, political, and sociological explanations for policy orientations in organized labor. Most of these will be found inadequate; none alone gives us an accurate explanation of local policy orientations. But a few will prove valuable in highlighting some pertinent associations and thus in beginning to sort out the conditions under which large industry promotes radical policy orientations in the Italian labor movement.

The logic of comparison employed in the analysis presented in this chapter is straightforward. As we have seen, two of the provinces con-

1. Sidney Webb and Beatrice Webb, *Industrial Democracy* (London: Longmans, Green, 1920), xxiv.

sidered are characterized by moderate policy orientations, two by radical orientations. Testing hypotheses across all four provinces entails rejecting those that do not correlate systematically with these outcomes. Only after having done this will I move to integrate these correlations with the intentions and goals of the actors themselves.

Provincial Economic Conditions

In Italy, as in the other OECD counties, the rhetoric of austerity was one of economic crisis. Its adoption was justified on the grounds that to save jobs in danger of being lost, to increase overall national employment levels, and to contain inflation, increases in the real earnings of the employed work force had to be held down. One might therefore reasonably imagine that unions in areas of the country most affected by economic crisis would also have been prone to accept austerity policies, whereas those in areas of the country where economic conditions were relatively good would have been likely to oppose them. A review of indicators of economic growth and disruption shows that this was not the case, however. There is no strong correlation between the extent of provincial economic disruption suffered during the 1970s and the union movement's responses to austerity recommendations.

Table 8 presents figures on the structure of the labor force in the four provinces and nationally in the late 1970s. Unemployment is relatively low in all four, ranging from a mere 3 percent in Cuneo to 7 percent in

Table 8. Structure of the Labor Force in Four Provinces and in All of Italy, 1977–79

Area	Agriculture	Industry	Tertiary	Unemployed	Total Labor Force
Turin	45	523	378	76	1,023
	(4%)	(51%)	(37%)	(7%)	(99%)
Cuneo	70	86	86	8	251
	(28%)	(34%)	(34%)	(3%)	(99%)
Pordenone	16	52	43	6	116
	(14%)	(45%)	(37%)	(5%)	(101%)
Modena	44	127	99	13	283
	(16%)	(45%)	(35%)	(5%)	(101%)
Italy	3,084	7,648	9,467	1,605	21,804
	(14%)	(35%)	(43%)	(7%)	(99%)

Source: Unpublished data collected in quarterly survey of the labor force, courtesy of ISTAT, Rome.
Note: Figures in thousands; averages for 1977–79.

Table 9. Industrial Growth from 1971 to 1981 in Four Provinces and in All of Italy

Area	Number of Plants, 1971	Number of Plants, 1981	Work Force, 1971	Work Force, 1981	Increase or Decrease in Number of Plants, 1981/1971	Increase or Decrease in Work Force, 1981/1971
Turin	23	35	517	457	+50%	−12%
Cuneo	10	13	69	87	+40%	+26%
Pordenone	4	7	49	56	+56%	+14%
Modena	13	21	103	141	+60%	+36%
Italy	714	950	6,284	7,071	+33%	+11%

Source: ISTAT, *Sesto censimento generale dell'industria, del commercio, dei servizi e dell'artigianato (26 ottobre 1981),* reported in Aris Accornero, Fabrizio Carmignani, and Nino Magna, "La geografia industriale tra due censimenti," *Ricerche CeSPE,* supplement to *Politica ed Economia,* no. 6 (June 1982), 42–43.
Note: Figures in thousands. Percentages calculated using exact numbers. Work-force figures include employed and self-employed, blue- and white-collar. Figures on plants include industrial firms and artisanal workshops for all industrial sectors.

Turin, just the national average. Even 7 percent is low compared with the levels of unemployment found in the south of Italy. Unemployment in Lazio, Campania, the Abruzzi, the Molise, Puglia, Basilicata, and Calabria averaged over 10 percent annually between 1977 and 1979. Both Modena (where labor endorsed austerity) and Pordenone (where it did not) had unemployment rates of 5 percent; there is no direct correlation between levels of unemployment and union responses to austerity.

As table 8 also shows, all four provinces are relatively industrialized, though Cuneo is still somewhat more agricultural than Italy as a whole. Provincial levels of industrialization—measured by the proportion of the labor force employed in industry—do not correlate strongly with union responses to austerity.

Table 9 presents data on the number of industrial plants and the number of industrial employees in the four provinces and nationally between 1971 and 1981. The data show that in all four the number of industrial firms expanded dramatically during that decade. This was also the case nationally; the diffusion of small industry in the 1970s was one of the surprising aspects of Italy's dynamic response to the dual shocks of, first, the hot autumn and, later, the international oil crisis.[2] Industrial employ-

2. See for instance Augusto Graziani, "Aspetti strutturali dell'economia italiana nell'ultimo decennio," in *Crisi e ristrutturazione dell'economia italiana: diciotto interventi,* ed.

ment, too, continued to grow nationally during the 1970s, though not at the same rate as it had in the 1950s and 1960s. As table 9 shows, there was an increase of 33 percent in the number of industrial firms and an increase of 11 percent in the size of the industrial work force nationally during the 1970s.

All four provinces saw expansion of their industrial structures well above the national average during the 1970s. In 1981 there were from 40 to 60 percent more plants in each than there had been ten years earlier. In three of the four this permitted an expansion in the number of persons employed in industry. The only province that experienced a decline of its overall industrial employment was Turin, which had some 12 percent fewer industrial employees in 1981 than a decade earlier. Yet in Turin both the FLM and the CGIL-CISL-UIL were particularly vocal opponents of an austerity policy. Despite their losses in industrial employment, the Turinese unions refused to endorse policies whose ambitions included the provision of new employment.

Another indicator of industrial disruption in the 1970s—the average annual hours of temporary layoffs for industrial employees—likewise speaks to a low correlation between external economic pressures and responses to austerity. Table 10 shows the average annual number of hours each industrial employee was temporarily suspended from work between 1971 and 1977, through use of the *cassa integrazione guadagni* (CIG), a form of nominally temporary layoff in which government guarantees most of an employee's wage. Only Cuneo fell below the national average, with an annual mean of twenty-six hours per employee. Pordenone ranked ninth nationally, with an annual average of seventy-eight hours of temporary suspension per industrial employee, owing to the massive recourse Zanussi made to the CIG for restructuring during the 1970s. Yet the FLM in Pordenone, far from embracing policies whose ostensible major goal was protecting jobs, rejected them.

The two indicators just examined—industrial decline and use of the CIG—rank Turin and Pordenone as the two provinces examined that were most affected by economic dislocation and disruption during the 1970s. Yet these union movements repeatedly dissented over austerity policies.

Augusto Graziani (Turin: Einaudi, 1975); Riccardo Varaldo, "Introduzione," in *Ristrutturazioni industriali e rapporti fra imprese: ricerche economico-tecniche sul decentramento produttivo,* ed. Riccardo Varaldo (Milan: F. Angeli, 1979). In English, see Michael Piore and Charles Sabel, *The Second Industrial Divide: Possibilities for Prosperity* (New York: Basic Books, 1984).

Table 10. Temporary Industrial Layoffs in Four Provinces and in All of Italy, 1971–77

Area	Average Annual Hours per Industrial Worker (1971–77)[a]	Rank Order Nationally
Turin	33	51
Cuneo	26	63
Pordenone	78	9
Modena	42	35
Italy	33	—

Source: Fabrizio Carmignani, ed., "Immagine socio-economica delle province italiane," *Congiuntura Sociale,* no. 2 (February 1979), 16, table 8; based on data from ISTAT and INAIL.
[a]Refers to average annual number of hours of legally registered industrial workers (as of 1975) in cassa integrazione guadagni between 1971 and 1977.

In fact, however, unionists from all four provinces repeatedly remarked in interviews that, at least until the early 1980s, austerity was a particularly difficult policy to present to the rank and file because of the perceived *absence* of any real signs of local economic crisis. In all four provinces officials used this to explain the rank and file's passive, unenthusiastic responses to the policy recommendations. The data suggest that differences in the extent of economic disruption during the 1970s were not sufficient to pressure local trade unions into supporting austerity. Economic disruption in the 1970s is not directly and causally linked to trade unions' responses to the adoption of austerity policies, and external economic variables are inadequate in predicting union behavior.

Wages, Collective Bargaining, and Militancy

Italian austerity policies explicitly aimed at altering collective bargaining practices. Specifically, they were meant to reduce the rate of increase of real earnings of the most highly paid industrial workers by containing wage demands in articulated and national collective bargaining. Furthermore, they aimed at increasing productivity by making unions more amenable to negotiating, rather than simply rejecting, internal mobility (the transfer of employees from one section to another), interfirm and intersectoral mobility (the transfer of workers from one firm or one sector to another in cases of permanent personnel reduction), the performance of overtime, and so forth.

Unions representing relatively highly paid employees should thus have been most likely to object to the adoption of austerity. Additionally, unions that had previously been most intensively engaged in supporting various forms of labor "rigidity" should have been most likely to manifest such dissent. Finally, unions linked to the most conflict-prone constituencies should have been especially reluctant to endorse austerity recommendations. None of these hypotheses are borne out by the data.

Wages and Earnings

Table 11 presents information on the relative earnings of industrial workers and on the wages of metalworkers in the four provinces and nationally. Both Turin and Modena ranked well above the national average in daily earnings in industry in 1977. Yet the responses made to austerity by the union movements in the two provinces were dissimilar. Likewise, Cuneo and Pordenone were well below the national average on this indicator, and once again their responses to austerity were not alike. There is no systematic correlation between real earnings and trade unions' response to austerity proposals. Unions that could have expected to be pressured into implementing some real containment of wages, such as the Modenese, nonetheless appeared genuinely reconciled to austerity. Although a full test of this hypothesis would require data on individual earnings rather than aggregated provincial data, the findings suggest that

Table 11. Blue-Collar Industrial Earnings and Metalworking Wages in Four Provinces and in All of Italy, 1976–77

Area	Average Daily Earnings in Lire: Industry (1977)	National Rank Order	Average Annual Wages in Lire: Metalworking Sector (1976)[a]
Turin	16.445	9	4,632
Cuneo	14.438	46	4,124
Pordenone	14.453	44	3,999
Modena	16.527	7	4,443
Italy	15.103	—	—

Sources: Industrial earnings and rank order: Fabrizio Carmignani, ed., "Immagine socio-economica delle province italiane," *Congiuntura Sociale,* no. 2 (February 1979), 18, table 9; based on data from INAIL and ISTAT. Metalworking wages: Federmeccanica, *Indagine sulla situazione dell'industria metalmeccanica (CCNL 1 Maggio 1976–Disciplina Generale, Sezione Prima-Rapporti Sindacali-Art. 1, paragrafi A e C). Dati al 31 ottobre 1976* (Rome: Federmeccanica, 1977), various volumes.

Note: Figures refer to blue-collar workers only.

[a]Includes various bonuses along with base pay but is not equivalent to total earnings.

local wage levels were not directly relevant in influencing reactions to austerity recommendations.

Neither is there a systematic correlation between actual collective bargaining as regards shop-floor rigidity and responses to wage moderation policies. The provincial trade union that refuses dramatically to corroborate this hypothesis is Pordenone's. Collective bargaining at Zanussi during the 1970s and 1980s reveals that something similar to a "producers' alliance" had been created in the province, linking labor to business (and both to government) in economic collaboration. Despite local tripartite cooperation, the union movement in Pordenone refused to sanction national policies of moderation.

The Producers' Alliance in Pordenone

Collective bargaining at Zanussi exhibited the concrete correlates of an austerity policy since 1971. During the 1970s and into the 1980s, bargaining revolved around wage restraint in exchange for the maintenance of employment levels and informal coresponsibility in the firm's productive choices. Moreover, beginning in 1978 the Pordenonese CGIL-CISL-UIL put its name to a series of extremely innovative provincial triangular accords with the purpose of directing local profits toward refinancing smaller ailing enterprises, and these accords signaled that labor "accepted mobility from job to job."[3] In short, no other province in Italy better fits what the Federazione Unitaria meant when it said, in February 1978: "The Federazione CGIL-CISL-UIL holds that, given substantial guarantees concerning the orientations of the government with respect to the growth of public investments, special interventions . . . and a policy of industrial reconversion, it is possible and necessary for the union to assume, autonomously, a line of behavior with respect to the issues of wages and nonmonetary benefits that is coherent with the general objectives of the equality of wages and benefits, control of inflation, and the growth of employment, which are the pivots of its bargaining strategy."[4]

In 1971 Zanussi was experiencing serious market and financial difficulties. On 20 June 1971, with the help of the minister of labor, Zanussi and the FLM signed an accord following some 140 strike hours per worker.

3. Federazione Unitaria Provinciale (Pordenone) CGIL-CISL-UIL, "Relazione: l'iniziativa sindacale attorno ai problemi generali e locali per rispondere ai mutamenti della società, della struttura e dei processi produttivi," 19, Consiglio Generale, Pordenone, internal document dated September 1978, courtesy of CGIL Pordenone.

4. Federazione Unitaria CGIL-CISL-UIL, "Per una svolta di politica economica e di sviluppo civile e democratico," il documento definitivo approvato dall'Assemblea nazionale, Roma, 13–14 febbraio 1978, *Rassegna Sindacale* 24 (23 February 1978), xxvii.

Management agreed not to fire any workers because of restructuring at least through the end of 1972, not to effect transfers except within geographically circumscribed areas, and to guarantee 85 percent of real hourly wages to workers temporarily suspended, through the cassa integrazione guadagni.[5] The accord was hailed as a national triumph for labor. The slogan of the negotiations had been "the guaranteed wage," and the accord paved the way for the nearly total maintenance of wage levels for Italian workers temporarily suspended.[6] In line with the goal of protecting jobs and the wage levels of suspended workers, the wage demands won were minimal.

In 1974 a second important accord was signed at Zanussi. The firm agreed to initiate a program of product diversification while maintaining its commitment to current levels of production for existing products. The commitment to product diversification was premised on public financing for the requisite research and development for developing new product lines. The thrust for product diversification came directly from the unions, whereas the local PCI's initial reaction had been far from enthusiastic.[7] The accord initiated what one observer has labeled the period of "technical compromise" between the firm and organized labor.[8]

In the same year, the FLM won its first integrated provincial accords. That is, the union bargained directly with Zanussi and Savio, the province's two largest employers in the metalworking industries. The rest of the firms in Pordenone were dealt with collectively: the small knife-making factories in the Maniagno area all negotiated together, as did all firms in general mechanics, the latter either through the Associazione Industriale (AI) or the Associazione Piccole Industrie (API). As a result, smaller firms received equal union protection, gradually diminishing disparities of wages and other benefits among them. Some small firms continued to enjoy factory bargaining as well; integrated territorial bargaining guaranteed that in the others wages and benefits would not fall dramatically behind.[9] Collective bargaining of this type continued with the integrated provincial accords of 1977 and 1980.

5. Accordo Gruppo Industrie A. Zanussi S.p.A.-FIM-FIOM-UILM, 20 June 1971, 1. Copy of accord courtesy of FLM Pordenone.

6. Interview no. 94, CISL Pordenone (Secretariat), 3 March 1981. For the interconfederal accord that followed, see Lauralba Bellardi and Elena Pisani, eds., *Sindacati e contrattazione collettiva in Italia nel 1975* (Milan: F. Angeli, 1978), 77–82, 127–28.

7. Interview no. 86, FLM Pordenone (Secretariat), 27 February 1981.

8. Roberto Diemoz, *Dal decollo industriale alla crisi dello sviluppo: il caso della Zanussi* (Bologna: Il Mulino, 1984), 91.

9. The first accords of this type in the province are dated spring 1974. The accords with API and AI include the issues of the inquadramento unico, working hours, breaks, over-

Finally, in 1978 the first triangular accord in the province was signed. The region Friuli-Venezia Giulia agreed to provide public financing for failing firms in order to avoid further unemployment in depressed zones of the province. A 1980 report on provincial firms in crisis suggested that the whole gamut of solutions had been used. Some firms had public financing of one sort or another; some received direct financing from Zanussi, which had initially inspired the agreement; a few simply went under. According to available figures, as of 1980 some 27,000 million lire had been dispersed in the province to save failing firms. Zanussi itself had directly provided 9,000 million lire, 7,500 million had been given by the region Friuli, and 6,500 million by the local business association.[10] In consequence, Pordenone has been marked, in the eyes of both the local Communist party and the CGIL-CISL-UIL, by "extremely positive" relations among the largest employer in the province (Zanussi), the various business associations, the unions, local government, and the parties.[11] In the words of a spokesman of the Associazione Industriale in the province: "Let me say right away that, luckily, in our province every effort has been and is being made both by the unions and by industrialists to attempt to maintain labor relations within the bounds of rational discourse rather than violent confrontations. In relations with the union one should favor, more than in the past, the dialectical rather than the conflictual aspect."[12]

By the late 1970s, wages were significantly lower at Zanussi than in smaller metalworking firms in the province and lower than in comparable firms in other areas of Italy.[13] Similarly, the firm's labor force had shrunk

---

time, union rights, and wages; FLM Pordenone, "La contrattazione integrativa nella provincia: i testi integrali degli accordi con l'Associazione Piccole Industrie (A.P.I.) e l'Associazione Industriale (A.I.)," internal document dated March 1974, courtesy of FLM Pordenone.

10. The situation as of 1980 is detailed, firm by firm, in an untitled and undated internal document, courtesy of CGIL Pordenone. An April 1980 chart details the financial operations performed vis-à-vis eighteen firms in the province, mainly in ceramics, wood, and textiles; chart also courtesy of CGIL Pordenone.

11. Interviews no. 82, PCI Pordenone (Secretariat), 26 February 1981 and no. 95, CGIL Pordenone (Secretariat), 3 March 1981.

12. Giacomo Brusadin, remarks in the Amministrazione Provinciale di Pordenone, *Atti della 3ª conferenza economica provinciale,* Pordenone, 27 ottobre 1979 (Pordenone: Amministrazione Provinciale, 1981), 45. The PCI was included in the provincial government only between April 1979 and June 1980; thus, good triangular relations existed even under monocolor DC administration.

13. This was reported by numerous local unionists. For some comparisons with other Italian manufacturers of household appliances, see PCI, Comitati regionali del Veneto e del Friuli-Venezia Giulia, "Zanussi e governo," leaflet for Zanussi workers, [1980], courtesy of PCI Pordenone.

during the decade. In partial compensation, Zanussi's management had been instrumental in establishing a series of useful triangular relationships in the province with the primary aim of protecting local jobs. The most recent triangular accord, from April 1983, gave the union the right to prior consultation with management and the regional government on all programs of financial assistance,[14] and it was signed despite the local PCI's initial opposition.[15]

Despite the affinities between this situation and the precepts of national confederal austerity recommendations, trade unionists in Pordenone were visibly unenthusiastic about national austerity policies. Opposition to austerity could not, therefore, have stemmed from the desire to protect collective bargaining practices in contradiction with the guidelines of national policy, nor was it the product of historically poor labor management relations. Collective bargaining and industrial relations are not irrelevant to austerity, but the impacts of these external activities is indirect. Like economic phenomena in general, the experiences of collective bargaining and labor management relations are filtered and mediated by organization: by representational structures, ideologies, patterns of internal decision making and influence, and the collective memory of officials and militants. Because complex organizations have both habits and conscious strategies, they do not respond automatically to external stimuli. Rather, they define and incorporate external pressures into their own relatively autonomous logics of organizational behavior. Policy orientations cannot be predicted on the basis of external pressures or opportunities.

Industrial Militancy

A final economical hypothesis concerns strike rates and union responses to austerity. Given that austerity policies require control of industrial militancy, it is plausible to imagine that unions in provinces with especially high levels of strike activity would be more reluctant than others to endorse austerity policies. Unfortunately, data are not available to permit examining strike rates in the provinces for the metalworking industries only. Nor are data available that would permit an analysis of anything other than overall strike volume; thus, examining strike duration, size, and frequency is precluded.[16] Table 12 reports a data analysis of strike volume for all industrial sectors taken together.

14. Interview no. 111, UIL Pordenone (Secretariat), 19 December 1983.
15. Interview no. 112, PCI Pordenone (Secretariat), 19 December 1983.
16. See chapter 2 for a discussion of these indicators.

Table 12. Average Annual Volume of Industrial Conflict in Four Provinces and in All of Italy, 1958–80

	Turin	Cuneo	Pordenone	Modena	Italy
Industrial strikes, 1958–80	15.10	5.22	—[a]	13.75	11.43
1958–68	8.25	3.12	—	10.86	9.00
1969 (hot autumn)	59.73	12.77	81.94	41.83	37.70
1970–80	17.90	6.62	21.33	14.10	11.46
1975–80					
Industrial strikes	17.59	4.47	17.77	11.69	9.58
Political strikes	2.95	1.55	7.32	6.08	4.22

Sources: Strike hours 1958–65: ISTAT, *Annuario di statistiche provinciali* (Rome: ISTAT, various years). Strike hours 1966–74: ISTAT, *Annuario di statistiche del lavoro* (Rome: ISTAT, various years). Strike hours 1975–80: courtesy of ISTAT, Rome. Industrial labor force: linear extrapolation using industrial census data: 1951, reported in ISTAT, *Annuario di statistiche provinciali, 1959* (Rome: ISTAT, n.d.), table 25; 1961, reported in ISTAT, *Annuario di statistiche provinciali* (Rome: ISTAT, 1974), vol. 13, table 88; 1971 and 1981, see table 10. Volume is the annual ratio of thousands of strike hours per thousand employees. See appendix B for further details.

[a]Pordenone acquired provincial status only in 1968, and figures for the province are not available before then.

Between 1970 and 1980, Turin, Modena, and Pordenone all manifested strike volumes above the national average, whereas Cuneo's volume was below, as the table indicates. The same is true for the period from 1958 as a whole. Strike volume was especially high in Pordenone and in Turin, where organized labor resisted austerity efforts, but was still considerably above the national average in Modena, where it did not. There is, in short, no systematic relationship between provincial strike volume in industry and the policy orientations of the union movement.

At least as revealing as strike averages for the twenty-three years considered is the effect—or lack thereof—of the hot autumn on the intensity of industrial conflict in the four provinces. In Modena and Cuneo, the hot autumn did not entail radical changes in patterns of industrial conflict. Cuneo's annual average volume of industrial conflict was well below the national average before 1969, and so it subsequently remained. In contrast, Modena's was above the national average before 1969, as it has continued to be. The average annual volume of conflict in Modena increased by about 30 percent between 1958–68 and 1970–80, more or less as it did nationally. In Turin, however, a radical break is discernible. Before 1969 industrial conflict was, on average, *below* the national level; the only exceptions were 1962 and 1965. But after 1969 the province's status altered dramatically. Excluding only 1970 and 1978, the volume of conflict was higher in Turin than nationally for every year since 1970, propelling its unions into a spearheading role for Italian labor in general. The average annual volume of conflict between 1970 and 1980 was eighteen hours per worker in Turin and only eleven hours nationally. Data are not available for Pordenone, but they would undoubtedly tell the same story.[17] The reversal from below to above the national average in the volume of conflict is one of the clearest indicators of the rupture in working-class collective action that occurred with the hot autumn. In Modena and Cuneo, on the other hand, there has been an underlying continuity to the patterns of conflict uninterrupted by the hot autumn.

Finally, data on the volume of conflict in Fiat plants in the three of the four provinces in which the firm has located—Turin, Cuneo, and Modena—permit a second kind of comparison of strike activity. The data are limited to the years between 1975 and 1980 and refer to manual workers only; thus they are not comparable with the figures presented above on overall provincial industrial conflict. Table 13 presents the volume of conflict in Fiat plants in the three provinces for the years 1975 to 1980.

The oscillations of volume are identical in plants across the three provinces, with the single exception of Turin in 1980, when, owing to the thirty-five-day Fiat strike, an exceptional number of strike hours occurred. The variations in conflict at Fiat plants in different provinces tend to resemble each other more strongly than they resemble variations in industrial conflict generally at the provincial level. At the enterprise level, articulated bargaining appears of clear importance in generating conflict: conflict rises and falls in similar measure across Italian Fiat plants owing to the coordinating abilities of the national FLM. But the overall volume of conflict differs significantly among the plants in each of these three provinces. In the province of Cuneo, where overall industrial conflict is relatively low, the volume of conflict at Fiat is relatively low. In Modena and Turin, where the overall volume of industrial conflict is relatively high, the volume of conflict at Fiat plants is relatively high.

Although national union strategies for articulated bargaining may determine the pattern of conflict in plants widely dispersed across Italy, the overall volume of conflict is more nearly a reflection of local strike habits,

17. This supposition drawns on two aspects of provincial class history. First, industrialization was rapid and extensive in Pordenone only in the 1960s. Relatively unindustrialized or newly industrializing areas are unlikely to display particularly high levels of industrial conflict. Second, the extremely high level of conflict in 1969 in Pordenone, along with what is known of the character of militancy there at the time (see chap. 7 for details), suggests that conflict must have been relatively low before 1968–69.

Table 13. Annual Volume of Conflict in Fiat Plants in Modena, Cuneo, and Turin, 1975–80

Year	Turin	Cuneo	Modena
1975	26.09	36.15	32.24
1976	59.26	77.87	74.93
1977	54.48	58.90	67.85
1978	10.10	11.94	23.53
1979	82.69	80.92	102.06
1980	138.84	40.02	59.70
Average	61.91	50.97	60.05

Source: Courtesy of Fiat, S.p.A., Turin. See appendix B for further details.
Note: Turin: Mirafiori Presse, Lingotto Presse, Rivalta Presse, Costruzione Stampi, Mirafiori Meccanica, Rivalta Meccanica, Mirafiori Carrozzaria, Lingotto Carrozzaria, Rivalta Carrozzaria, Direzione Attività Internazionali, Gruppo Automobili-Direzione, Direzione Ricambi, Filiale di Torino, Centro Diretto di Vendita. Cuneo: Società Ferroviaria Savigliano. Modena: Fiat Trattori. Volume is annual ratio of number of strike hours to number of manual employees.

provincial trade union mobilization capacity, and provincial industrial relations. These variations in strike volume at the local level indirectly corroborate the important role of local union officials; although the national FLM may set the timing of Fiat's collective bargaining—and hence determine the timing of its strikes—local conditions have an important effect in determining the overall relative volume of conflict. Between 1975 and 1980, Fiat workers in all three provinces struck a good deal more often than workers employed in industry as a whole, attesting to the spearheading role still entrusted to Fiat by the national FLM. But Fiat workers in Cuneo struck less often than those in Modena and Turin, as did industrial employees there generally. National elites experience structural difficulties in imposing uniformity on the behaviors of actors in widely varying environments.

Levels of industrial action per se appear unsystematically related to provincial strategy orientations. The most militant labor environments are not necessarily characterized by unions that display radical policies, as the Modenese case in particular shows. Rank-and-file militancy and union policy orientations are distinct, and militant labor movements did not necessarily repudiate austerity recommendations. Radical trade union movements, however, have been blessed with militant rank and file in Turin and Pordenone since the hot autumn: indeed, it was the pattern-setting burst of militancy in 1969 that propelled these labor movements into consolidating their preexisting radical tendencies into relatively enduring strategic orientations and logics of organizational behavior. Chapter 7 will show just how this happened.

The Sociology of Union Functionaries

It is frequently asserted, and is perfectly plausible, that union leadership groups that emerged during and after the hot autumn were more likely to favor conflict over administrative activities than were previous generations. The "generation of '69" was said to lay particular stress on the importance of factory councils and on strike activity. It was, by almost all accounts, a generation largely inclined toward radicalism: indeed, many blamed it outright for its supposed blanket repudiation of incomes policies in the late 1970s and early 1980s. A sociological version of this argument leads us to expect clear and relevant differences in the age and recruitment of the FLM's functionaries in the two provinces that accepted austerity and the two that rejected it.

Table 14 presents the relevant data. They do not coincide with what a generational hypothesis would lead us to expect. In all four provinces, most full-time political functionaries in the FLM were between twenty-six and thirty-six years of age (as of 1980), thus clearly falling into the "generation of '69." Indeed, Turin, which repeatedly manifested most dissent over austerity recommendations, had a greater proportion of older, and presumably pre–hot autumn, functionaries than the other three provinces, with a full 43 percent older than thirty six years. Average age was lowest in Pordenone (thirty-one years) and highest in Turin (thirty-seven years); the two provinces do not even fall at the same end of the generational spectrum.

Neither does an analysis of recruitment patterns corroborate a generational hypothesis. As of 1980, in all four provinces at least one-quarter of full-time officials had been recruited within the previous two years. In Modena, a full 60 percent had been recruited during that period. Turin had the highest proportion of functionaries who had been full time since before 1968, but even this was only 6 percent. Average time as a full-time functionary ranged from three to six years, with Turin again at the opposite end of the spectrum from Pordenone. Most local functionaries had been brought in as full-time union officials only recently, and union movements that accepted austerity recommendations did so despite being overwhelmingly staffed by members of the "generation of '69."

In short, neither age nor recruitment confirms that provincial unions rejecting austerity were distinctly characterized by the hot autumn genera-

Table 14. Age and Recruitment Patterns of FLM Functionaries in Four Provinces, 1980–81

	Cuneo	Modena	Turin	Pordenone
Number	8	22	105	9
Age				
< 26 years	0	2 (9%)	1 (1%)	0
26–36 years	6 (75%)	16 (73%)	58 (55%)	8 (89%)
> 36 years	2 (25%)	4 (18%)	45 (43%)	1 (11%)
Average	34 years	33 years	37 years	31 years
Missing	—	—	1	—
Years as full-time functionary				
< 3	4 (50%)	13 (59%)	25 (24%)	5 (56%)
3–12	4 (50%)	8 (36%)	71 (68%)	4 (44%)
> 12	0	1 (5%)	6 (6%)	0
Average	4 years	3 years	6 years	3 years
Missing	—	—	3	—

Sources: Courtesy of FLM Turin, Cuneo, Modena, and Pordenone.
Note: Refers to political functionaries only; technical and secretarial staff are excluded.

tion. Although the influence of the hot autumn on subsequent union policy orientations is not negligible, a narrowly formulated generational explanation is simply too mechanical to capture the ways the earlier cycle of militancy altered union structures and strategies. The hot autumn bred a new generation of trade union functionaries everywhere in northern Italy, all of whom may equally well have shared individual predispositions toward radicalism. But only selected local environments and organizations consolidated individual preferences into official behavior.

Union Strength

Drawing on Michelsian theories of size and bureaucracy, numerous studies have suggested a relationship between union size or strength and policy. The most extensive and systematic empirical research on the union's responses to the hot autumn found that "the most significant factor influencing the union's response to demands coming from the rank and file was . . . the *level of union strength* in a specific situation. *The weaker the union, the more it is led to accept or promote conflictual thrusts of the rank and file; the stronger it is, the more it is led to contain them.*"[18] In a similar vein, Claus Offe and Helmut Wiesenthal have posited two polar types of union organization: the small and militant and the large but bureaucratic.[19] They argue that after a certain point increasing size becomes dysfunctional for labor organizations because it encourages bureaucratization and member apathy, which undercut the organization's ability to mobilize its constituency to strike. Contrariwise, small unions are expected to be particularly militant promoters of rank-and-file conflict as they seek to expand membership.

Table 15 presents data on industrial unionization rates in the four provinces and in the metalworking industries. We might take 40 percent as the cutoff for distinguishing weak from strong organizations in settings without closed or union shops, and in which no one can be required to join a union. Unionization in the metalworking industries was a mere 35 percent in Cuneo in 1981 and 38 percent in Turin; both FLMs should be classed as relatively weak. In Pordenone, unionization in the metalworking sector was 47 percent, compared with 60 percent in the province of Modena. Both of these FLMs may be considered relatively strong. The data on unionization in the metalworking sector thus do not support the argument that union radicalism is a function of organizational weakness, which would have required that unionization in both Turin and Pordenone be relatively weak (see also tables 16–19 below).

Neither do the data presented in table 15 on overall industrial unionization rates corroborate this interpretation. Industrial unionization rates are over 40 percent in Turin, Pordenone, and Modena, whereas corroboration would have entailed that only Modena and Cuneo's levels of industrial unionization be relatively high. There is no direct correlation between union strength and a trade union strategy aimed at protecting the organization's future ability to engage in militant behavior. Indeed, as I have already demonstrated, militant trade unionism may emerge and endure in contexts of either relative strength or relative weakness, and militancy is not a direct function of membership levels.

18. Alessandro Pizzorno, "Le due logiche dell'azione di classe," in *Lotte operaie e sindacato: il ciclo 1968–1972*, ed. Alessandro Pizzorno et al., vol. 6 of *Lotte operaie e sindacato in Italia: 1968–1972*, ed. Alessandro Pizzorno, 6 vols. (Bologna: Il Mulino, 1978), 24–25. Emphasis in the original.

19. Claus Offe and Helmut Wiesenthal, "Two Logics of Collective Action: Theoretical Notes on Social Class and Organizational Form," in *Political Power and Social Theory: A Research Annual*, ed. Maurice Zeitlin, 1 (Greenwich, Conn.: JAI Press, 1980). The "two logics" of the title refer to business and labor associations; the distinctions drawn between types of labor organizations are secondary to the thrust of the essay.

Table 15. Industrial and Metalworking Unionization in Four Provinces and in All of Italy, 1981

	Turin	Cuneo	Pordenone	Modena	Italy
Union members in industry by confederation					
CGIL	88,827 (48%)	12,034 (50%)	9,635 (48%)	54,368 (86%)	1,757,954 (55%)
CISL	43,863 (24%)	8,474 (35%)	8,094 (40%)	5,006 (8%)	950,560 (30%)
UIL[a]	52,447 (28%)	3,404 (14%)	2,448 (12%)	4,090 (6%)	481,947 (15%)
Total	185,137 (100%)	23,912 (99%)	20,177 (100%)	63,464 (100%)	3,190,461 (100%)
Industrial employees	438,748	66,829	45,610	105,348	5,870,648
Industrial unionization	42%	36%	44%	60%	54%
FLM members	110,526	5,963	9,351	21,016	1,037,265
Metalworkers	289,872	16,972	19,776	35,353	1,952,988
Metalworking unionization	38%	35%	47%	59%	53%

Sources: National CGIL, CISL, UIL industrial members: reported in Guido Romagnoli, "Sindacalizzazione e rappresentanza," in *Le relazioni Sindacali in Italia: rapporto 1981*, ed. Guido Baglioni, Ettore Santi, and Corrado Squarzon, Centro di Studi Sociali e Sindacali (Rome: Edizioni Lavoro, 1982), 177, table 3. Provincial industrial union members: courtesy of the Uffici Organizzativi of the CGIL, CISL, and UIL, Rome. FLM members: courtesy of FLM, Rome. Numbers of employees: ISTAT, *Sesto censimento generale dell'industria, del commercio, dei servizi e dell'artigianato, 26 ottobre 1981*, vol. 1: *Primi risultati sulle imprese e sulle unità locali (dati provvisori)*, book 1: *Dati nazionali, regionali e provinciali* (Rome: ISTAT, 1983), unpublished tables, courtesy of ISTAT, Rome. For additional details, see appendix B.

[a]Provincial UIL figures for industrial members are from 1980.

If we turn to tables 16–19, which present membership figures for these four provincial FLMs between the early 1970s and the early 1980s, we can evaluate the same issue in a different way. First, it is important to note that the unionization rates shown in these tables differ from those reported in table 15 because the number of relevant employees has been estimated differently. Whereas table 15 utilized industrial census data from 1981, which included all employees in all metalworking plants, the data used in tables 16–19 were obtained from the FLMs themselves and estimate only the number of employees in plants where the union has some members (and thus is able to obtain—from its own members—an estimate of the

Table 16. Metalworking Unionization: Cuneo, 1971–83

Year	FLM Members	Employees	Unionization (%)
1971	3,203	n.a.[a]	n.a.
1972	3,670	n.a.	n.a.
1973	3,895	n.a.	n.a.
1974	4,452	n.a.	n.a.
1975	5,095	n.a.	n.a.
1976	5,295	n.a.	n.a.
1977	5,693	9,568	59
1978	5,712	9,703	59
1979	6,154	10,123	61
1980	6,095	10,771	57
1981	5,763	n.a.	n.a.
1982	5,758	11,315	51
1983	6,628	10,798	52

Source: Courtesy of FLM Cuneo. All data refer to close of membership drive at official end of year.
Note: Figures refer only to those employed in firms in which union is present.
[a]N.a. = not available.

total number of employees). These unionization rates, in other words, reflect the proportion of the unionized work force only in plants where the union has been established. As a general rule, this excludes very small plants, including what are legally classified as artisanal firms—in which the right to organize is not protected by law.

We may first briefly compare these figures with those reported in table 15. FLM members as a proportion of all metalworkers constituted 38 percent in Turin, 35 percent in Cuneo, 47 percent in Pordenone, and 59 percent in Modena in 1981. In the same year, FLM members as a proportion of metalworkers in organized plants were roughly equivalent in Turin and Pordenone, some 5 percent higher in Modena, and nearly 20 percent higher in Cuneo. Particularly interesting is the difference between the two figures for Cuneo, where organizational density across the sector as a whole is low, thanks to the large number of very small plants without any union representation, but where the FLM is surprisingly strong in those plants it has been able to penetrate. Such data attest both to the relative weakness of unionism in a predominantly Catholic and still relatively agricultural province and to the considerable ability of organized labor to attract members once it gets a foot in the door.

More revealing are the rates of growth for union membership in the

Table 17. Metalworking Unionization: Modena, 1971–83

Year	FIM	FIOM	UILM	SSC	Total	Employees
1971	2,204 (15%)	11,424 (78%)	1,065 (7%)	0	14,693	n.a.[a]
1972	2,194 (14%)	12,029 (79%)	1,065 (7%)	0	15,288	n.a.
1973	2,330 (13%)	13,031 (75%)	1,050 (6%)	867 (5%)	17,278	n.a.
1974	2,503 (13%)	14,071 (75%)	1,120 (6%)	1,123 (6%)	18,817	n.a.
1975	2,532 (13%)	15,034 (77%)	1,120 (6%)	900 (5%)	19,586	n.a.
1976	2,515 (12%)	16,047 (78%)	1,120 (5%)	978 (5%)	20,660	n.a.
1977	2,616 (12%)	16,657 (78%)	936 (4%)	1,080 (5%)	21,289	n.a.
1978	2,743 (13%)	16,997 (78%)	889 (4%)	1,202 (5%)	21,831	n.a.
1979	2,879 (13%)	17,434 (77%)	938 (4%)	1,439 (6%)	22,690	n.a.
1980	2,883 (12%)	17,997 (77%)	912 (4%)	1,657 (7%)	23,449	36,568 (64%)
1981	2,777 (12%)	17,838 (77%)	881 (4%)	1,662 (7%)	23,158	n.a.
1982	2,471 (12%)	16,620 (77%)	760 (4%)	1,630 (8%)	21,181	32,662 (65%)
1983	2,371 (12%)	15,219 (77%)	689 (3%)	1,449 (7%)	19,728	30,823 (64%)

Source: Courtesy of FLM Modena. All data refer to close of membership drive at official end of year.
Note: Figures refer only to those employed in firms in which union is present.
[a]N.a. = not available.

1970s. In Pordenone, the number of FLM members increased by only 8 percent between 1973—the first year for which data were available—and 1979, the peak year for metalworking membership in the province. This figure disguises the very important difference between union growth at Zanussi and that characterizing the rest of the metalworking firms in the province. In Zanussi plants, membership began falling as early as 1977, as a function of declining employment in the firm. In other metalworking plants in Pordenone, however, membership increased by 52 percent between 1973 and 1979. Almost all of the FLM's membership growth in the province came from firms other than Zanussi, corroborating arguments made by FLM officials there—to be reviewed in the next chapter—that

Table 18. Metalworking Unionization: Pordenone, 1973–83

Year	Zanussi	Other	Total
1973 employees	n.a.[a]	n.a.	
FLM members	7,884	2,864	10,748
Unionization			
1974 employees	n.a.	n.a.	
FLM members	8,212	3,285	11,497
Unionization			
1975 employees	12,141	7,148	19,289
FLM members	8,369	3,400	11,769
Unionization	69%	48%	61%
1976 employees	11,975	7,695	19,670
FLM members	8,096	3,193	11,289
Unionization	68%	41%	57%
1977 employees	11,977	7,948	19,925
FLM members	7,725	4,211	11,936
Unionization	64%	53%	60%
1978 employees	11,818	8,534	20,352
FLM members	7,271	4,134	11,405
Unionization	62%	48%	56%
1979 employees	n.a.	n.a.	
FLM members	7,271	4,354	11,625
Unionization			
1980 employees	n.a.	n.a.	
FLM members	6,985	4,284	11,269
Unionization			
1981 employees	10,236	n.a.	
FLM members	6,493	4,148	10,641
Unionization	63%		
1982 employees	n.a.	n.a.	
FLM members	5,483	4,072	9,555
Unionization			
1983 employees	n.a.	n.a.	
FLM members	n.a.	3,638	
Unionization			

Sources: Courtesy of FLM Pordenone. Number of employees reported in Marzio Strassoldo, ed., *Ricerche socio-economiche per la provincia di Pordenone, 1972–1979* (Pordenone: Camera di Commercio Industria Agricoltura e Artigianato, 1980), 66.
Note: Figures include only industrial firms with at least five employees.
[a]N.a. = not available.

Table 19. Metalworking Unionization: Turin, 1972–83

Year	Fiat	Other	Total
1972 employees	142,241	157,395	299,636
FLM members	31,556	69,716	101,272
Unionization	22%	44%	34%
1973 employees	141,685	157,480	299,165
FLM members	38,350	77,466	115,816
Unionization	27%	49%	39%
1974 employees	134,791	154,610	289,401
FLM members	37,350	79,304	116,700
Unionization	28%	51%	40%
1975 employees	134,551	157,566	292,117
FLM members	36,983	76,670	113,653
Unionization	30%	49%	39%
1976 employees	132,263	149,520	281,783
FLM members	43,901	75,800	119,701
Unionization	33%	51%	42%
1977 employees	142,932	145,293[a]	288,225
FLM members	43,388	73,836	117,224
Unionization	30%	51%	41%
1978 employees	147,893	144,732	292,625
FLM members	47,529	72,757	120,286
Unionization	32%	50%	41%
1979 employees	150,238	143,621	293,859
FLM members	51,723	71,828	123,551
Unionization	34%	50%	42%
1980 employees	155,402	140,689	296,091
FLM members	51,028	71,119	122,147
Unionization	33%	50%	41%
1981 employees	n.a.[b]	n.a.	
FLM members	42,873	64,942	107,815
Unionization			
1982 employees	121,835	136,050	257,985
FLM members	34,524	58,155	92,679
Unionization	28%	43%	36%
1983 employees	108,799	137,558	246,357
FLM members	26,328	56,150	82,478
Unionization	24%	41%	33%

Source: Courtesy of FLM Turin. All data refer to close of membership drive at official end of year.
Note: Figures include only industrial firms with at least five employees.
[a]Employees in 3[a] Lega estimated.
[b]N.a. = not available.

unionization in Zanussi plants was relatively high even before the hot autumn.

The situation in Turin is a mirror image of that in Pordenone. The FLM's membership increased by 21 percent between 1972 and the provincial peak of 1980, but in fact membership during these years in Turinese Fiat plants increased a full 64 percent compared with the modest 6 percent in all other firms in the province. Almost all membership growth in Turin was in the Fiat works. In Modena, membership increased by 60 percent between 1971 and the provincial peak of 1980. In Cuneo, finally, membership nearly doubled between 1971 and 1979, increasing by an astonishing 92 percent.

These calculations show that rates of provincial union growth do not seem particularly germane for understanding variations in policy orientations in organized labor. The sheer ability to generate new members is not necessarily related to radical propensities, since all these FLMs proved extremely successful in enrolling new members in the 1970s, even if new enrollments were not spread evenly across large and small industry. Radicalism was not an outgrowth of a newly organized rank and file.

The Influence of the Communist Party

Between 1976 and 1979, the Italian Communist party had a particularly strong interest in promoting austerity in order to convince the DC and the middle classes both that it was committed to democracy and that its cooperation was indispensable in managing the economic crisis. After 1979, with the party's move back into the opposition, the PCI had an equally strong interest in demonstrating its ability to forestall the incomes policy supported by a center-left government. Traditional interpretations of union/party relations in Communist-oriented labor movements—especially various versions of the "transmission belt" hypothesis—lead us to expect that union responses to austerity would follow party directives in contexts where the party's presence in organized labor was strong. The argument is patently inaccurate, since provincial union responses to austerity were stable over time despite the changes in the party's national policies. But it is worth exploring in some detail how the structure of relations between the party and the union movement at the local level may have nonetheless had an impact on union responses to austerity policies.

There are a number of possible measures with which to capture party influence over organized labor. One is sheer electoral strength; where the PCI dominates electorally, its general political influence is likely to be powerful, and this will be especially true for its relations with organized labor. Table 20 presents electoral results in the four provinces and nationally for the Chamber of Deputies since 1958.

The data show that both Pordenone and Turin are competitive party systems.[20] In Turin, neither major Italian party has obtained more than 40 percent of the popular vote in any election since 1958. In the most recent elections reported, the PCI won 33 percent of the vote against the DC's 23 percent. In Pordenone, the PCI increased its share of the vote from 17 percent in 1968 (the first national elections in which the province participated as an entity distinct from Udine) to 27 percent in 1976, falling to 22 percent in 1983. Although the DC still remains politically vital, its share of the vote has fallen below 40 percent. The once-dominant Catholic subculture there is disintegrating. Indeed, in 1978 and 1979 the PCI controlled the provincial government, and in early 1981 it administered nineteen out of fifty-two communes in the province, or more than a third.[21]

Cuneo and Modena, by contrast, may be characterized as stable and one-party dominated—Cuneo by the DC, Modena by the PCI. In Cuneo, the DC won 43 percent in 1983, below the stable 55 percent it won in 1958, 1963, and 1968, but still monolithic compared with the PCI's shallow 14 percent. In Modena the PCI has become even stronger over the decades. Its share of the vote grew from 41 percent in 1958 to 53 percent in 1983. These provinces are still relatively intact one-party subcultures. Although the PCI is extremely weak in Cuneo—and extremely powerful in Modena—in both provinces the union movement responded similarly to austerity policies. Below, I begin to discuss why unions in subcultural environments (whether red or white) exhibit similar strategies. In the meantime, it is worth noting that sheer electoral hegemony on the part of the PCI is not a good predictor of the union movement's policy orientation.

Table 21 provides additional measures of the PCI's provincial strength by presenting data on the ratio of party members to voters in 1979 as well as the ratio of members to residents as of 1981. Nationally, there are thirty-three Italian residents for each PCI member. In Modena, however, where the party's strength is monolithic, the ratio of inhabitants to members falls to a mere seven to one, ranking the province fourth nationally. Contrariwise, in Cuneo it rises to 137 residents per member, a good indicator of the PCI's extreme weakness compared with the DC there.

20. For empirical definitions of competitive and subcultural party systems, see p. 32, above.

21. Reported in interview no. 82, PCI Pordenone (Secretariat), 26 February 1981.

Table 20. Electoral Results in Four Provinces and in All of Italy, 1958–83 (Percentages)

Year	Turin	Cuneo	Pordenone	Modena	Italy
1958					
PCI	20	6	—[a]	41	23
DC	37	55		32	42
1963					
PCI	25	8	—[a]	45	25
DC	32	55		28	38
1968					
PCI	29	9	17	48	27
DC	32	55	48	28	39
1972					
PCI	29	9	18	49	27
DC	33	54	46	28	39
1976					
PCI	39	17	27	53	34
DC	32	53	44	29	39
1979					
PCI	33	14	25	53	30
DC	30	50	42	28	38
1983					
PCI	33	14	22	53	30
DC	23	43	39	23	33

Sources: For 1958 and 1963: PCI, Ufficio Elettorale e di Statistica del PCI, *Il PCI nelle elezioni e nel Paese, 1946–1976* (Rome: PCI, 1977), and PCI, Ufficio Elettorale e di Statistica del P.C.I., *I voti della DC: quanti sono, da dove provengono, chi li ha espressi, 1946–1976* (Rome: PCI, 1978). For 1969 through 1979: PCI, Ufficio Elettorale, *Elezione politiche del 3–4 giugno: prima documentazione sui risultati delle elezioni della Camera dei Deputati e del Senato della Repubblica* (Rome: PCI, 1979). For 1983: PCI, Sezione Elettorale, ed., *I risultati della elezione della Camera dei Deputati (relativi alle province) del 26 giugno 1983* (Rome: PCI, 1983). All the above are internal documents courtesy of PCI, Rome.

Note: Refers to elections to the Chamber of Deputies.

[a]Results for Pordenone not available.

Both Turin and Pordenone, finally, are above the national average, with fifty-four and sixty-seven residents, respectively, for every PCI member. These are historically weak party organizations embedded in increasingly volatile electoral environments. Again, the data attest to the subcultural dominance of the PCI in Modena and of the DC in Cuneo, and to the relatively fluid political environments found in Turin and Pordenone.

Table 21. Communist Organizational Strength in Four Provinces and in All of Italy, 1979–81

Measure	Turin	Cuneo	Pordenone	Modena	Italy
Voters per PCI member (1979)	11	15	11	3	6
National rank order	87	94	80	4	—
Residents per PCI member (1981)	54	137	67	7	33
National rank order	50	87	65	4	—

Sources: 1979: PCI, Sezione centrale di organizzazione, *Organizzazione dati statistiche,* XVI Congresso nazionale del Partito comunista italiano (Rome: PCI, 1983), 143–46. 1981: PCI members: ibid., 9–12. Resident population: ISTAT, *Dodicesimo censimento generale sulla popolazione: 25 ottobre 1981,* vol. 1, *Primi risultati provinciali e communali sulla popolazione e sulle abitazioni (dati provvisori)* (Rome: ISTAT, 1982), 8–9, table 7. Rank orders are my calculations.

The figures on PCI voters per member reveal similar effects. Modena falls well below the national average, with about three voters per party member, again ranking the province fourth nationally. Cuneo falls at the other extreme, with fifteen voters per member, or more than twice the national average; this is the worst ratio in the country. Turin is only slightly better off than Cuneo, with twelve voters per member. Although the PCI may now win elections there, its organizational structures are still notoriously weak. Pordenone, finally, with eleven voters per member, reveals an organizational structure commensurate with the party's still weak but expanding social attraction. Both indicators highlight the PCI's subcultural strength in Modena and its subcultural weakness in Cuneo, as well as the general absence of subcultural networks in Pordenone and Turin.

Finally, table 22 shows the percentage of the PCI's members who are working class in the four provinces and nationally. Approximately 60 percent of the party's membership in Turin and Pordenone is blue collar, while Cuneo and Modena are both slightly below the national average of 40 percent. If blue- and white-collar employees are combined, Pordenone and Turin still rank well above the national average. So does Cuneo, which has an exceptionally high proportion of white collar and technical party members, almost three times the national average. These figures correspond only in part to the industrial environments of the four provinces. In Turin and Pordenone, the labor force is concentrated in industry (see table 8), and it is thus unremarkable that the PCI should be prevalently blue collar. In Modena, however, where 45 percent of the labor force in found in the industrial sectors, only 39 percent of the party's membership is blue collar, attesting to the PCI's traditional ability to

Table 22. Proportion of Blue- and White-Collar PCI Members in Four Provinces and in All of Italy, 1977

	Turin	Cuneo	Pordenone	Modena	Italy
Percentage blue-collar	59	39	63	39	40
Percentage white-collar and technical	11	18	4	5	7
Percentage blue- and white-collar	70	57	67	44	47

Source: PCI, Sezione centrale di organizzazione, *Dati sull'organizzazione del partito,* XV Congresso nazionale del Partito comunista italiano (Rome: PCI, 1979), 38–43.

enroll members from a variety of social classes in areas of its subcultural dominance.

In provinces in which three out of every five of the PCI's members are manual workers, the constituencies of the party and of the unions necessarily overlap more than in those in which only two out of five members are blue collar. And it is counterintuitive that the more union and party constituencies overlap, the more likely the union is to be radical, since historically the PCI's national policy orientation has been relatively moderate since World War II. Indeed, we would expect the party to keep the union on reformist tracks where both share large proportions of constituents. Nonetheless, the union movements in Turin and Pordenone—where the PCI is disproportionately blue-collar—are distinctly radical, unlike their moderate counterparts in Modena and Cuneo. I advance an explanation for this situation below.

Another way to get at the extent of party influence over organized labor is to look at the proportion of full-time union officials who are members of the PCI. The incomplete data available on this show, however, that among members of the secretariats of the four FLMs under consideration, Communists occupy a disproportionate number of posts only in Modena.[22] In fact, partisanship among full-time officials is generally regulated by triorganizational agreements and bargaining, which explicitly preclude—except in cases of Communist subcultural hegemony—giving more than a minority of full-time positions to Communists.

An alternative but perhaps more useful measure of Communist influence over union decision making is the proportion of shop-floor union activists who are party members. If the party's ability to influence the union movement via full-time officials is relatively restricted, it may continue to exercise greater political sway over its rank-and-file militants. Fortunately, relatively good data are available for three of the four prov-

22. This is an estimate using incomplete data courtesy of the FLMs of the four provinces.

inces under examination. If Communist party influence is relevant to the policy orientations of organized labor, moderation should correlate with a greater proportion of shop-floor delegates who are also members of the PCI.

In Cuneo, there were 291 FLM delegates in 1983, of whom 52 were also members of the PCI, or approximately 18 percent, according to full-time FLM officials there.[23] In Modena, a recent survey of 100 metalworking delegates from eight firms found that 55 percent were members of the PCI.[24] Although the reliability of the sample is open to question, the finding is eminently plausible and may be used as a rough estimate of Communist affiliation among FLM delegates in the province. In Piedmont, a survey of 1,840 delegates from ninety-six industrial firms found that half were Communist party members. This is likely to overestimate PCI affiliation, however, since the survey was biased toward delegates enrolled in industrial unions affiliated with the CGIL.[25] More useful, perhaps, is the finding that some 62 percent of the CGIL's delegates were also Communist;[26] if we apply this to the number of FLM delegates affiliated with the FIOM-CGIL in Turin (see table 23 below), we estimate that some 23 percent of the FLM's Turinese delegates are Communist, though this excludes the small number of Communists found in the FIM and the UILM, along with those without confederal affiliation altogether. Finally, no precise data are available for Pordenone, but FLM officials there figure that some 30 percent of their delegates are Communist, a plausible estimate.[27]

These data are certainly imprecise. They accord, however, with what we would expect: only in Modena, where the party maintains sociopolitical hegemony, are a majority of the FLM's factory delegates also members of the Italian Communist party. In the other three provinces, Communists probably constitute between 20 and 30 percent of metalworking

23. Data courtesy of FLM Cuneo. The information was obtained by asking full-time officials how many of the delegates in their comprensorio were Communists. Given the small numbers involved and the fact that the officials normally know all their delegates personally, the data are likely to be relatively reliable. In one comprensorio, data were obtained from a Communist who reported, with some embarrassment, that a mere 8 percent of his delegates were members of the PCI, indicating that the figures are unlikely to be inflated.

24. Maura Franchi and Vittorio Rieser, *Esperienza e cultura dei delegati: un'indagine nella realtà metalmeccanica modenese* (Reggio Emilia: Bonhoeffer, 1984), 30.

25. IRES-CGIL Piemonte, ed., *Delegati in Piemonte: una ricerca in cento fabbriche*, Formazione e cultura FIOM-CGIL Piemonte (Milan: F. Angeli, 1986), 50, table 12.

26. Ibid., 51, table 13.

27. Interview no. 119, FLM Pordenone (Secretariat), 21 December 1983.

factory delegates. This indicator, too, fails to correlate with union policy orientations or with responses to austerity recommendations.

It is curious, however, that the PCI's presence among FLM delegates in Cuneo is statistically so low (18 percent overall and 28 percent in the FIOM), because union officials there perceive the situation quite differently. Functionaries in all three confederations—not just the FIOM-CGIL and not just Communists—reported that a disproportionate number of the FLM's delegates were members of the PCI, even though most workers in the province do not vote for the party.[28] This suggests either that there may be a substantial number of delegates who, though not formally inscribed in the PCI, somehow "act" Communist because of their sympathies for the party or that Communist delegates exercise a disproportionate influence because they are more visible, more active in union affairs, and more likely to serve as rank-and-file spokesmen than non-Communist delegates. In fact, both are probably true. One way of resolving this discrepancy between statistical fact and union perceptions is to examine briefly the relative weights of the three confederations among FLM delegates in the four provinces.

Table 23 shows that the FIOM-CGIL has more delegates than either the FIM-CISL or the UILM-UIL in each of the four provinces. The relative weight of the FIOM differs considerably across the four, however. In Modena and Cuneo, well over half of the FLM's delegates were enrolled in the FIOM in 1983—86 percent in the former and 65 percent in the latter. In Pordenone and Turin, by contrast, fewer than 40 percent of delegates were members of the FIOM-CGIL, while large numbers (35 percent in Turin and 27 percent in Pordenone) were not affiliated with any of the three confederations.

In the two provinces where the union movement is characterized by radical propensities, a substantially smaller proportion of metalworking factory delegates is enrolled in the Communist and Socialist CGIL than in the two provinces where the union movement tends toward moderation. This resolves the Cuneese discrepancy to the extent that delegates affiliated with the FIOM-CGIL identify and are identified by others with the PCI, even when they may not have formally taken out party cards. In Cuneo, as in Modena, Communist-identified factory delegates exercise a disproportionate influence in the FLM because of the hegemony of the FIOM among metalworking delegates.

28. Interviews 64, CISL Cuneo (Secretariat), 14 January 1981; no. 63, UIL Cuneo (Secretariat), 14 January 1981; no. 105, FLM Cuneo (Secretariat), 15 December 1983; and no. 108, PCI Cuneo, 15 December 1983.

Table 23. Distribution of FLM Delegates by Organization in Four Provinces, 1983

Province	Total Delegates	FIM	FIOM	UILM	SSC or Nonmembers
Cuneo	291	55 (19%)	188 (65%)	19 (7%)	29 (10%)
Turin	4,568	640 (14%)	1,724 (38%)	604 (13%)	1,600 (35%)
Fiat plants	1,387	235 (17%)	592 (43%)	222 (16%)	338 (24%)
Other plants	3,181	405 (13%)	1,132 (36%)	382 (12%)	1,262 (40%)
Modena	1,098	90 (8%)	941 (86%)	33 (3%)	34 (3%)
Pordenone	328	92 (28%)	121 (37%)	28 (9%)	87 (27%)
Zanussi plants	142	38 (27%)	70 (49%)	11 (8%)	23 (16%)
Other plants	186	54 (29%)	51 (27%)	17 (9%)	64 (34%)

Sources: Courtesy of FLM Cuneo, Turin, Modena, and Pordenone.
Note: Figures as of December 1983 for Cuneo and Turin; August 1983 for Modena; December 1982 for Pordenone.

This correlation between shop-floor partisanship and union policy orientations indicates that the structure of local relations between the Communist party and organized labor is likely to be important in shaping the strategic preferences of the union movement, even though national party policy appears to bear little direct relation to local trade union policy positions. I shall return to some of the implications of this after considering a final plausible explanation of union responses to austerity, one involving the degree of union unity.

Interorganizational Union Relations

A final hypothesis that might explain union policy orientations at the provincial level concerns the union unity, or interorganizational relations more generally. One plausible argument holds that the greater the unity among the three organizations and the less pronounced the rivalry among them, the less likely they should have been to agree to austerity recommendations. In settings where interorganizational rivalry is low and there is little competition for new members, many have suggested, the organizations concerned will manifest low levels of interest in recruiting new members.[29] They posit further that, in consequence, these unionists will devote their resources to maintaining factory councils and promoting industrial conflict rather than to traditional bureaucratic tasks. The hypothesis predicts a close connection between the demise of traditional interorganizational rivalry and the growth of a new kind of union radicalism.

One measure of the degree of interorganizational rivalry is the extent of joint FLM members in relation to membership in the FIM, the FIOM, and the UILM. With the establishment of the FLM in 1972, competition for members among the three component organizations was formally abolished and only joint FLM membership was officially permitted. Each provincial FLM was instructed to freeze its membership using commonly agreed-upon quotas. New members could enroll only in the FLM, and the quotas would determine the purely nominal divisions of members for the administrative and financial requirements of the three confederations.[30] Confirmation of the hypothesis requires that a relatively greater share of nonconfederal membership (the senza scelte confederali) be found in those provincial unions that opposed austerity. Table 24 provides the relevant data.

The data on Turin, Modena, and Pordenone confirm the hypothesis. In Turin and Pordenone, where the FLM manifested dissent over austerity recommendations, close to 60 percent of the FLM's members are not associated with any of the three confederations. In Modena, where the FLM was reconciled to the policy, only 7 percent of the FLM's members are SSC. The case that apparently confounds the hypothesis is Cuneo. There the union neglects to compile other than administrative membership figures: figures, that is, that reflect the purely nominal quotas agreed upon in 1972 by the FIM, the FIOM and the UILM. However, Cuneese unionists all reported that no confederal membership cards had been distributed since 1971 except to delegates, for whom confederal membership was still deemed necessary.[31] Since union membership nearly doubled between

29. See, for instance, Rino Fasol, "Una provincia del nord a prevalenza CISL," in *La sindacalizzazione tra ideologia e pratica: il caso italiano, 1950/1977*, ed. Guido Romagnoli, Centro Studi Nazionale CISL Firenze (Rome: Edizioni Lavoro, 1980), vol. 2, especially 31–32. This argument is widely diffused among Italian unionists.

30. For some examples of these agreements, see FLM, "Alcune iniziative unitarie provinciali," in FLM, *Esperienze FLM/2*, I lavori del primo convegno di organizzazione FLM, Bellaria, 28–30 novembre 1974 (Rome: FLM, n.d.).

31. Interviews no. 34, FLM Cuneo (Secretariat), 14 July 1980; no. 60, FLM Cuneo (Secretariat), 14 January 1981; and no. 62, FLM Cuneo (Secretariat), 14 January 1981.

Table 24. Proportion of Nonconfederal Membership (SSC) in Four Provincial FLMs, 1972–83

Year	Cuneo	Turin	Pordenone	Modena
1972 membership	3,670	101,272	n.a.[a]	15,288
SSC	n.a.	19,734	n.a.	—
% SSC		19		0
1973 membership	3,895	115,816	10,748	17,278
SSC	n.a.	40,694	2,674	867
% SSC		35	25	6
1974 membership	4,452	116,700	11,497	18,817
SSC	n.a.	54,463	4,482	1,123
% SSC		47	39	6
1975 membership	5,095	113,653	11,769	19,586
SSC	n.a.	57,387	4,907	900
% SSC		50	42	5
1976 membership	5,295	119,701	11,289	20,660
SSC	n.a.	67,629	4,901	978
% SSC		56	43	5
1977 membership	5,693	117,224	11,936	21,289
SSC	n.a.	69,120	5,194	1,080
% SSC		59	44	5
1978 membership	5,712	120,286	10,405	21,831
SSC	n.a.	70,764	n.a.	1,202
% SSC		59		6
1979 membership	6,154	123,551	11,625	22,690
SSC	n.a.	79,158	5,906	1,439
% SSC		64	51	6
1980 membership	6,095	121,147	11,269	23,449
SSC	n.a.	70,386	6,462	1,657
% SSC		58	57	7
1981 membership	5,763	107,815	10,641	23,158
SSC	n.a.	n.a.	n.a.	1,662
% SSC				7
1982 membership	5,758	92,679	9,555	21,181
SSC	n.a.	n.a.	5,606	1,630
% SSC			59	8
1983 membership	5,628	82,478	n.a.	19,728
SSC	n.a.	49,115	n.a.	1,449
% SSC		60		7

Sources: Courtesy of FLM Cuneo, Turin, Pordenone, and Modena.
[a]N.a. = not available.

1971 and 1979 (see table 16), the majority of the province's 6,000–odd members are therefore SSC.

However, the same is not true of the FLM's delegates in Cuneo, as table 23 shows. Delegate figures provide a far more accurate indicator of real interorganizational relations and rank-and-file sentiments than do membership figures, since the latter fulfill predetermined quotas. As of 1983 the FLM had 291 factory delegates in Cuneo's three comprensori, of which only 10 percent were not affiliated with any of the parent confederations. The comparable figure for Modena is also extremely low: a mere 3 percent. Both situations contrast sharply with those found in Pordenone and Turin, where a full 27 and 35 percent of factory delegates were not affiliated with any of the three confederations in 1982–83. In Turin and Pordenone, delegates are more unitary in their orientations and therefore may be less subject to control from above. Not being affiliated with any of the three union confederations, they appear relatively autonomous as a body.

Note that relatively fewer unaffiliated delegates are found Turin and Pordenone's two major firms, Fiat and Zanussi. Data made available by the FLM in the two provinces but not reported here show that the proportion of unaffiliated delegates in these two firms shrank considerably after the mid-1970s, because the organizations involved felt under increasing pressure to enroll delegates in the confederations. At Fiat Mirafiori, for instance, some 33 percent of delegates were SSC in 1976, but this figure had fallen to 23 percent by 1983 (see table 30, p. 240). Even so, a quarter of delegates at Turinese Fiat plants were SSC in 1983, as were one-sixth of Zanussi's delegates.

These indicators point to a number of pertinent conclusions. First, in the two provinces in which radically oriented unions opposed austerity, the unions in the metalworking industries are more unitary, more equally weighted, and less dominated by the FIOM, and the delegates may be more independent of union control. In the two provinces where moderate union movements endorsed austerity, by contrast, the union movement in the metalworking sector is largely dominated by a single organization—the FIOM-CGIL—and plausibly is subject to greater Communist influence via the delegates, who themselves may be more subject to union control. Partisanship appears more salient for unions that supported austerity, whereas rank-and-file autonomy appears to characterize unions that resisted. The implications of these findings for organizational identity and patterns of reproduction will be elaborated in the next chapter.

Industrial Concentration

In examining the FLM's reactions to austerity proposals in the four provinces, the stories recounted in the previous chapter—especially that concerning the 1982 consultazione—spoke directly to the important role of large industry in generating antiausterity sentiments. We saw that when anything resembling visible rank-and-file dissent over austerity surfaced, it did so principally in large industry and it typically took the form of nonparticipation by the rank and file in union assemblies. It would be overinterpreting the data to imagine that this constituted genuine rank-and-file rebellion over austerity, but it certainly singled out large industry in locating the external correlates of antiausterity sentiment. Below, I report data attesting to the degree of industrial concentration in Pordenone and Turin, on the one hand, and industrial fragmentation in Modena and Cuneo, on the other.

Table 25 presents data on sectoral industrial concentration in the four provinces as well as nationally. Industrial employment in both Turin and Pordenone is highly concentrated in the metalworking industries, which account for between 40 and 60 percent of their entire provincial industrial work force. In Pordenone, one out of every five industrial jobs is in a

Table 25. Distribution of Industrial Work Force in Four Provinces and in All of Italy, 1981

Area	Metalworking Industries	Chemicals, Ceramics, Plastics	Textiles, Food, Wood, Furniture	Construction	Total Industrial Work Force[a]
Turin	304,492 (63%)	32,616 (7%)	100,581 (21%)	37,138 (7%)	485,387
Cuneo	20,627 (24%)	7,714 (9%)	38,321 (45%)	15,937 (19%)	84,350
Pordenone	22,038 (40%)	4,775 (9%)	16,962 (31%)	10,377 (19%)	54,893
Modena	42,946 (30%)	27,950 (20%)	49,499 (35%)	19,190 (14%)	141,281
Italy	2,208,281 (31%)	868,831 (12%)	2,654,151 (37%)	1,190,013 (17%)	7,140,326

Source: ISTAT, *Sesto censimento generale dell'industria, del commercio, dei servizi e dell'artigianato (26 ottobre 1981),* provisional figures reported in ISTAT, *Annuario statistico italiano 1983* (Rome: ISTAT, 1983), 170–73, table 168.

[a]Total industrial work force also includes energy, gas, and water. Figures include employees and employers (*occupati dipendenti e indipendenti*).

Table 26. Average Plant Size by Industrial Sector in Four Provinces and in All of Italy, 1981

Area	Chemicals, Ceramics, Plastics	Metalworking Industries	Textiles, Food, Wood, Furniture	Construction	All Industry[a]
Turin	22	27	9	3	13
Cuneo	13	8	10	3	6
Pordenone	18	17	10	3	8
Modena	34	10	5	3	7
Italy	19	12	7	4	7

Source: See table 25. My calculations.
[a]Total industrial work force also includes energy, gas, and water.

metalworking plant; in Turin the same figure rises to three out of five. In both, the metalworking industries constitute the single largest industrial sector. In Cuneo and Modena, by contrast, these industries provide considerable numbers of industrial jobs but are in no way dominant. Only a quarter to a third of the Cuneese and Modenese industrial work force is engaged in the metalworking industries, less than the numbers engaged in textiles, food, wood, and furniture.

Along with sectoral concentration, Turin and Pordenone are also subject to considerable plant concentration within the metalworking sector. Table 26 examines average plant size for four major industrial sectors in 1981. Although the average metalworking plant in Italy has a work force of twelve, in Turin the equivalent figure jumps to twenty-seven and in Pordenone it is seventeen. In Cuneo and Modena, by contrast, plant size is below the national average.

Table 27 further explores the importance of large industry in the four provinces. In Turin nearly half (46 percent) of the province's metalworkers hold jobs in plants employing at least 1,000 persons. Pordenone, similarly, finds some 43 percent of its metalworkers in plants of at least 1,000 persons.[32] Cuneo, on the other hand, has a mere 5 percent of its metalworkers in large plants. Modena, finally, is characterized by the diffusion of very small industry. Just over 10 percent of Modenese metal-

32. This figure would rise to just over 60 percent were we examining firm size rather than plant size. The three plants that provide all metalworking employment in the 500–999 range are owned by Zanussi, which has six plants in the province. The only other plant with more than 1,000 employees in Pordenone is the Savio (with 1,663 employees in 1978), part of a state holding company.

Table 27. Percentage of Industrial Work Force in Large Plants by Sector in Four Provinces and in All of Italy, 1981

Area	Chemicals, Ceramics, Plastics	Metalworking Industries	Textiles, Food, Wood, Furniture	All Industry[a]
Turin	20	46	19	35
Cuneo	0	5	22	11
Pordenone	0	43	0	17
Modena	5	11	0	4
Italy	20	22	4	11

Source: ISTAT, *Sesto censimento generale dell'industria, del commercio, dei servizi e dell'artigianato: 26 ottobre 1981*, vol. 1, *Primi risultati sulle imprese e sulle unità locali (dati provvisori)*, book 1, *Dati nazionali, regionali e provinciali* (Rome: ISTAT, 1983), various tables. My calculations.
Note: "Large plants" are as those with more than 999 employees.
[a]Total industrial work force also includes construction and energy, gas, and water. Figures include employees and employers (occupati dipendenti e indipendenti).

workers are employed in large industry. In Modena and Cuneo small and medium-sized industry predominates, whereas Turin and Pordenone are greatly dependent on large industry.

Finally, table 28 shows the percentages of industrial and metalworking jobs provided by Turin's and Pordenone's largest firms, Fiat and Zanussi. In Pordenone, more than a fifth of all industrial employment was provided by Zanussi in 1981, and more than half the employees in the metalworking industries were concentrated in this firm. In Turin, similarly, a third of all

Table 28. Fiat and Zanussi Employment in Turin and Pordenone, 1981

Province	All Industrial Employees	Metalworking Employees	Fiat[a]/Zanussi Provincial Employees	Fiat/Zanussi as Percent of Industrial Employees	Fiat/Zanussi as Percent of Metalworking Employees
Turin	438,748	289,872	155,402	35	54
Pordenone	45,610	19,776	10,236	22	52

Sources: Figures on industrial and metalworking employees: ISTAT, *Sesto censimento generale dell' industria, del commercio, dei servizi e dell'artigianato: 26 ottobre 1981*, vol. 2, book 1, unpublished tables courtesy of ISTAT, Rome. Fiat employees: courtesy of FLM, Turin. Zanussi employees: FLM Pordenone, *Bilancio '81: struttura organizzazione tesseramento* (February 1982), special internal bulletin, 10.
[a]Figures from December 1980.

industrial employment in the province came from Fiat, which accounted for more than half of metalworking employment.

In both provinces, then, employment is highly concentrated in the metalworking industries; within the metalworking industries, it is concentrated in large industry; and within large industry, it is concentrated in single firms. In neither Modena nor Cuneo, on the other hand, is there any single firm capable of playing the same role. In Modena, for instance, the largest plant in the metalworking industries is a Fiat tractor factory, which employed some 3,900 persons in 1980, or about 11 percent of the sector's jobs. Similarly, Cuneo's largest plant is a Fiat-owned train factory, which employed 1,080 persons in 1980, or a mere 5 percent of all metalworkers.[33]

Associations Are Not Explanations

Although it might appear possible to build on this evidence and construct an argument for how large industry generates union radicalism, such an endeavor would entail seriously forcing the data. For one thing, as we have seen, rank-and-file reactions to austerity recommendations exhibited more geographic variation than could plausibly be accounted for with reference to plant size.

Although much of what passed for rank-and-file dissent was concentrated in large plants, and dissent there certainly attracted most public notice, workers in large plants did not necessarily dissent. Thus far we have no way of discriminating between large plants in which workers did or did not appear especially reluctant to approve wage moderation policies. Evidence presented in the last chapter suggests that how union officials presented austerity recommendations to the rank and file was critical in shaping the latter's reactions, and that it was union officials more than workers who rebelled over policies of wage moderation. If this is true, then we require an independent account of the policy orientations of union officials. Data presented in this chapter reveal too that radicalism and moderation in provincial FLMs correlate with factors other than industrial concentration. As chart 2 shows, union policy orientations also corresponded to the presence or absence of a dominant political subculture; the presence or absence of a break in rank-and-file collective action during the hot autumn; the degree of union unity; the relative weight of the

33. Figures on employment in these plants courtesy of FLM Modena and Cuneo.

Chart 2. Correlates of Local Policy Orientations

	Moderate	Radical
Political environment	Stable subculture	Competitive parties
Industrial environment	Fragmented	Concentrated
Working-class collective action: impact of hot autumn	Continuous	Interrupted
Degree of union unity (% SSC of FLM delegates)	Low (below 10%)	High (above 25%)
Party influence over union delegates (% FIOM delegates in FLM)	High (above 60%)	Low (below 40%)
Social composition of PCI	Supraclass (40% blue collar)	Class specific (60% blue collar)
Union responses to austerity policies (1978 and 1982)	Reconciled	Opposed

FIOM in the FLM; and the social composition of the PCI's membership. The mere association of large industry with a radical trade unionism neither provides an explanation in and of itself nor tells us why these other factors should also appear consistent with union policy orientations.

I began with the stricture to "cherish all hypotheses." The analysis thus far has served to discard a series of plausible hypotheses meant to account for variations in organized labor's policy orientations at the local level. We do not yet have an explanation, however; we merely have some interesting empirical associations. How do we move from association to explanation?

"The Document, Personal Observation, and the Interview" are what the Webbs advised as the next step.[34] If we listen long and carefully enough, and if we devise sensitive ways of interpreting what they say, labor movement participants should themselves be able to provide coherent accounts of their policy orientations. In the following chapter we shall listen to them turn associations into explanations.

34. Webb and Webb, *Industrial Democracy*, xxv.

7

The Historical and Organizational Dynamics of Provincial Unionism

How do labor movements construct policy orientations out of historical and environmental opportunities? Policy orientations are, we have seen, relatively stable, reflecting how contextual factors get worked into the organizational life of the union movement—how unionists experience and think about their environments and how they develop organizations designed to work on the external world. In this chapter I show that union organizations in the two types of provincial environments we have identified understood the militancy of the hot autumn in two distinct ways and initiated pattern-setting organizational alterations in correspondingly distinct ways. These alterations subsequently generated two identifiable logics of organizational behavior: one in which the union movement acts as if rank-and-file loyalty is largely based on instrumental calculations directed at visible benefits, another in which it acts as if loyalty is primarily a function of expressive and global identification with a project of social transformation. I identify these divergent logics of organizational behavior with two systems of organizational reproduction: how the union movement solicits rank-and-file support from day to day. These two logics of organizational behavior, I argue, also are consistent with and reflect variations in the sources of union legitimacy: either external and partisan derived or internal and intrinsic. Finally, this chapter puts these historical and organizational patterns of behavior together with the story of austerity, attempting to explain what repeatedly drove unions in certain provinces to resist its adoption while others supported it.

Working Class Collective Action and Union Responses to the Hot Autumn

We saw in the previous chapter that there were significant differences in the effects of the hot autumn on patterns of working-class collective action at the provincial level. Turin and Pordenone had been marked by reversals, or ruptures, in their patterns of collective action, whereas Modena and Cuneo were characterized by continuity. To substantiate this argument, I examined the extent and type of change in the volume of provincial industrial conflict compared with the national volume of conflict (see table 12).

Rank-and-file mobilization is not, however, a phenomenon whose pattern is determined only from below. Over time it is institutionalized, channeled, encouraged or dampened, guided, and directed by trade unions. Industrial militancy peaked across Italy in 1969, more or less when it exploded in most of the Western European countries. But in most settings, both in Italy and in the rest of Western Europe, rank-and-file action did not permanently alter union strategy and structure. This was an exceptional response, one possible in Italy owing to the weakness of the PCI in conjunction with the aggressivity and imagination of organized labor.

Below I make a parallel argument, one reformulated for application to the provincial level. I demonstrate that the extent of continuity in working-class collective action and the subsequent reorganization of union structures were functions of the stability or instability of the local political subculture. I thus link political context with self-conscious organizational behavior. The argument is worth pursuing in some detail because, though plausible, it is probably not the most immediately compelling explanation for changes in patterns of collective action and union reorganization during the hot autumn.

In assessing the changes wrought by the hot autumn, scholars have focused largely on plant-level variables, especially plant size. In their account of why it proved so difficult to effect economic adjustment in the 1970s, for instance, one group of observers noted that "the unions helped convert shop-floor militancy into firmly entrenched plant unions, and large companies were unable to eliminate plant-level union activity after the 'Hot Autumn.'"[1] This account suffers from two weaknesses. First, it

1. Robert J. Flanagan, David W. Soskice, and Lloyd Ulman, *Unionism, Economic Stabilization, and Incomes Policies: European Experience* (Washington, D.C.: Brookings Institution, 1983), 500.

fails to recognize that the appropriate level of analysis for union responses to militancy is not the plant or the firm but the province. Since Italian unions are organized not by plant but rather geographically and by sector, the relevant actor is not plant specific. Nor are provincial unions the sum of the factories they organize. Second, such an explanation fails to distinguish large plants in which militancy generated enduring transformations of union structures from those where it did not. In all cases, commissioni interne were replaced by factory councils. But, as we shall see below, reorganization proceeded in distinct ways according to the political context in which it occurred, with distinct consequences for subsequent union policy.

The Impact of the Hot Autumn in Modena and Cuneo

In both Modena and Cuneo 1969 marked a high in industrial strike volume, as was commonly the case across Italy. In neither province did events between 1968 and 1972 lead to radical or thorough organizational transformations, however. Continuity in the union's habits and pattern of linkages to the rank and file went hand in hand with continuity of the working class's pattern of collective action. Underlying this was the fundamental stability of the political subcultures of the two provinces.

As two Cuneese FLM unionists reported, 1969 "was another thing here."[2] "We lived a little off the movements of others," another explained, assessing the impact of the hot autumn.[3] Although rank-and-file militancy in the province increased in 1969, it still remained radically below the national average and well below that found in most of the rest of northern Italy, as table 12 shows.

Before 1968, category unions as distinct organizational entities were unknown in the Cuneese CGIL. A look at membership figures there explains why. Although the CGIL boasted more than 16,500 Cuneese members in 1949, by the mid-1960s the confederation had only 4,551 members in the entire province. In 1961 the CGIL's full-time functionaries consisted of a mere four persons, responsible for everything from textiles to

2. Interviews no. 61 and 62 (held simultaneously), FLM Cuneo (Secretariat), 14 January 1981.

3. Interview no. 59, CGIL Cuneo (Secretariat), 13 January 1981. Unionists in the province are fond of lamenting that events regularly take two years to reach Cuneo from more dynamic areas of Italy. Another unionist, confirming the more detailed analysis below, admitted that most changes that affected the union's organization and strategy in Cuneo in the 1970s were "copied" from those that had already occurred elsewhere. Interview no. 64, CISL Cuneo (Secretariat), 14 January 1981.

food workers.[4] In 1968, following trends long evident elsewhere, the CGIL of Cuneo established its various category unions,[5] and a year later it initiated discussion of the conversion from the commissione interna to the consiglio di fabbrica. The first formal joint CGIL-CISL-UIL meetings were not held until 1970, and the decision to constitute the CdFs was made "with considerable delay";[6] only in late 1970 did the Cuneese metalworkers' unions announce that they would no longer conduct elections for CIs and begin establishing CdFs in their stead.[7] The CGIL, apparently, was internally divided on the question, as was the PCI. Both viewed the shift with apprehension, since the outcomes of CdF elections were potentially "uncontrollable," unlike those of the CIs, mainly because CdFs are elected using write-in procedures rather than chosen from preselected union candidates. "We ourselves created the councils here," one unionist said, with no push from below and, indeed, against the open opposition of workers and shop-floor cadres.[8] The decisions to establish the FLM and to offer nonconfederal joint membership in it were enforced by national directives. The recruitment of a younger, more militant, and less divisive generation of CGIL and CISL unionists did not began until about 1973; until then, change was nationally imposed and dutifully, if somewhat reluctantly, implemented.[9] Similarly, generational turnover of the PCI's local leadership took place only in 1979 and 1980, a full six years after "it could have happened." Under the older leadership, weekly meetings between the PCI Federation's and the CGIL's general secretaries had been the norm.[10]

The absence of much impetus for establishing new linkages with the rank and file was only one aspect of the general sociopolitical stability characteristic of Cuneo. Table 20 shows that the DC's electoral hegemony has still not been seriously contested there; equally, its dominion over

4. Data courtesy of CGIL Cuneo.

5. In 1964 the FIOM did hold a provincial "congress" consisting of five or six full-time CGIL functionaries and militants who met one Sunday morning. This was the first congressional meeting of any category union of the CGIL in Cuneo within living memory.

6. Interview no. 59, CGIL Cuneo (Secretariat), 13 January 1981.

7. Reported in *Sindacato Nuovo*, giornale unitario FIM-FIOM-UILM Cuneo, no. 1 (November–December 1970).

8. Interview no. 59, CGIL Cuneo (Secretariat), 13 January 1981.

9. Interviews no. 60, FLM Cuneo (Secretariat), 13 February 1981, and nos. 61 and 62 (held simultaneously), FLM Cuneo (Secretariat), 14 January 1981.

10. Interview no. 65, PCI Cuneo (Secretariat), 15 January 1981. Even in 1981 important leaders of the local CGIL lamented the official breakdown (owing to the incompatibility regulations) of such close ties with the PCI but claimed to participate as much as possible—informally—in the life of the local Federation.

society has not been challenged. Subcultural stability is extremely high in Cuneo. In consequence, new institutions for mobilizing working-class social and political action appeared only as a result of the gradual, forced implementation of extraneous national directives.

The hot autumn did not exert a direct or immediate radicalizing effect on union structures in Modena either. The only important instance of "unpredictable" rank-and-file militancy in the province took place at a Fiat tractor factory, one of the few Modenese metalworking plants where the CISL was roughly the equal of the CGIL. The delegates who emerged were strongly supported by the FIM in an effort to displace the FIOM.[11] The provincial decision to replace the CIs with CdFs encountered "internal resistance" in the CGIL, which feared losing the overwhelming majority it held in most commissioni interne.[12] Moreover, thanks to the CGIL's strength, itself primarily a function of the PCI's subcultural penetration, the CIs had proved relatively active and effective bargaining agents in the 1960s, and it was difficult for the FIOM to see the need to replace them with CdFs.[13] In consequence, as a delegate in an important local metalworking plant put it: "The delegates were formed in 1970, after the contractual battle. The initiative came from the national leaders of the union."[14] The decisions to endorse the new factory councils and to begin holding the open shop-floor assemblies required for electing delegates were made by the PCI and then communicated to the union.[15] When delegates were elected, the same CI activists by and large moved into the CdFs.[16] Moreover, the Modenese FIOM never enforced the federation's national directives regarding nonconfederal membership for delegates, so that in 1983 a mere 3 percent of metalworking delegates there was not affiliated with any of the three parent confederations.[17] As the FIOM's

11. Interviews no. 77, FLM Modena (Secretariat), 20 February 1981, and no. 78, FLM Modena, 21 February 1981.

12. Interview no. 71, CGIL Modena (Secretariat), 9 February 1981.

13. I am grateful to an FLM official for pointing this out to me, in an effort to correct the incomplete interpretation offered in my "L'austerità e i rapporti base-vertice nel caso dei metalmeccanici," *Laboratorio Politico* 2 (September–December 1982), 59–77. Interview no. 123, FLM Modena (Secretariat), 27 December 1983.

14. FIOM delegate at the Fonderia Corni (Modena), quoted in Fabrizio D'Agostini, *La condizione operaia e i consigli di fabbrica* (Rome: Editori Riuniti, 1974), 207.

15. Interview no. 79, ex-PCI Modena (Secretariat), 21 February 1981.

16. Interview no. 78, FLM Modena, 21 February 1981.

17. Data reported in FLM Modena, "Situazione delegati provincia di Modena-agosto 1983 raffronto con giugno 1980," unnumbered table included in FLM-Modena, "Note su tesseramento," prepared for the Conferenza di organizzazione FIOM-CGIL [modenese], 14–15 novembre 1983 (Modena, 30 October 1983), internal document courtesy of FIOM-CGIL Modena.

general secretary explained: "The Modenese FIOM has never accepted this position [i.e., requiring delegates to remain SSC] because it would have been an error to expropriate from the delegates one of their basic tasks, that of proselytism and [securing the] adhesion of workers to the union."[18]

This picture is consistent with how other scholars have described relations between the union movement and the Communist party in the strongly Communist zones of Italy.[19] Even before 1969, unionization in Modena was extremely high, dominated by the CGIL, and more a function of Communist party subcultural penetration than of independent trade union activities.[20] In a context of high subcultural stability, institutional changes in the trade unions were painstaking, piecemeal, and channeled by the PCI itself. One unionist, who used the word "courageous" to characterize the decision made in the early 1970s to extend the delegate structure and articulated bargaining to the smaller firms in the province,[21] argued that this extension had been possible for three reasons. First, it had been assumed only following a "political choice" made by the union: thus, far from being automatic or pushed from below, it had been carefully prepared and long debated. Second, the peculiar "political-union history" of the province and the "will of the working class to involve itself in the union and the party" made success probable from the outset, since long-established subcultural communication networks already linked employees in small firms to the PCI and thence to the union. Finally, the "presence of a vast network of democratic associations"—of Communist-oriented managerial associations, specifically—meant that the instinctive reluctance of the *padroncini* (literally, "little bosses": the owners of very small firms, as they are called in the area) could be mediated by the PCI itself, which had the credibility to guarantee the union's behavior.[22] This

18. Lauro Setti, "Le lotte del 1969—e la nascita della F.L.M.," relazione, 80 Anniversario F.I.O.M. [Modena], undated internal document [ca. September 1982], courtesy of FIOM-CGIL Modena.

19. For instance, Stephen Hellman, "The PCI's Alliance Strategy and the Case of the Middle Classes," in *Communism in Italy and France*, ed. Donald L. M. Blackmer and Sidney Tarrow (Princeton: Princeton University Press, 1975), especially 407–8.

20. See Guido Romagnoli and Maurizio Rossi, "La sindacalizzazione in Italia fra ciclo economico, conflitto e facilitazioni istituzionali," in *La sindacalizzazione tra ideologia e pratica: il caso italiano 1950/1970*, ed. Guido Romagnoli, Centro Study Nazionale CISL Firenze, 2 vols. (Rome: Edizioni Lavoro, 1980), vol. 1, especially chap. 2.

21. Because of the potential impact on the PCI's electoral support from small plant owners. See the discussion below on artisans.

22. Interview no. 71, CGIL Modena (Secretariat), 9 February 1981.

is an archetypal example of the bases of political change in the province: decisions are reached within leadership groups, not because of unexpected rank-and-file behavior; a multiplicity of local actors is involved, all mediated by the PCI; and change is relatively painless to implement thanks to the PCI's strength as a subcultural actor.

Thus, although the volume of labor conflict was particularly high in 1969 and though it has historically been above the national average in Modena, it has not disrupted well-established political and union structures. Not only was the "essential stability" of relations between the PCI and the union unaffected by the hot autumn,[23] the party managed to use the growth of industrial unrest to reinforce its own primacy over the union and its direct ties to the rank and file. The PCI regularly intervened in shop-floor problems after 1969 in order to maintain direct links with the working class.[24] At the height of the hot autumn, the party demonstrated its primacy, and the union never acquired the independent bases for initiatives and legitimacy that rank-and-file militancy provided elsewhere.

In neither Modena nor Cuneo did radical and permanent changes in working-class collective action occur during the hot autumn. The responses of the FLM in both provinces were extremely cautious, even wary. Institutional changes in union organization, including the provision of joint membership cards, the construction of factory councils, and the introduction of extensive articulated bargaining, were implemented slowly, from above, and over considerable initial local resistance. Political subcultures retained high levels of stability, and any changes in relations between the unions and the party system were gradual rather than dramatic, tempered rather than violent. The union movement's fundamental source of legitimacy remained the PCI, and organized labor never developed a significant capacity for autonomy and self-legitimation.

The Impact of the Hot Autumn in Pordenone and Turin

Events in Pordenone and Turin differed sharply from those in Cuneo and Modena. Radical transformations took place in the patterns of working-class collective action; important changes in the unions' organization were instituted rapidly and with enthusiasm. In consequence, relations between the FLM and the rank and file were deeply and permanently altered. Such changes occurred in the context of profound subcultural

23. Interview no. 72, PCI Modena (Secretariat), 12 February 1981.
24. Interview no. 79, ex-PCI Modena (Secretariat), 20 February 1981.

political instability in which the party system proved incapable of channeling social change.

The Pordenonese union movement was relatively weak before 1969, mainly as a result of the rapid industrialization Pordenone underwent during the 1960s. In 1961, for instance, some 48 percent of the province's labor force was employed in industry, while fully 26 percent remained in agriculture. By 1971 agricultural employment had shrunk to 14 percent whereas industry accounted for 52 percent of the labor force.[25] To put it more vividly, industrial employment rose from some 27,000 persons in 1961 to 50,000 in 1971, increasing by 83 percent, considerably higher than the national rate of industrial growth.[26]

Industrial development in the province largely coincided with the growth of the Industrie Zanussi, S.p.A., founded in 1916 and by the 1960s the province's largest employer and Europe's largest manufacturer of household appliances. (The firm was bought in 1984 by its Swedish competitor, Electrolux.) As the local chamber of commerce noted: "The branch of the mechanical industries in the province, passing from 7,256 employees in 1961 to 20,955 in 1971, has in ten years provoked an increase in the industrial labor force of some 13,699 persons; an increase that represents the true flywheel of provincial economic growth."[27] As opposed to what occurred in other industrial sectors in the province, the growth of the metalworking industries in Pordenone was not associated with a diffusion of small industry but rather with the expansion of large industry, notably Zanussi.[28] In 1956 the firm employed some 1,300 persons. By 1961 employment had nearly doubled, rising to 2,000. And a decade later Zanussi employed some some 13,386 persons in the province, or 27 percent of all provincial industrial employees.[29]

The firm's original work force was recruited both from the surrounding countryside and from the city of Pordenone, which boasted a traditional

25. Giorgio Bazo, ed., *Demografia e forze di lavoro,* vol. 2 of *Ricerche socio-economiche per la provincia di Pordenone*, ed. Giorgio Bazo, 4 vols. (Pordenone: Camera di Commercio Industria Agricoltura e Artigianato, 1978), 397.

26. Giorgio Bazo, ed., *Le attività produttive*, vol. 3 of ibid., 64–65. For an analysis of industrial development in the region Friuli-Venezia Giulia, see Pierluigi Grandinetti and Roberto Grandinetti, *Il caso Friuli: arretratezza o sviluppo?* (Udine: Cooperativa "Il Campo," 1975). The authors examine industrial growth in the region as a variant of the decentralized industrialization model. While this may characterize the province of Udine, it is not apt for Pordenone, where industrialization has been both concentrated and led by large industry.

27. Bazo, ed., *Attività produttive*, 119.

28. Ibid.

29. Ibid., 123, 81, 66.

urban and largely Communist working class isolated in an overwhelmingly Catholic and rural area. Strikes at Zanussi are known to have taken place as early as 1955, though most hiring at the time was done through ecclesiastical channels and production was still only seasonal.[30] The CGIL maintained a majority in the CI in the middle of the decade—electing six members to the CISL's three —but union activity was hampered by the collaborationist behavior of the latter and the authoritarian style of management. By 1960, however, the CISL began to sever its ties to both management and the church, and a younger, more militant leadership group gradually gained power in Zanussi's FIM-CISL.

1965 marks a turning point in the history of the labor movement at Zanussi. First, the only separate accord in the history of the firm was signed that year, an accord that excluded the FIOM.[31] Second, the CISL gained a majority in the CI, electing seven members to the CGIL's five. By then, an enormous expansion of the work force had taken place: in 1964 alone some 1,400 new workers had been hired. Predominantly of Catholic peasant extraction, they seem to have literally overwhelmed the red urban cadres who had previously provided the CGIL with such strength. These new members of the work force took out union cards upon joining the firm, and as early as the mid-1960s, 60 to 70 percent of the manual work force and 40 percent of white-collar workers were unionized at the firm's largest plant in Porcia. Thanks to a strong tradition of agricultural militancy, there was a direct transfer of hostility from the landowner to industrial management, immediately sparking bitter and even violent industrial conflicts, particularly acute given the extremely repressive atmosphere in the factory, the long work hours (for many years Saturdays were regular workdays, while Sunday overtime was a virtual condition of employment), and the low wages relative to other firms in the province and also to other firms in the sector elsewhere in Italy. Low levels of education combined with the lack of urban or industrial traditions meant, however, that these new workers made few distinctions between the three union organizations, and they apparently joined whichever union happened to approach them first. They were also susceptible to religiously defined divisiveness; Catholic anti-Communism was a potent force dividing workers.[32]

30. The early demand for stoves rose during winter.

31. Also reported in Roberto Diemoz, *Dal decollo industriale alla crisi dello sviluppo: il caso della Zanussi* (Bologna: Il Mulino, 1984), 208–9. Diemoz claims that the CISL already had a majority in the CI by 1962, however (206).

32. The history above was recounted by one of the most important figures in the battle to extricate the CISL at Zanussi from its subordination to church, party, and management in

For a variety of reasons, then, the hot autumn at Zanussi was especially hot. Delegates emerged in late 1968 and rapidly received strong union support, generating one of Italy's earliest factory accords granting them recognition. Bargaining was virtually continuous and swelled collective enthusiasm: at one point management was forced to conduct negotiations—over wages and the formal recognition of delegates—in the middle of the factory courtyard, surrounded by striking workers.[33] A traditionally weak PCI followed in the union's wake. The PCI had only one very small factory section at Zanussi at the time and, owing to the party's virtual absence on the shop floor, proved unable to influence union choices concerning delegates one way or another.[34] The subsequent expansion of the PCI's shop-floor membership in the 1970s was, according to unionists I interviewed, a secondary consequence of the union's expansion.

The radical changes in working-class collective action in Pordenone, especially at Zanussi, and the permanent transformations of union struc-

---

the 1950s (interview no. 89, CISL Pordenone [Secretariat], 28 February 1981), and by two FIM-CISL members of the factory council executive, Zanussi (Porcia) (interview no. 90, 1 March 1981). A review of the composition of the labor force at Zanussi and of conflicts over working conditions in the 1960s is Silvio Valdevit, "Fine di un mito neocapitalistico: organizzazione del lavoro e condizione operaia nel complesso Zanussi," *Classe* 3 (June 1971), 233–44.

33. Interviews no. 89, CISL Pordenone (Secretariat), 28 February 1981, and no. 86, FLM Pordenone (Secretariat), 22 February 1981. The incident is also reported in Diemoz, *Decollo industriale alla crisi dello sviluppo*, 68. The Zanussi accord formally recognizing delegates, signed in June 1969, after an earlier accord in 1968, is reprinted under REX (Pordenone) in Eugenio Guidi, ed., "Analisi e valutazione degli accordi sui delegati," *Quaderni di Rassegna Sindacale* 7 (December 1969), 67–68. See also Silvio Valdevit, "La Rex di Pordenone e la Zoppas di Treviso," *Quaderni di Rassegna Sindacale* 7 (December 1969), 91–94. According to this author, the UILM at Zanussi (as at Fiat) initially refused to endorse the new delegates, whereas the FIM and FIOM immediately supported them.

For a marvelous description of the innovations in the strike forms used at Zanussi during the hot autumn, see Ottaviano Del Turco, "Una tipologia delle forme di lotta oggi in Italia," *Quaderni di Rassegna Sindacale* 8 (March 1970), 66–67. Del Turco writes: "The workers brought their alarm clocks to their work posts, and the simultaneous ringing in the sections gave the signal for the beginning of a strike. All the clocks had been set to go off at the hours planned for articulated strikes, which had been announced by the union and posted outside the factory." When management too began watching the announcements and reorganizing production in anticipation of the articulation of strikes, the delegates changed their procedure: "The signal for the beginning of a strike would be given by the delegates with the trill of a whistle. Now the damage to the firm was not confined merely to the hours of strikes actually effected. The tension that accumulated in the sections while waiting for the delegates to give the signal (no one, not even the workers, knew the exact hour for the beginning of a strike) provoked a slowdown of production. The delegate became everyone's reference point" (66–67).

34. Interview no. 86, FLM Pordenone (Secretariat), 27 February 1981.

tures that resulted were part of a more general disintegration of the province's traditionally white subculture. The initial appearance of radical and militant trade unionism at Zanussi was the product of a severance of ties between the FIM-CISL and the DC in the early 1960s. Over that decade, the DC gradually lost its ability to condition the union's behavior and to channel social change. By 1969 the FIM-CISL at Zanussi retained only residual links to the DC and was known as one of the more politically independent and radical of Italy's provincial Catholic-oriented unions. After 1969 subcultural instability became increasingly pronounced in Pordenone: the DC's electoral performance fell from 48 percent in 1968 to 39 percent in 1983 and can only be expected to decline further (see table 20). By the early 1980s, the CGIL had close to an absolute majority of industrial union members—48 percent to the CISL's 40 percent and the UIL's tiny 12 percent (see table 15). The province began evolving rapidly from a relatively stable white political subculture into a competitive party system and simultaneously from the political monopolization of social change to the development of independent and powerful social actors.

The Turinese case resembles the Pordenonese to the extent that a radical transformation of working-class collective action took place with the hot autumn and a new pattern of linkages emerged between the FLM and the rank and file. It differs in that Turin has never experienced a stable political subculture. As one of Italy's early industrializers and an important urban center for at least the past century, Turin has never been conducive to the establishment of sociopolitical subcultural networks.

The fascinating history of Turinese unionism in the 1950s and 1960s cannot be presented here, but it is nonetheless relevant to the contemporary situation. The FIOM-CGIL was defeated in Fiat in 1955 when, in a stunning reversal, it lost its majority in the CI. The UILM-UIL was discredited as a "yellow union" in 1962, when it tried to sign a separate accord with Fiat's management. In 1958 the FIM-CISL too underwent serious internal travail after a failed attempt by the majoritarian current of its local leadership to turn Fiat's FIM into a company union. In consequence, 105 of the CISL's 115 members of the CI at Fiat were expelled.[35]

Two consequences of these vicissitudes stand out: the relative equality

35. See Renzo Gianotti, *Trent'anni di lotte alla Fiat (1948–1978): dalla ricostruzione al nuovo modo di fare l'auto* (Bari: DeDonato, 1979), 101–2. Those expelled established what later became the *Sindacato Italiano dell'Automobile* (SIDA), still a small company union at Fiat. According to company sources, the SIDA at present accounts for some 10 percent of unionized workers in Fiat plants across the country; Fiat External Relations Department, ed., *FIAT 80* (Turin: Fiat, 1980), 267.

among the three unions that resulted, and the rapid generational turnover of leadership groups. Even in the 1980s, unionists in Turin argued that because of the 1955 defeat of FIOM, the 1958 schism of the FIM, and the 1962 discrediting of the UILM, the three organizations met the hot autumn in "an equality of weakness."[36] So although the FIOM holds a plurality of the FLM's provincial membership, it cannot exercise hegemony over the FIM and the UILM. Neither can its relative strength compensate for the weakness of all three organizations together, a weakness illustrated by the 18 percent unionization in the metalworking industries in 1968.[37]

There were also important consequences for the unions' leadership recruitment. The Turinese FIOM was de-Stalinized in the mid-1950s, even before the thorough de-Stalinization of the PCI there, and it was launched on the new factory-oriented strategy well in advance of national actors.[38] The FIM expelled its most damaging company union advocates and initiated its search for a new generation of militants and leaders well before significant changes occurred nationally. In both cases new leaders were quickly installed—new leaders who did not have to fight rearguard battles against the previous generation. In Turin, unlike many other provinces, battles within each component and between the local metalworkers' unions and their local confederal offices could be avoided. Given the relative importance of the metalworking industries in the province's economic structure, these rapid and thorough changes in the unions' leadership groups permitted equivalent changes to take place in the local horizontal structures at a relatively early date. The defeats of the 1950s thus ensured that the metalworkers' unions would devote themselves to years of patiently preparing the ground for an eventual resurgence of militancy.

36. Interview no. 24, FLM Turin (Secretariat), 9 July 1980.

37. Membership figures are available in FLM Turin, *1ª conferenza organizzativa dei delegati metalmeccanici torinesi,* Torino, 5–7 giugno 1975 (Turin: FLM, 1975), 14. The size of the work force in the metalworking industries was taken from Maria Cristina Cavallo Perin, "Analisi quantitativa della sindacalizzazione dei metalmeccanici a Torino (1961–71)," *Quaderni di Rassegna Sindacale* 18 (January–February, 1980), 175. The figure refers only to blue-collar workers, thus overestimating unionization. Perin's very useful analysis, concentrated on the FIOM, is taken from her thesis, "La sindacalizzazione dei metalmeccanici nella provincia di Torino: anni 1961–1971" (unpublished Tesi di Laurea, Università di Torino, Facoltà di Lettere e Filosofia, [ca. 1975]), which should also be consulted for the period.

38. See Paola Agosti Ronza, "Appunti sulla contrattazione articolata: l'elaborazione della Fiom torinese (1960–1962)," *Classe* 3 (June 1971), 109–41, and idem, "Appunti sulla contrattazione articolata: la Fiom e la svolta sindacale alla Fiat (1955–1962)," *Classe* 5 (July 1973), 351–86.

By 1968, then, the Turinese FIOM and FIM were eager to propel the rapidly emerging rank-and-file militancy, especially at Fiat. The twenty-one members of Mirafiori's CI—representing 50,000 employees—met daily with local full-time union officials to tell them what was happening on the shop floor and to continue the work of making ready for an explosion of militancy, an explosion "patiently prepared and constructed" by the union movement itself.[39] In March of that year the first successful strike since 1953 over specifically firm issues—not national collective bargaining—took place at Fiat.[40] For the first time in fifteen years, Fiat workers directly confronted their own management. In December the first successful internal strike took place at Fiat; internal because, rather than laying down their tools and abandoning the workplace, striking workers marched through the plant encouraging others to join them.[41] In the spring of 1969 the first shop-floor delegates came into being.[42] The response of the union was immediate. In July the general secretary of the CGIL's Camera del Lavoro in Turin pronounced that "the decisions made by assemblies of workers and by section delegates or delegates on the [assembly] line must be binding on our union organization,"[43] a position substantially in advance of the confederal reaction to the emergence of CdFs.

39. Remark by Giampiero Carpo, in *La presa di coscienza. Classe operaia e sindacato: una strategia per gli anni '80* Francesca Romana Libertini, ed. (Turin: Stampatori, 1979), 80.

40. Emilio Pugno and Sergio Garavini, *Gli anni duri alla Fiat: la resistenza sindacale e la ripresa* (Turin: Einaudi, 1974), 13–15. The issues were working hours and piecework rates. On events at Fiat during the spring and summer of 1968, see PSIUP torinese, Gruppo di lavoro, ed., *Per un movimento politico di massa: raccolta di documenti della lotta di classe e del lavoro politico alla Fiat* (Turin: Musolini, 1969).

41. Del Turco notes that "a procession of workers up a street or across a square shouting slogans is a pretty normal event in periods of tension and conflict. But a procession inside the factory, which passes through the sections and the courtyards, which ends up underneath management's windows and holds its protest there—that's an exceptional event." "Tipologia delle forme di lotta," 69.

42. On the emergence of delegates in Fiat, see Angelo Dina, "Un'esperienza di movimento politico di massa: le lotte interne alla Fiat (fine 1968–giugno 1969)," *Classe* 2 (February 1970), 133–50; the chapter on Fiat in Giuseppe Bianchi et al., *Grande impresa e conflitto industriale. Ricerca su quattro casi di conflitto sindacale: Fiat-Pirelli-Marzotto-Italcantiere,* Quaderni ISRIL (Rome: Coines Edizioni, 1970); Luciana Castellina, "Rapporto sulla Fiat," *Il Manifesto* 1 (July–August 1969), 12–25; Pino Ferraris, "Strategie a confronto," *Il Manifesto* 1 (September 1969), 18–21; Diego Novelli, "Gli operai dell'Officina 32," *Rinascita* 26 (12 September 1969), 13–14; Adalberto Minucci, "La lotta operaia alla FIAT e a Torino," *Rinascita* 26 (18 July 1969), 11–13; "Colloquio alla Mirafiori," *Il Manifesto* 2 (January 1970), 28–33; and the various interviews with shop-floor activists at Fiat reported in D'Agostini, *Condizione operaia,* part 2.

43. Emilio Pugno, "L'unità nella lotta," *Rinascita* 26 (18 July 1969), 14.

The support given new forms of shop-floor representation by the unions was rivaled by that emanating from the PCI. "In front of the factory gates, the young members of the FGCI [the PCI's youth organization] were saying things that were partially different from and more 'left wing' than those the union was saying."[44] Like the FIOM, the PCI had suffered greatly at Fiat in the 1950s and through the 1960s.[45] In 1965, for instance, there were only some 1,100 PCI members at Fiat, or less than 1 percent of the work force. In the 123 factories in the province in which some organized party presence remained, the PCI enrolled only 1.7 percent of the work force compared with, for instance, Milan, where the PCI's members constituted 3.8 percent of the work force in plants where factory sections existed.[46] In 1967 there were only thirty-seven factory sections throughout Piedmont: before 1969 there was no significant Communist presence in the larger Turinese enterprises.[47] Not surprisingly, the PCI's Turinese Federation joined with the unions, and especially with the FIOM-CGIL, to promote rank-and-file militancy in the late 1960s even though this implied continuing to direct the party's resources to organized labor. The party expected that eventually it would accrue enormous benefits and indeed it did.[48]

In Turin, as in Pordenone, the breakthrough in rank-and-file militancy in the absence of any hegemonic political subculture proved decisive in determining the union's responses to the hot autumn. There were no stable existing channels for expressing social change and conflict. The unions stepped into a virtual political void; in so doing, they temporarily legit-

44. Vittorio Rieser, "Cronaca delle lotte alla Fiat," *Quaderni Piacentini*, no. 38 (July 1969), 12–13. See the entire article for careful reporting on the period. The PCI's strong initial support for the establishment of the new delegate structures at Fiat was confirmed in interview no. 69, PCI Turin (Secretariat), 30 January 1981.

45. On the liquidation of the PCI in the major Turinese firms, see Romano Alquati, "Torino: il partito nella città-fabbrica" (1965), reprinted in his *Sulla FIAT e altri scritti* (Milan: Feltrinelli, 1975). Cf. Stephen Hellman, *Italian Communism in Transition: The Rise and Fall of the Historic Compromise in Turin, 1975–1980* (New York: Oxford University Press, 1988).

46. Reported in Alquati, "Torino: il partito nella città-fabbrica," 232. Cf. the regional figures covering 1950 through 1964 in Fausto Anderlini, "La cellula," in *Il partito comunista italiano: struttura e storia dell'organizzazione, 1921/1979*, ed. Massimo Ilardi and Aris Accornero, vol. 21 of *Annali Fondazione G. Feltrinelli, 1981* (Milan: Feltrinelli, 1982), 207, and those for 1968–70 in Celso Ghini, "Gli iscritti al partito e alla FGCI," in ibid., 290.

47. Stephen Hellman, "Il PCI e l'ambigua eredità dell'autunno caldo a Torino," *Il Mulino* 29 (March–April 1980), 272–73.

48. For an empirical analysis of the long term consequences of the hot autumn on the PCI's organization in Turin, see ibid.

imized the structural primacy of the union in politically representing working class interests. Wedded to new forms of rank-and-file democracy, these unions successfully constructed institutional mechanisms for high levels of autonomy and self-legitimation, mechanisms capable of carrying radicalism.

Legitimacy and Types of Linkage with the Rank and File

In Modena and Cuneo, which did not experience radical changes in their patterns of working class collective action in 1969, the FLM instituted internal organizational changes after the hot autumn only with caution and reluctance. In Turin and Pordenone, on the other hand, where there were ruptures in the patterns of working-class collective action, powerful, militant, and innovative grass-roots actions joined with union organizations enthusiastic about translating them into permanent and enduring transformations. In these two provinces, militancy generated organizational alterations capable of carrying radical strategies.

These two responses coincided with the extent of subcultural political stability in the four provinces. In stable contexts, neither breakthroughs in working-class collective action nor changes in union structures occurred except reluctantly and as a result of national directives. In unstable contexts, both types of changes took place with a rapidity and thoroughness greater than national policy would have warranted. Where political subcultures were weak, the union movement took advantage of collective mobilization to reconstruct its own organization along lines suitable for sustaining radical policy orientations.

These two patterns of responses to the hot autumn endured throughout the 1970s and into the 1980s in the form of two logics of organizational behavior. One sought to retain rank-and-file loyalty as if it were a function of instrumental calculations aimed at visible benefits. The other treated rank-and-file support as if it were instead a product of expressive and symbolic identification with a broad project of social transformation. These logics constituted substantially different mechanisms of organizational reproduction: distinct patterns by which the union movement maintained its linkages with the rank and file and typically recruited members and militants. These two types of linkages speak to different sources of trade union legitimacy. In the former case, legitimacy was extrinsic and partisan derived; in the latter, it was intrinsic and linked to the mobilization of rank-and-file conflict itself. These two types of linkages with the rank and file were thus tied to different patterns of working-class collective action and expressed through the systematic pursuit of different organizational goals. They were replicated in two diverse understandings of the political role of Italian unionism and two different conceptions of the proper relationship between the political arena and collective bargaining. They involved, moreover, systematically different kinds of relations with friendly political parties—in this case the PCI. They resulted, finally, in different outcomes when organized labor was forced to confront policy proposals of the sort embodied in austerity recommendations. The rest of this chapter examines how union officials from the four provinces understood their organizational goals, how they described the inner workings of their organizations, and how the internal politics of trade unions was related to external pressures.

Mechanisms of Organizational Reproduction

Although trade unions everywhere must be concerned with organizational maintenance and reproduction, the tasks involved may be performed in a wide variety of ways. Even when union membership is entirely voluntary and maintenance is a more pressing daily concern than when union membership is obligatory, there is no uniform approach. The most obvious aspects of organizational reproduction, particularly the recruitment of new members, are not necessarily important union activities per se; other ways of linking the organization to the rank and file may be used instead. Even the same industrial union may perform these tasks differently in different contexts. As a study of trade unionism in a northern Italian province found, "membership activity does not always and necessarily present itself as an explicit organizational interest; only under certain conditions can one speak of recruitment policy as an expression of organizational policy."[49]

The research presented thus far has identified two distinct patterns of organizational reproduction characteristic of the Italian union movement in this period. Moderate union movements are characterized by their relatively great expenditure of organizational resources on recruitment, membership, and services—all those tasks typically associated with organizational reproduction, which appeal to workers on the basis of instrumental calculations of the visible benefits loyalty may generate. Union movements that pursue radical strategies, by contrast, relegate such tasks to the

49. Rino Fasol, "Una provincia del nord a prevalenza CISL," in Romagnoli, *Sindacalizzazione tra ideologia e pratica,* 2:45.

periphery. Rather than explicitly devoting a relatively large share of resources to activities such as recruitment, radical union movements use a series of indirect forms of organizational reproduction, which in turn encourage a kind of fusion with the social movements whose interests they express. Resources are concentrated on maintaining shop-floor structures—the consigli di fabbrica—and on organizing strikes. Of course these unions are concerned with the actual benefits their activities obtain for workers. But they conceive of rank-and-file loyalty in terms that transcend such benefits; they act as if loyalty were largely a function of an expressive identification with the broad sociopolitical goals of the workers' movement as a whole. In summary, moderate union movements aim resources at recruiting members, whereas radical union movements focus instead on recruiting activists and militants. The first may be characterized as an instrumental logic of behavior, the second as expressive. Both seek to interweave strategy and structure so as to guarantee the survival of the organization itself.

The four cases examined fall into two categories. In Modena and Cuneo, the union behaves according to an instrumental logic and exhibits moderate policy orientations similar in many ways to those evidenced by the national confederations. In Pordenone and Turin, on the other hand, an expressive logic of behavior predominates, one linked to a radical orientation resembling that characteristic of the national FLM. This is evident in the ways FLM officials in these four provinces talk about their own activities.

The Logic of Organizational Behavior in Cuneo and Modena

The primary activities of the FLM's officials in Cuneo are recruitment and the provision of benefits to individual members, or "assistance," as it is called. Although I attended only about half a dozen union meeetings in the province,[50] in one-third (those that included union delegates) the problem of membership recruitment was extensively, though by no means exclusively, discussed. This contrasts sharply with Turin, where I witnessed more than two dozen meetings of all kinds and never heard the problem of membership explicitly mentioned once (except in PCI meetings with Fiat workers). Cuneese unionists reported that recruitment is

50. None was for FLM functionaries only. The full-time staff is so small and on such close personal terms that formal meetings within the FLM are almost superfluous. The various meetings I observed were all shop-floor assemblies of various types and meetings with delegates from larger firms.

considered so central an issue that it is brought up at every assembly regardless of the topic under formal consideration.[51]

The success of Cuneese unionists in enrolling new members in the 1970s was, according to the union's functionaries, closely bound up with their ability to provide services to individual members. "Workers want assistance here"; the union is seen as an "instrument for [obtaining] personal services"; "full-time functionaries here do everything, not just the inspiring stuff, but also membership, keeping lists"; "the union here is an institution, not a [mass] movement"—all these are common complaints,[52] reflecting the belief that rank-and-file loyalty is based mainly on instrumental calculations about the concrete benefits the union can provide. Bureaucratic and service tasks are viewed as the only way to communicate with, and gain the support of, the rank and file, and they dominate organizational activities. The FLM's local officials justify such concerns on their intrinsic and utilitarian merits, yet clearly they would prefer it otherwise. If individual attitudes could determine organizational behavior, the FLM in Cuneo would be just as radical and as conflict oriented as that in Turin. Instead it is so routinized and minimally militant that it cannot convince the rank and file to conduct articulated strikes in lieu of all-out factory blockades.[53] One functionary summed up the Cuneese position when, at a meeting of an important factory council, he argued: "Membership is the only way we have of evaluating our relationship with the workers and it is how management measures our strength."[54] In a province where the union has only weak shop-floor bodies to mobilize militancy, membership levels are the alternative mea-

51. Interviews no. 60 and no. 62 (held simultaneously), FLM Cuneo (Secretariat), 15 January 1981).

52. Interviews no. 62, FLM Cuneo (Secretariat), 16 July 1980; no. 63, UIL Cuneo (Secretariat), 14 January 1981; and nos. 60 and 62 (held simultaneously), FLM Cuneo (Secretariat), 15 January 1981.

53. In July 1980 I witnessed a strike that had broken out in a small firm in the province, with a labor force of about one hundred. The strike was nominally compact. Even half of the forty-odd white-collar workers joined, quite unknown in the firm's history. The workers absolutely refused to follow the suggestion made by full-time officials that some sort of articulation take place. Instead they insisted on halting all production simultaneously for the full afternoon shift for the rest of the week. The unionists were unable to convince them that employing this strategy would result in workers' losing more pay through striking than they could hope to gain in the raise they were negotiating. Apparently it was psychologically easier not to return after the lunch break than to have to walk off the floor, in a very small group, for an hour or two and then reenter production.

54. FLM official (Secretariat) at a meeting of the consiglio di fabbrica, Michelin (Cuneo), 15 January 1981, observed by the author.

sures of the strength of the rank and file's consensus and of organizational legitimacy.

Modenese unionists repeatedly spoke of a "shared myth of organization" that dominated both the CGIL and the CISL.[55] As in Cuneo, the union "puts a lot of emphasis on" membership recruitment. Aside from the annual provincial drive to expand membership in firms where the FLM has already been established, a month's campaign (using delegates from other firms) is conducted annually to organize the very small industrial and artisanal firms.[56] I attended the meeting of the CGIL's provincial Comitato Direttivo in February 1981 which formally opened the membership drive for that year. The CGIL's national secretary for organization spoke, lauding the Modenese for their organizational virtues and their ability to expand membership among the employed even as it was falling in industrial centers such as Milan.[57]

Two Modenese unionists argued that these levels of unionization made the union in Modena "a prisoner of its own strength." It is so strong that it often does not need to strike: collective bargaining may succeed even in the absence of industrial action. The union movement thereby has little occasion to test and solidify its relationship to the rank and file. Members remain loyal even if the only contact they have with the organization occurs with the annual membership drive. It is a union movement so well self-financed that it has to invent ways to spend its money, and it receives such strong recognition from management that it cannot use all the available hours off for its RSAs.[58] This union, as two other FLM officials put it, "doesn't need to waste its strength": collective bargaining strikes, except in the few large plants or in confrontations with unusually recalcitrant management, are brief and infrequent.[59] The primary linkage between the rank and file and the organization is membership, not militancy.

This takes place in a context in which political loyalties remain largely traditional: individual workers in the red belt vote for and join the PCI because their fathers did, and they join the CGIL because that comes with identifying with the PCI. At the same time, both the PCI and the CGIL are highly performance oriented in these contexts, acting as though traditional

55. Interview no. 78, FLM Modena, 21 February 1981.

56. Interview no. 74, FLM Modena (Secretariat), 19 February 1981.

57. Closing remarks by Rinaldo Scheda, Comitato Direttivo CGIL Modena, 5 February 1981, observed by the author.

58. Interview no. 74, two FLM Modena (one Secretariat), 18 February 1981.

59. Interviews no. 70 and no. 75 (held simultaneously), FLM Modena (Secretariat), 18 February 1981.

subcultural loyalties can be retained only if actual benefits continue to reinforce and perpetuate them. Given the precarious position of the Left nationally, these organizations do not believe that a minority opposition tradition is or can be self-sustaining; rather, they employ instrumental strategies to recreate it anew daily. The unions, for instance, are extremely sensitive to how well they have actually been doing for their constituents, turning out unusually frequent and extremely detailed studies of collective bargaining, wages, health and safety conditions, and factory accords.[60] They treat the traditional basis of rank-and-file loyalty as residual, and their logic of organizational behavior is principally instrumental in its construction of mass support.

The Logic of Organizational Behavior in Pordenone and Turin

In Pordenone, by contrast, "we don't bother much" with strictly organizational issues, one local leader reported.[61] Other officials explained that the union's reduced emphasis on routine organizational issues was the product of both material and ideological factors. On the one hand, since most Pordenonese industrialization had occurred only in the mid-1960s, the organizational traditions of each confederation were weak. Workers perceived few if any differences between the three organizations, having lived with an FLM that had mainly engaged in joint activities, and this discouraged membership drives. Second, the work force at Zanussi had shrunk during the 1970s, and few younger workers had been hired. Older workers were either already union members or highly unlikely to take out membership.[62]

Unionists reported that there were three ways relations with the rank and file were maintained in lieu of routine bureaucratic activities: factory assemblies, personal relations, and strikes. Factory assemblies are held

60. See FLM Modena, ufficio sindacale, ed., "La contrattazione aziendale dal CCNL a oggi: riepilogo in cifre," and "Primi dati dell'indagine su salari qualifiche occupazione," internal documents dated 30 September 1977; "Dati definitivi dell'indagine su salari qualifiche occupazione," internal document dated July 1978; "La contrattazione aziendale nell'ultimo anno (dal settembre 1977 al settembre 1978): riepilogo in cifre," internal document dated 10 August 1978; "Dati definitivi dell'indagine nel settore metalmeccanico nella provincia di Mo [Modena] su: salari qualifiche occupazione," internal document for 1978; and "Dati riassuntivi: contrattazione articolata nella provincia di Modena," internal document for 1979–80, all courtesy of the FLM Modena. Similar studies have been conducted and published by the FLM Bologna.

61. Interview no. 86, FLM Pordenone (Secretariat), 27 February 1981.

62. Interview no. 90, two members of Executive of consiglio di fabbrica, Zanussi (Porcia), 1 March 1981.

with extraordinary frequency in the province, averaging one per month per firm.[63] Personal relations, especially with shop-floor delegates, are also of great importance. Delegates need and expect direct contact with full-time provincial union officials, to the extent that it is incumbent on the latter to sit through long dinners at the homes of their delegates until well into the night.[64] Finally, strikes play an important role in maintaining contact with the rank and file. They must be for concrete and realizable goals, one official reported, they must engage the work force in issues of tangible importance, and they must be regular. Any relatively long-term attempt to depress conflict (two to three years was the figure mentioned, with implicit reference to the period of national unity) could seriously undermine relations with the rank and file.[65]

In Turin, too, routine organizational issues receive only nominal attention. Since the FLM is much larger, it does boast an organizational office, but according to one of the functionaries engaged there, organizational and membership issues are among the FLM's lowest priorities, and few resources are devoted to them by most local unionists.[66] Indeed, the union in Turin did not place any particular emphasis on organizational issues throughout the 1970s. Rather than expending energy on membership problems per se, the FLM prefered to "act politically."[67] That is, extensive resources are devoted to the maintenance of the factory councils and to conflict, as in Pordenone. Membership increased in Turin after the hot autumn only as a secondary effect of these primary activities. Even its continued relative weakness did not induce the organization to take up the matter on its own merits.

In Turin organizational weakness is a potent factor reinforcing the FLM's radical orientation. A local unionist explained this well when he said that the FLM at Fiat was a union "of the avant-garde and of opinion." It has always tried to use "political proposals" (messages concerning general social change) to organize mass movements, but this strategy had never produced greater organizational strength or stability. Writing in 1967, a leader of the FIOM in Turin commented: "In Fiat, in fact, the class movement in Italy has its weakest point: within the union, the FIOM (CGIL) has an extremely limited number of adherents and an extremely

63. Interview no. 91, FLM Pordenone (Secretariat), 2 March 1981.

64. Interview no. 92, FLM Pordenone (Secretariat), 3 March 1981. Personalism in relations with delegates and the rank and file was also discussed in interview no. 95, CGIL Pordenone (Secretariat), 3 March 1981.

65. Interview no. 86, FLM Pordenone (Secretariat), 4 March 1981.

66. Interview no. 67, ex-FLM Turin, 21 January 1981.

67. Interview no. 1, FLM Turin (Secretariat), 24 December 1980.

shallow factory organization. One could say that it leads a movement of opinion more than a mass movement."[68] Nearly twenty years later, local leaders were apt to use almost the same words in describing the current situation. Indeed, the union in Turin "doesn't want" to build any real organization; it simply has not chosen to consolidate its gains in that fashion.[69] The enormous emphasis placed on factory councils in Turin, to the detriment of the issue of recruitment, works to reinforce low levels of unionization.

Despite the fact that much of this is post hoc rationalization for an extremely precarious organizational situation, Turinese unionists are also genuinely apprehensive of what greater membership strength would carry with it. One important local leader said, jokingly, "If we had 60 percent [membership] at Fiat, we would be a moderate union." Although admitting that "in the long run" this stance was untenable, he said that for the moment the FLM still preferred weakness and radicalism.[70] Turinese trade union officials deeply believe that they are more radical than their counterparts elsewhere, and they tend to equate this with organizational weakness. "Why are we more left wing" than the union movement in most other Italian provinces? asked a local unionist. "Not because we're better; or not only because we're better. But because we're weaker."[71] In Turin officials from all three confederations act on this belief, discouraging changes in organizational practice that could achieve greater stability.

Union officials in Turin and Pordenone do not believe that workers fail to evaluate their organizations on utilitarian and instrumental grounds. They know that collective bargaining, for instance, is a central task they must perform as effectively as possible. But they do believe that, fundamentally, their activities are and should be directed to broader goals. They correspondingly conceive of their constituents as a militant or potentially militant collective social movement, whose loyalties can be obtained at least as well if not better by elaborating strategies aimed at general social transformation.

Organizational Behavior in Historical Context

Two distinct types of union behavior emerge as we examine the FLM in the four provinces. One, characterized by its moderate policy orientation,

68. Paolo Franco, "La Fiat e i sindacati," *Problemi del Socialismo*, nos. 19–20 (1967), 791.

69. Interview no. 68, CGIL Turin (Secretariat), 26 January 1981.

70. Interview no. 1, FLM Turin (Secretariat), 24 December 1980.

71. Interview no. 14, CGIL Turin (Secretariat), 1 April 1980.

devotes a relatively large share of its resources to membership recruitment and to providing services to members. The other, whose strategy is radical, expends its resources on maintaining its delegate and factory council structures and on organizing militancy. Both spend most of their time and resources on activities involving collective bargaining, as is common to unions in the highly industrialized north of Italy. The salient differences between unions in different environments do not involve the extent or content of collective bargaining, but rather concern their choices regarding daily organizational priorities.

As part of their two very different logics of organizational behavior, there are also differences in leadership styles between moderate and radical union movements. It would be difficult to devise precise indicators of leadership styles, but extensive fieldwork revealed what appear to be systematic differences. Radical unions enjoy charismatic leaders: men—for they are almost all male—who are unforgettable, whose characters are forceful enough to remain imprinted on one's memory. Individual style seems especially important; factory delegates and lower-level officials speak of their attachments to particular leaders in highly personal terms. In moderate contexts, on the other hand, individual charisma seems less salient. In recruiting full-time officials, expertise and experience—along with sheer availability—appear to be of greater importance. It is not that these men are necessarily "grey and tactful functionaries,"[72] but that personality and character seem to be less important for getting their work done. They can be effective even without style; after all, their tasks, as they describe them, are nearly all routine and entirely routinized. Although charismatic leaders may occasionally surface in moderate unions, their charisma is superfluous. Radical union movements, by contrast, engage in nonroutine activities much of the time and thus require leaders able to respond instinctively to sudden turbulence, disruption, unpredictability—leaders able to get up before a thousand angry workers and explain a particularly unpleasant piece of union news, able to forge close ties to relatively independent, self-conscious, and often distrustful factory delegates. The organizational tasks of radical and moderate union movements differ, and so do the skills and capabilities of their officials.

These two patterns of organizational behavior coincide with the union's

72. The characterization is used by historian Eric Hobsbawm to describe national confederal unionists in their ability to coordinate more radically inclined industrial unions in Britain. See "The 1970s: Syndicalism without Syndicalists?" (1979), reprinted in his *Worlds of Labour: Further Studies in the History of Labour* (London: Weidenfeld and Nicolson, 1984), 278.

pattern-setting responses to the hot autumn. In contexts where the FLM initiated changes in its own structures early and without hesitation, a logic of organizational behavior linked to rank-and-file militancy predominated even into the 1980s. Where the FLM resisted structural changes at the turn of the decade, a logic of organizational behavior appropriate to a calculating rank and file remained characteristic. Where linkages with the rank and file were reestablished in the 1960s, the union as an organization was profoundly and permanently altered. Strategy became locked into structure; policy orientations reflected internal organizational logics.

This suggests that organizational and mobilizational habits of trade unions persist over time unless subjected to severe external shocks. In the case under consideration, this shock was provided by the sudden burst of rank-and-file militancy that occurred with the hot autumn, which acted as a pattern-setting catalyst for union organizations. The persistence of organizational habits also implies that provincial union responses to austerity policies were unlikely to have been arbitrary or unpredictable, providing it can be shown how these responses were rooted in enduring organizational habits. It also suggests that even strong pressures emanating from the confederations would have been unlikely to succeed in forcing provincial union offices to accept policy directives if such policies ran flagrantly against the grain of organizational habits. The rest of this chapter will elaborate these arguments by tracing the connections between organizational habits and provincial responses to austerity policies, detailing how strategy has become a function of structure.

Explaining Provincial Policy Orientations

The moderate union devotes a considerable share of its resources to such tasks as recruiting members and providing services, whereas the radical union emphasizes its shop-floor actors and conflict. These two logics depend on different historical sources of trade union legitimacy and patterns of working-class collective action and therefore entail varying degrees of internal union autonomy and self-legitimation. The relation between these logics of organizational behavior and strategic orientations is not only historical, however. Extreme industrial concentration continues to shape union strategy in Pordenone and Turin, whereas subcultural political stability conditions it in Modena and Cuneo. Extreme industrial concentration gives shop-floor union actors a very real influence over the way the union is linked to the rank and file, the issues it emphasizes, the organizational priorities it sets, and the extent of its autonomy from partisan and confederal pressures. This union, much like the national FLM, derives its legitimacy above all from its council structures and through the exercise of conflict. It is thus likely to oppose moderate policies that necessarily contain conflict and undercut the importance of autonomous union activities. Vice versa, in highly stable political subcultures, the party system itself largely determines the way the union is linked to the rank and file, the issues it emphasizes, the organizational priorities it sets, and the extent of its autonomy from partisan and confederal pressures. Much like the national confederations, this union derives its legitimacy from the party system that surrounds it. It thus is able to reconcile itself to moderate policies that contain conflict and seek to shift union resources to the political arena.

Provincial unions responded similarly to national austerity recommendations in 1978 and 1982, despite the changes that had occurred in the national political context. In 1978 the PCI's proximity to power gave it a strong reason to promote austerity, whereas by 1982 its withdrawal to the opposition made it suspicious of moderation. The national metalworkers' federation and the union movements in Pordenone and Turin opposed austerity in both cases, while the three confederations and the union movements in Modena and Cuneo largely approved it. Whatever direct pressures the PCI may have attempted to apply to organized labor were thus largely ineffective in influencing union responses to austerity. Instead, despite changes in the party's national strategy, provincial relations between the party and the union movement remained intact and relatively stable across the two periods.

Industrial Fragmentation and Political Subcultures in Modena and Cuneo

Tables 25–27 present data on sectoral and industrial concentration in Modena and Cuneo. The industrial structures of these two provinces are highly fragmented both with respect to the relative weights of different sectors and, within the metalworking sector, with respect to plant size. Sectoral fragmentation prevents the metalworkers' unions from playing any particularly important role in provincial union decision making. The labor force employed in this sector accounts for only a quarter of the province's total industrial employment; other sectors rival its importance. The FLM therefore enjoys no special role in forming provincial union policy.

The major consequence of fragmentation within the metalworking sector is that factory councils likewise cannot play particularly significant roles within the FLM. They barely constitute a distinct organizational entity and are unable to act independently to condition provincial decision making. The FLM's officials deal directly with the rank and file at least as much as with delegates and may occasionally even bypass the delegates entirely in dealing with their mass base. The delegates, meanwhile, devote their energies to recruiting members and to collective bargaining. As an indicator of their relative lack of autonomy, they are less likely to be unaffiliated with any of the three confederations than delegates in highly concentrated environments, as table 23 shows.

In Cuneo, for instance, the largest factory in the metalworking industries is Fiat Ferroviara. In December 1983 its CdF, the largest in the province, comprised twenty-four members. Given the 299 delegates spread across the sixty-five plants organized by the FLM (another twenty-eight plants were without either delegates or RSAs), Fiat accounted for only 8 percent of all Cuneese metalworking delegates. Excluding this factory, the average number of delegates per plant was four.[73] Most delegates are extremely isolated and lack regular channels of communication among themselves. They thus cannot effectively condition provincial union activities.

Industrial fragmentation undercuts the union's ability to establish intrinsic trade union legitimacy because it denies the necessary bases for organizational autonomy in the workplace. The strength of working-class subcultural attachments to the PCI, even in a predominantly Catholic area, lends Communist militants a disproportionate influence over union affairs, particularly since their militancy is primarily partisan based. We have seen that the FLM in Cuneo is largely dominated by the FIOM-CGIL, and though Communist delegates are nominally scarce, their influence is exaggerated by the FIOM's hegemony. The lack of genuine electoral competition in Cuneo and the persistence of Christian Democratic subcultural mechanisms for ensuring sociopolitical consensus interweave with industrial fragmentation to account for the FLM's persistently moderate policy orientation there.

Table 20 shows the overwhelming strength and stability of the DC's control of the province of Cuneo. It received 43 percent of the vote in the national elections held in 1983—a full 10 percent above its national showing. According to local trade union and Communist party officials, the DC's principal mechanisms for ensuring political consensus are the Coltivatori Diretti (the DC-sponsored small farmers' association) and the

73. Data courtesy of FLM Cuneo.

church, along with its control over the local governments and the banking and credit systems.[74] The DC's direct involvement in trade union and labor affairs is extremely limited. Although the general secretary of the CISL is a member of the DC—not the case in either Turin or Pordenone—even he admitted that his party could continue winning local elections without bothering much with organized labor. Instead the working class—or what there is of one, since nonindustrial traditions and landownership are still high except in the more urbanized areas of Bra-Savigliano—is left to the unions and the PCI.[75] The 1972 FIM-FIOM-UILM quotas, for instance, allotted 30 percent of overall membership to the FIM, 55 percent to the FIOM, and 15 percent to the UILM, hardly an indication of a DC controlling the province's union movement. Indeed, the CISL derives few resources from the party except, ironically, that of not being too closely associated with it. The CGIL, however, derives considerable benefit from its association with that political party commonly viewed as most representative of working-class interests. Unionists across the three organizations reported that the CGIL's factory militants were typically the best prepared, most active, and most influential delegates and that a disproportionate share of the CGIL's cadres were members of the PCI. In fact, I have shown that statistically this is not the case; if it is believed by both Communist and non-Communist unionists, this testifies to the activism and influence of Communist delegates in a Catholic environment. In fact, the perception makes sense in political context. Given that there are nearly 140 residents per party member in the province (see table 21), that nearly

74. Interviews no. 63, UIL Cueno (Secretariat), 14 January 1981; no. 65, PCI Cuneo (Secretariat), 15 January 1981; and no. 64, CISL Cuneo (Secretariat), 14 January 1981. On the Coldiretti, see Agopik Manoukian, ed., *La presenza sociale del PCI e della DC*, vol. 4 of *Ricerche sulla partecipazione politica in Italia*, by Istituto di Studi e Ricerche Carlo Cattaneo (Bologna: Il Mulino, 1968), 442–65.

75. Similar findings are reported by Robert Evans in his study of a DC village in the Veneto. He writes that "People see the unions as an instrument of defense in the case of a grievance rather than an instrument of pressure that could play a local political role. Thus the mayor had no qualms in advising Antonio Tiberto, who had been laid off following a disagreement with his foreman, to seek counsel and defense through the CGIL which is far more aggressive than its DC counterpart. All in all, opposition parties and unions in [the village studied] find it extremely difficult to act as agents of political socialization because they are perceived as evil." And he quotes a factory worker as saying: "I vote for the CISL to keep the reds out, but if I have a grievance I'll go to the CGIL: they're more efficient"; Robert Evans, *Life and Politics in a Venetian Community* (Notre Dame: University of Notre Dame Press, 1976), 152, 153. The similarities with Cuneo are striking: in both cases the unions are perceived as service providers, anti-communism is all-pervasive, and the CGIL is generally seen as the more active and efficient union.

one of every five metalworking delegates is a Communist does reveal the disproportionate influence of the party in the union movement—even in an overwhelmingly white province. "Ours are just the best," a PCI official explained, without indulging in any false modesty.[76] The CISL agreed that the CGIL was far and away the most visible and active capillary organization within the working class.[77]

A subculture of opposition derives certain advantages from its weaknesses. For Communist workers in Cuneo the party is absolutely primary to the union. Activities in the union are filtered through this prior political commitment. As a result, "the union itself has no intrinsic legitimacy." Rather, "relations between the union and its base pass through the PCI."[78] And this is the case despite the PCI's modest attention to working-class issues and the union movement in the province. In 1977, 39 percent of the PCI's provincial membership was blue collar, as table 22 shows. As an extremely weak but subculturally based party, the PCI in Cuneo sees its principal political role as building relations with other social strata, virtually leaving the factories to the unions.[79] The disporportionate influence it already exercises in the union movement—through Communist union functionaries and especially via the delegates—frees up for other tasks what shallow resources the Federation possesses. Relations between the Federation on the one hand and the CGIL and FIOM on the other are relatively regular, with little role distinction, and the perennially short-staffed PCI often tries to move skilled organizers out of the union. But this is a party that has never won more than 17 percent of the province's vote in national elections, a party with few resources and little political influence except the historically residual sway it implicitly holds over union affairs.

In reacting to confederal austerity recommendations in 1978 and 1982, the FLM in Cuneo thus found itself without an adequate basis for opposition. In 1978 the PCI's own parallel austerity policy meant that potential dissidents in Cuneo lacked the critically necessary support of their factory militants. In 1982, despite the national party's objections to austerity, the consultazione was left to the union movement—a movement that predictably followed confederal directives. The FLM found itself too isolated to emulate the opposition manifested in Turin and by the national offices of the federation.

76. Interview no. 65, PCI Cuneo (Secretariat), 15 January 1981.

77. Interview no. 64, CISL Cuneo (Secretariat), 14 January 1981.

78. Interviews no. 62, FLM Cuneo (Secretariat), 16 July 1980, and no. 61, FLM Cuneo (Secretariat), 13 January 1981.

79. Interview no. 108, PCI Cuneo (Secretariat), 15 December 1983.

The Modenese case is a strong variant on the Cuneese theme. In Modena, as in Cuneo, industrial fragmentation and the overwhelming hegemony of the dominant party—in this case the PCI—combine to produce a union surprisingly reminiscent of the Cuneese. Although considerably stronger, the Modenese FLM is both partisan dominated and highly routinized in its relations with an overwhelmingly Communist rank and file.

Modena, like Cuneo, is marked by sectoral and industrial fragmentation, as I have shown in tables 25–27. Large industry plays little role in directly shaping union structures. Similarly, the metalworking industries do not dominate the labor market. In consequence, a relatively clear demarcation exists between the activities of the horizontal and vertical union offices, and the former tends to dominate the latter. As a result, the FLM is not able to gain hegemony over union activities in the province. Within the FLM factory delegates are without the cohesion and autonomy that would ensure them powerful roles in decision making. The largest metalworking plant in the province is a Fiat tractor factory, which employed some 3,600 persons at the end of 1983. Its CdF was composed of 50 delegates, out of a total of 1,098 in the metalworking sector. The overwhelming majority of delegates are thus scattered across the 348 factories organized by the FLM, and the average size of a CdF is a mere three.

Modena is also one of the strongest Communist-dominated provinces in Italy, not merely with respect to electoral support but also as regards member voter and inhabitant member ratios, as table 21 shows. The Modenese PCI is the archetypal subcultural party, historically rooted and the architect of a relatively successful system of cross-class alliances.

The precise nature of Communist rule in Emilia has been the object of considerable controversy. In the early 1970s, the Bolognese metalworkers' unions launched an attack on the PCI's supraclass alliance strategy, arguing that Emilia's small owners were just as oppressive as Italy's large capitalists. Emilia has historically been characterized by small plant size, and the number of small firms was growing rapidly. Unionists argued that the flowering of small firms was intimately linked to the needs of large capital, to which the former were linked by "productive subordination." Productive decentralization, in turn, was interpreted as a political response by large industry to the gains the organized working class had won with the hot autumn—as a way to escape union control, relatively high wages, better working conditions, and high levels of conflict in large industry.[80]

80. For the first statement of this interpretation, see FIM-CISL, FIOM-CGIL, UILM-

The debate that followed was often highly technical, revolving around the definition of "productive subordination" and around problems of measurement.[81] But the political implications were far from academic. The FLM's reading of Emilia's political economy threatened the PCI's alliance strategy, which depended on a clear demarcation between the interests of large and small capital. The labor movement, as one of the party's most important national leaders argued, should view owners of small firms as potential political allies and adopt a bargaining strategy that would give them greater latitude in matters of wages and working conditions in order to allow them to stay in business.[82]

The most sophisticated sociopolitical analyses to have emerged from this debate touched more directly than the union dared on the PCI's exercise of political power in Emilia. Salvatore Sechi, for instance, argued that Emilian society and politics were a kind of social democracy in miniature, characterized by a series of trade-offs between lower wages and less industrial conflict in exchange for the better social services provided by local left-wing administrations.[83]

This view is inaccurate. Wages are not lower in Emilia than elsewhere

---

UIL Emilia-Romagna, *Atti: convegno regionale sulle piccole e medie aziende metalmeccaniche industriali e artigiane* (Bologna: FIM-CISL, FIOM-CGIL, UILM-UIL, 1972), especially the "Relazione introduttiva svolta dal compagno Claudio Sabattini, Segretario Responsabile della FIOM di Bologna, a nome delle Segreterie Provinciali della FIM-FIOM-UILM della Regione." The report was based on the findings of a union-conducted study of over half of the existing Bolognese firms with between twenty and one hundred employees. See also Francesco Garibaldo, Tiziano Rinaldini, and Agnese Zappelli, "Un'analisi sull'impresa minore in Emilia—Ristrutturazione capitalistica e sfruttamento operaio," *Fabbrica e Stato* 1 (March–April 1972), 29–33.

81. See the criticisms of the Bolognese study by Sebastiano Brusco, "Organizzazione del lavoro e decentramento produttivo nel settore metalmeccanico," in *Sindacato e piccola impresa: strategia del capitale e azione sindacale nel decentramento produttivo*, ed. FLM Bergamo (Bari: DeDonato, 1975).

82. Giorgio Amendola, "Conclusioni," in *La piccola e media industria nella crisi dell'economia italiana*, ed. Carlo Catena, Atti del convegno tenuto a Milano, 4–5 novembre 1974, Istituto Gramsci-CeSPE, 2 vols. (Rome: Editori Riuniti, 1975), 2:397–418.

83. See Salvatore Sechi, "Partito e blocco sociale in Emilia" (1978), and "Partito delle alleanze ed egemonia" (1978), both reprinted in his *La pelle di zigrino: storia e politica del PCI* (Bologna: Cappelli, 1980). Similar arguments have been advanced by Franco Piro, "Utopia e realtà del modello emiliano" (1976), reprinted in Stefania Conti, Raffaela Lungarella, and Franco Piro, *L'economia emiliana nel dopoguerra* (Venice: Marsilio, 1979); in part by Valerio Evangelisti, "Micro-azienda, programmazione e proletariato precario in Emilia-Romagna," *Il Mulino* 29 (September–October 1980), 770–803; and by Sebastiano Brusco, "Il 'modello Emilia': disintegrazione produttiva e integrazione sociale," *Problemi della Transizione*, no. 5 (1980), 86–107.

in the country, nor is industrial conflict. Indeed, the region is one of the more conflict prone in Italy. This is true not merely in Modena, for which data have already been presented in table 12, but for the whole of the region.[84] The volume of labor conflict in Emilia is higher than the national average and has been for decades. Industrial wages have also been higher than the national average at least since the mid-1970s, if not longer.[85]

Both phenomena are products of the exceptional mobilizational capacity of the Emilian PCI and through it of the unions. They should be considered within the framework of the changing responses of a locally hegemonic PCI to a national government dominated by the opposition.[86] So long as it remains carefully controlled and free of elements of micro-conflict, a high volume of industrial militancy gives public voice to the PCI's social consensus by exhibiting its ability to mobilize an objectively fragmented working class. When thousands of workers across thousands of artisanal firms turn out in support of the national labor contract for artisans—even though many of these very same workers already enjoy all the pertinent benefits because of earlier bargaining with Communist artisans—the PCI sends an important political message to Rome about the unity of the Italian working class and the party's own capacity for mobilization. The Emilian labor movement has little strategic interest in inducing a long-term depression of labor conflict in the area, though it does need to ensure that this conflict remains controllable.

Despite a high volume of industrial conflict, the strength of the Communist subculture in Modena restricts the unions there to a subordinate status. Modenese unionists reported, for instance, that there had never been a strike against any of the (Communist-controlled) local government bodies in the province.[87] Such an event would be virtually unthinkable—if not doomed to failure from the outset. Furthermore, union and party officials in Modena—as well as leaders of other Communist-oriented voluntary associations in the province—uniformly perceive industrial mil-

84. See the data provided by Fabrizio Carmignani, ed., "Immagine socio-economica delle province italiane," *Congiuntura Sociale*, no. 2 (February 1979), 18. The argument that industrial conflict is lower in Emilia than in the rest of Italy was based on a single year's observation (1971) taken from Arnaldo Bagnasco and Marcello Messori, *Tendenze dell'economia periferica* (Turin: Editoriale Valentino, 1975), 52.

85. Differences in wage levels still exist according to firm size, but it is far from clear to what extent they are due to differences in the skill levels of the labor force. The relevant data for Modena are available in the documentation referred to in n. 60, above.

86. An interpretation of regional politics along these lines is Marco Cammelli, "Politica istituzionale e modello emiliano: ipotesi per una ricerca," *Il Mulino* 27 (September–October 1978), 743–67.

87. Interview no. 71, CGIL Modena (Secretariat), 9 February 1981.

itancy as extremely contained there. They were invariably taken aback, in fact, when I asked why the volume of conflict was so high; they consider it low. And such a perception is not as far off as it might seem: the area's large strike volume is principally a function of massive strike size, not frequency or duration. Size, in turn, is primarily a function of the Communist political culture. Unionists reported that strikes for collective bargaining were frequently unnecessary, both because the union's strength made the mere threat of conflict effective, and because there were alternative channels for mediating conflict.

These channels flow from the PCI Federation. A local party functionary offered a telling illustration. While employed in a small artisanal workshop, he and six other employees asked for a raise. Management countered with a lower offer, and a standoff ensued. The PCI decided to resolve the matter in short order. The workers, union officials, owner, and representatives of the Communist-affiliated artisanal management association were all called into Federation headquarters, where the issue was promptly settled.[88] The PCI regularly mediates labor disputes, limiting the damages wrought by open confrontation.

The proportion of Communist employers in the province is far from negligible. As of 1980, there were 27,000 legally registered artisanal firms in Modena. Of these, 17,000 were affiliated with the Confederazione Nazionale Artigianato (CNA) (National Artisans' Confederation), the PCI-affiliated artisanal association. Local government subsidizes the CNA in a variety of ways, including contributing financially to buying and selling cooperatives for these very small firms and multiplant luncheon halls for employees to shift the burden off individual employers. Local government also leases land to artisanal firms at favorable rates. The CNA is represented in the PCI's local decision-making organs and has national representatives in party bodies in Rome.[89] Because of the strength of Communist and Communist-affiliated local employers, the PCI is generally successful in mediating local labor conflicts. This reinforces the mobilizational capacity of the party itself.

The PCI also intervenes directly in the Modenese union movement in a number of other ways, all of which reinforce the party's primacy. It has considerable influence over the local CGIL's leadership recruitment[90] and

88. Interview no. 72, PCI Modena (Secretariat), 5 March 1981. Ironically, this was reported in an attempt to convince me that, even under Communist governance, class conflict still existed and "capitalism is still capitalism."

89. Interview no. 76, CNA Modena (Secretariat), 18 February 1981.

90. Interviews no. 70 and no. 75 (held simultaneously), FLM Modena (Secretariat), 18 February 1981.

over union shop-floor organizations, for instance. We have already seen that an absolute majority of the FLM's factory delegates in Modena are Communists. A striking example of the potential irony of Communist hegemony was provided by an important local Communist politician. In 1980, in a local medium-sized establishment, elections for union delegates were held. Seventeen Communists were elected. The PCI Federation immediately intervened, insisting that one of the newly elected delegates resign and a non-Communist be elected in his stead. An entirely Communist CdF was unacceptable because it would have denied representation to political minorities.[91] "I don't quite have a hot line direct to [the general secretary of the Modenese Camera del Lavoro]," explained one Federation functionary who dealt with labor problems, but communication is constant and the union simply does not make decisions without already having consulted the PCI.[92]

The FLM in Modena thus lacks any independent source of legitimacy for two interrelated reasons. First, extreme industrial fragmentation denies any internally legitimating role to the CdFs. Their tasks, as in Cuneo, are principally collective bargaining and recruitment. They do not guarantee the organization of conflict, which is sustained by the party. Second, the PCI's massive subcultural presence denies the unions much of an independent and autonomous role. The FLM represents the interests of labor, but labor is only one element in the PCI's supraclass social constituency. Conflicts among these groups are mediated by the party itself and thus kept manageable. The principal organizer of social conflict and consensus is the party. The FLM's linkages to the rank and file are mainly formal and institutional.

In both Cuneo and Modena the FLM behaves as a moderate, not a radical, union. Its major tasks are recruiting members and providing services, not organizing conflict. It is unable to use conflict as its principal linkage with its rank and file both because industrial fragmentation militates against it and because the relative strength of the PCI in organizing the working class renders such a strategy unnecessary. Both union movements lacked the will and the resources to challenge austerity policies. Nor did the PCI in 1982 pressure them to do so, despite the party's more radical rhetoric nationally. In both provinces the Communist party dominates organized labor without really trying; directly pressuring the union movement into assuming precarious policy stands would have been un-

91. Interview no. 79, ex-PCI Modena (Secretariat), 20 February 1981.
92. Interview no. 72, PCI Modena (Secretariat), 5 March 1981.

necessarily disruptive, introducing uncertainty into stable, predictable relations.

Industrial Concentration and Union Autonomy in Pordenone and Turin

The cases of Turin and Pordenone differ radically from those of Modena and Cuneo. With the hot autumn the FLMs in these provinces created their own independent sources of autonomy and self-legitimation—the factory councils. Throughout the 1970s they maintained their councils both through the regular use of industrial conflict and by permitting them considerable autonomy in day-to-day shop-floor negotiating. By the early 1980s, the councils were badly weakened but continued to absorb massive organizational resources. The PCI's lack of subcultural networks and its exposure to electoral competition have rendered the party's control over union affairs precarious even as the material importance of the working class in such highly industrialized areas makes the union movement central to party strategy. Union autonomy and a class-based party conjoin to create a certain amount of tension and rivalry between these two wings of the labor movement. The FLM in Turin and Pordenone could not sanction moderate policies entailing public commitment to long-term reductions in industrial conflict and a centralization of wage determination, regardless of their implications for the PCI's political future. Doing so would have jeopardized the union's relations with its CdFs and undermined trade union legitimacy.

Tables 25–28 present data on sectoral concentration and plant size in Pordenone and Turin. The industrial structures of both provinces are largely concentrated in the metalworking sector. This has had important consequences for the unions' activities there. The dominant position of the metalworking industries in the local labor market produces a poor demarcation between horizontal and vertical union activities and a fusion of their roles and powers. This fusion lends extraordinary weight to the FLM in shaping overall provincial union decisions and activities. As one unionist noted, "the FLM 'confederalizes itself.'"[93] It acts as the strategic leader in the provincial union movement, whereas the offices of CGIL-CISL-UIL have few tasks distinguishing them from the federation. At the extreme, "the horizontal level is defined on the basis of factory bargaining,"[94] a perversion of the horizontal organizational role.

93. Interview no. 94, CISL Pordenone (Secretariat), 3 March 1981.
94. Interview no. 68, CGIL Turin (Secretariat), 26 January 1981.

The importance of large industry not only within the metalworking sector but in the local economy generally reinforces the FLM's powers in the union movement's activities in the two provinces. It also produces a constant and nearly obsessive concern on the part of the *whole* of organized labor with the major firms involved. The bulk of the union's resources is dedicated to the gigantic firms that dominate their labor markets. In Turin and Pordenone the FLM *is* whatever it does at Fiat and Zanussi. Activities not relating to these firms tend to be sporadic, inadequate, and highly dependent upon lulls at Fiat and Zanussi. One of the most frequently repeated phrases of Turinese trade unionists, for instance, is, "But here, there's the Fiat." The firm functions as a deus ex machina in explanations of just about everything the union decides.

And not without reason. In Turin, nearly 40 percent of the FLM's membership was employed by Fiat in 1982. In Pordenone, nearly half of the FLM's members worked for Zanussi. As the largest single employers, the two firms thus necessarily play central roles for their respective unions, engendering concentrations of union resources as extreme as the industrial structures they mirror.

In 1982 Zanussi employed over 10,000 persons in Pordenone, while the Turinese Fiat plants had a work force of over 200,000. Firms of such dimensions cannot be managed with even a modicum of efficiency without shop-floor union representatives. Even regular communication with the rank and file would be virtually impossible without the union delegates. After 1969, maintaining the delegate structures in these firms had not surprisingly become the central organizational activity of the union, largely replacing those institutional tasks—recruiting members and providing individual services—so prevalent in Cuneo and Modena. Contact with the rank and file was necessarily filtered through the delegate structure, and every emphasis was placed on maintaining a good working relationship with the latter. The delegate had become the crucial intermediary in the linkage with the organization's mass base. And to recruit delegates, the union movement must continue to employ a largely expressive orientation.

The material basis propelling the concentration of resources on expressive goals is thus twofold. First, following the extraordinary mass enthusiasm of the hot autumn, there developed an acute shortage of individuals willing to serve as factory delegates. One recent study found, for instance, that 94 percent of factory councils complained of problems in finding people willing to run for the position.[95] Additionally, delegates in large

95. Ida Regalia, *Eletti e abbandonati: modelli e stili di rappresentanza in fabbrica* (Bologna: Il Mulino, 1984), 96–97.

plants are more likely to be motivated by expressive-ideological concerns than their counterparts in small plants, where pragmatic, instrumental, or individual motivations are more common.[96] Thus, in large plants the union movement successfully employs expressive, ideological mechanisms in recruiting delegates. Second, however, precisely because Italian unionism is not fundamentally plant based and full-time officials have no interest in allowing it to become so, delegates are socialized into the structures of unionism. This means that relations between delegates and full-time officials become structured such that "the goal . . . should be unanimous and rational consensus, not an optimal compromise between irreducibly opposed interests. The forum is not to be contaminated by the principles that regulate the market, nor should communication be confused with bargaining."[97] Union officials at all times seek the consensus of their factory councils.

In December of 1983 there were 4,562 FLM delegates and RSAs in Turin, of whom 1,387 were concentrated at Fiat plants.[98] Thus, nearly one-third of all metalworking delegates in the province represented Fiat workers. In Pordenone in January 1982, there were 162 Zanussi delegates and only 191 from all other firms organized by the federation. Approximately 46 percent of the FLM's delegates were from Zanussi.[99] These delegates exercise a disproportionate influence in provincial union decision making. The isolation and fragmentation of delegates from smaller firms renders them less than potent in dealing with the union offices. When they challenge union authority, as they occasionally do, they are generally passive and withdrawn.[100] They are unable to muster concerted and unified efforts, if only because group meetings are held at the union's discretion and are relatively infrequent.

In Pordenone, Zanussi's factory council is seen by full-time officials as

96. Ibid., 122–25.

97. Jon Elster, *Sour Grapes: Studies in the Subversion of Rationality* (Cambridge: Cambridge University Press, 1983), 35.

98. Data courtesy of FLM Turin.

99. Data courtesy of FLM Pordenone.

100. The most typical—if still rare—challenge involves signing factory accords that in some way would not meet official approval. The usual tactic in such a case is for the delegate to withdraw communication with the provincial or local trade union office and, if challenged, to refuse to show the full-time functionary a copy of the controversial accord. In smaller provinces, where full-time officials have less difficulty keeping track of the activities of their delegates and where the former are able to place considerably more informal pressure on the latter, such occurrences are relatively easy to reverse. The official can appeal directly to the rank and file and suggest that the delegate be recalled. I witnessed such a case in Cuneo.

"strong and autonomous, but always open to dialogue with the union."[101] An outside but interested observer even characterized relations between the CdF at Zanussi and the provincial union as "conflictual."[102] Shopfloor bargaining—excluding that affecting all Zanussi plants in the country—is conducted by the executive of the CdF in consultation with provincial officials, but not necessarily in their presence.[103] The CdF at the Porcia plant has been known to block union decision making for months at a time when dissatisfied with provincial or national proposals. The relative independence of the CdF is reflected in the high proportion of delegates without confederal affilation and in the inability of any of the three organizations to dominate decision making, as table 23 shows.

At Fiat the situation is complicated by the complexity of production sites and the intense interest of the FLM's national offices and the confederations in conditioning local activities. Table 23 shows that a large number of the FLM's delegates are without confederal affiliation and that none of the three organizations is able to dominate numerically. Both indicate the relative autonomy and independence of Fiat's CdFs. One graphic illustration corroborating the relative autonomy and strength of the CdF at Mirafiori, the largest factory in the country, came with the 1980 Fiat strike. In the fall of 1980, Fiat's management threatened to lay off workers because of poor market conditions. The eventual response of the union included a thirty-five-day strike at Fiat *ad oltranza:* that is, a total walkout rather than the more usual articulated strike pattern. Total walkouts are both rare and dangerous, since unions in Italy maintain no strike funds. At a number of points over the course of the strike, provincial, national, and confederal unionists, as well as functionaries from the Turinese PCI Federation, made strenuous but vain efforts to transform the strike ad oltranza into the more effective and potentially longer-lived articulated pattern. According to research conducted later, these efforts failed primarily, though not exclusively, because of the veto by the dele-

101. Interview no. 86, FLM Pordenone (Secretariat), 27 February 1981. In her study of factory councils, Regalia comments on the twofold and ambivalent meaning of "autonomy" when used by full-time officials to characterize a council: "Sometimes, one says a council is autonomous because it's capable of acting even without the help of the external union (a positive evaluation). And sometimes one says that a council is autonomous because it opposes, contests, tries to make do without the external union (negative evaluation)"; Regalia, *Eletti e abbandonati*, 267n.4.

102. Interview no. 82, PCI Pordenone (Secretariat), 26 February 1981.

103. Interview no. 90, two members of executive of CdF, Zanussi (Porcia), 1 March 1981. Within the CdF, the executive is the primary decision-making and bargaining agent and maintains most contact with the provincial offices.

gates, the same CdF that earlier had vetoed Fiat's requests for greater flexibility in the use of labor, thus provoking the firm's drastic threat of firing in the first place.[104] The strike ended only after some 40,000 angry Fiat workers—mainly white-collar workers and foremen—took to the streets in Turin demanding the "right to work." The accord that emerged was officially called "a partial victory," but the delegates' reaction was near total demoralization, disgust, and bitter defeat.[105] After 1980, unionization at Fiat plummeted a full ten points, from 34 to 24 percent (see table 19), and the number of delegates in Mirafiori dropped from nearly 800 in 1979 to about 600 in late 1983, as table 29 shows.

In both Turin and Pordenone, then, strong and concentrated factory councils are able to veto, at least for extended periods, provincial and even national union proposals. The behavior of the CdFs does not necessarily conform to the expectations or needs of provincial or national union officials. Because they are potentially uncontrollable, these CdFs exercise powerful influence over decisions. Decisions by provincial officials are adjusted in anticipation of the expected reactions of their largest CdFs.

In the eyes of his fellow workers, the delegate acquires status and legitimacy mainly to the extent that he is the visible intermediary in winning collective gains. He must bargain, and to bargain he must be able to ensure disruption of production. The key to the delegates' power, status, and influence within organized labor lies with the organization of the strike. "Power," one unionist acutely observed, in a phrase that unfortunately translates poorly, "rests with him who can guarantee conflict to the counterpart."[106] In large firms, only the CdFs guarantee factory peace. The union can call a strike, but the delegates organize it. The union can officially legitimate unexpected, spontaneous strikes, but the delegates provide the accurate and immediate information so vital to the continued credibility of the union as the recognized representative of conflict. It is the exercise of conflict itself that sustains the autonomy and organizational legitimacy of the delegate: "The tasks of the delegates normally tend to be reduced to those of organizational channel between the rank and

104. See Giuseppe Bonazzi, "La lotta dei 35 giorni alla Fiat: un'analisi sociologica," *Ricerche CeSPE,* supplement to *Politica ed Economia,* no. 11 (November 1984), 35.

105. Interviews no. 54, member of executive of CdF, Fiat (Mirafiori), 5 December 1980; no. 55, one member of executive of CdF Fiat (Mirafiori) and one union delegate (Mirafiori) then suspended by Fiat, 6 December 1980; no. 57, CISL Torino, 11 December 1980; no. 13, FLM Turin (Secretariat), 1 December 1980; and no. 69, PCI Turin (Secretariat), 30 January 1981.

106. Interview no. 88, UIL Pordenone (Secretariat), 27 February 1981.

Table 29. FLM Delegates by Organization at Fiat Mirafiori, 1976–83

Year	FIM	FIOM	UILM	SSC	Total
1976	132 (16%)	271 (34%)	121 (15%)	268 (33%)	804[a] (98%)
1977[b]	134 (17%)	274 (34%)	122 (15%)	266 (33%)	798 (99%)
1978	137 (17%)	294 (37%)	122 (15%)	240 (30%)	793 (99%)
1979	137 (17%)	306 (39%)	125 (16%)	225 (28%)	793 (100%)
1980	n.a.[c]	n.a.	n.a.	293 (38%)	766
1981	115 (15%)	302 (38%)	122 (15%)	249 (32%)	788 (100%)
1982	111 (16%)	290 (42%)	115 (17%)	171 (25%)	687 (100%)
1983	95 (16%)	264 (44%)	102 (17%)	135 (23%)	596 (100%)

Source: Courtesy of FLM Turin.
[a]Total higher than sum of components owing to missing data on twelve delegates.
[b]As of February 1978. Other data refer to official end of year.
[c]N.a. = not available.

file and union leadership for the firm, and assume greater autonomy only in the case of the organization of conflict."[107] A preliminary analysis of a 1980 sample survey conducted among manual workers in Turinese Fiat plants confirms the visible importance of the CdFs in organizing conflict. In answer to the question, "Who do you think normally makes the decision to call a workshop strike?" 36 percent of the respondents indicated "the CdF," compared with 26 percent who replied "the union."[108] Similarly, recent research on factory councils has shown that in large plants

107. Alessandro Pizzorno, "Le due logiche dell'azione di classe," in *Lotte operaie e sindacato: il ciclo 1968–1972,* ed. Alessandro Pizzorno et al., vol. 6 of *Lotte operaie e sindacato in Italia: 1968–1972*, ed. Alessandro Pizzorno (Bologna: Il Mulino, 1978), 29.

108. The other responses were "we workers" (17 percent), "the delegate" (17 percent), and "the executive" of the CdF (4 percent). Reported in Aris Accornero, Alberto Baldissera, and Sergio Scamuzzi, "Ricerca di massa sulla condizione operaia alla Fiat: primi risultati," *Congiuntura Sociale,* no. 2 (February 1980), 8.

these organs are engaged more in strike activity and less in reçruiting new members than in small plants.[109]

It is thus not surprising that the volume of industrial conflict tends to be higher in Pordenone and in Turin than the national average, as table 12 shows. Table 13 also shows that industrial conflict at the Turinese Fiat works is relatively high.[110] But conflict at Fiat in Turin is irregular and unpredictable, unlike industrial action at Zanussi. As one unionist metaphorically put it, the FLM exercises only "limited sovereignty" over the work force there.[111] The structure of Fiat's CdFs is perennially weak. The FLM has so much difficulty in finding workers willing to serve as delegates[112] and in recruiting young workers as activists[113] that in January 1980 only 14 percent of Mirafiori's delegates had been elected before 1976. Twenty-eight percent had served only since 1977.[114] In short, as unionists constantly lament in Turin, there is a tremendous turnover of factory delegates and an inability to recruit new groups of workers, to the detriment of organizational stability, continuity, and representativeness. The result, as one unionist put it, with a prescience that would acquire tragic proportions with the FLM's defeat in late 1980, is that "there's always the possibility" of a breakdown of relations between the union and the rank and file because the union "has no filter" of a stable organizational structure in the factory.[115] In the wake of the 1980 strike, what organization the union had established in Fiat between 1968 and the strike had

109. Regalia, *Eletti e abbandonati*, 248.

110. For figures on strike hours in Fiat plants between 1969 and 1977, see Paolo Buran, "La classe ostile: forme di conflitto e forme di soggettività operaia a Torino negli anni '70," *Laboratorio Politico* 2 (January–February 1982), 172. It is not clear which plants are included in the figures.

111. Interview no. 32, FLM Turin, 7 July 1980.

112. Interview no. 1, FLM Turin (Secretariat), 21 January 1981. This problem is of course common across Italy; the difference is the huge pool of potential delegates in Turin.

113. In 1978 and 1979 some 20,000 new, mainly young, workers were hired at Fiat in Turin; see the review of the literature on the sociological differences between them and older employees in Buran, "Classe ostile." Difficulties in recruiting newly hired workers to act as delegates were reported in a discussion with one of the officials who worked in the FLM's office responsible for Fiat Rivalta, where many of the new employees had gone to work, while a complete round of elections for delegates was in progress in the Turinese Fiat plants. Interview no. 7, FLM Turin, 11 March 1980. The problem was also discussed in a meeting of the Comitato Direttivo FLM Turin, 27 March 1980; the opening address reported that in the 1980 elections for delegates at Fiat there had been, on average, 95 percent voting participation, with some 50 to 55 percent new delegates elected, but that neither young employees nor women had been elected.

114. Data courtesy of FLM Turin.

115. Interview no. 68, CGIL Turin (Secretariat), 26 January 1980.

been badly crippled. Throughout the 1970s these organizational weaknesses had encouraged the FLM to devote vast resources to maintaining what organization it had in the factory. Without its delegates, strikes at Fiat fail, as the Turinese union movement learned quite well after its failed thirty-five–day strike.

Giving priority to maintaining factory delegate structures was a reasonable response to large factory size, though it may leave the union uncovered with respect to membership. After the hot autumn and the breakthroughs in the patterns of working-class collective action that took place at Fiat and Zanussi, the FLM in Pordenone and Turin pursued radical logics of organizational habits. *Once the CdF replaced membership enrollment as the principal linkage between the rank and file and the provincial union, conflict became the primary mechanism of consensus building.* The only way to test the continued loyalty of the base was to strike: alternative measures of consensus were virtually nonexistent. Every strike became a test and a measure of rank-and-file loyalty; strikes thereby become goals, not ends. And to retain the active support and involvement of the CdF itself, the provincial union must allow it to perform the few tasks for which it is suited and that allow it a measure of organizational autonomy: shop-floor bargaining and the organization of the strike. Structure perpetuates a persistently radical strategy: these conditions give organized labor a specific organizational interest in propelling industrial conflict beyond its nominal aims. Conflict attains a virtue of its own.

In neither Turin nor Pordenone are alternative bases of union legitimacy available. Table 20 shows the extent of electoral instability in the two provinces, and table 21 presents data on the PCI's weaknesses as a subcultural actor. The weaknesses of the PCI mean that partisan-based mechanisms for reproducing factory councils are largely absent. The first direct and formative politicizing experience for working-class militants is likely to come through the union: the union reproduces itself organizationally.

At Zanussi, only the PCI and the PSI maintain factory sections, and weak ones at that. At the Zanussi plant in Porcia—the firm's largest plant in the country, employing some 8,000 persons—there are only some 200 members (or 4 percent of the work force) in the PCI's factory section. All the Communist unionists I spoke with independently told me that if there were a "transmission belt" between the union and the party, it went the other way. The party's leaders frequently emerge out of the union; the CGIL and FIOM's officials often begin full-time union work before taking out a party card; union decisions are made by the "three or four people who count" and then communicated to the party; a significant proportion of full-time officials and militants in the FIM-CISL are Communist party members; party meetings over labor issues regularly include non-Communists. One full-time union functionary, not a PCI member, said that before assuming his post he had had some reservations about relations between the party and the union. Since working for the union and regularly attending party meetings involving unionists, his doubts had evaporated: it had become clear that the union ended up conditioning the party rather than the reverse.[116]

Over 60 percent of the party's provincial membership is blue collar (see table 22); the party's alliance strategy has not paid in Pordenone.[117] The problem, one Federation functionary said, is not the working class vote per se, despite the large proportion of the working class that votes for the DC, but relations between the working class and other social strata and the isolation of the former.[118] Given the centrality of the working class in the party's membership, it is not surprising that relations with organized labor are of considerable importance.[119] But given the political heterogeneity of the Pordenonese working class and the difficulties of dealing with a newly industrialized and militant work force concentrated in large industry, the PCI cannot take its class base for granted.

Turin has never experienced one-party subcultural domination, and the party system has been organizationally weak there throughout the postwar period. Nowhere is the perennial weakness of the PCI more apparent than in the factories. Table 30 presents data on the PCI's factory sections and the FLM's members at Mirafiori since 1972. Even next to the very low 20 percent unionization held by the FLM in 1983, the PCI's 3 percent is shocking. Out of a work force of nearly 52,000, the PCI had only 1,400 members. Admittedly, this was twice as many as the 700 members enrolled in Mirafiori in 1972, but it was still too few to render the PCI a viable workplace organization. As an attentive observer of the party there has noted:

> Almost all party militants in the factory are also union militants, and the very top cadres are inevitably union delegates . . . who are deeply caught up in union affairs. Because the unions have operated at arm's length from the parties in Italy—and particularly in Turin—for many years, there is by no

116. Interviews no. 81, CGIL Pordenone, 26 February 1981; no. 82, PCI Pordenone (Secretariat), 26 February 1981; no. 91, FLM Pordenone (Secretariat), 2 March 1981; no. 95, CGIL Pordenone (Secretariat), 3 March 1981; no. 86, FLM Pordenone (Secretariat), 27 February 1981; and no. 84, FLM Pordenone (Secretariat), 26 February 1981.

117. Interview no. 112, PCI Pordenone (Secretariat), 19 December 1983.

118. Interview no. 82, PCI Pordenone (Secretariat), 26 February 1981.

119. Interview no. 113, PCI Pordenone (Secretariat), 19 December 1983.

> means a harmony of interests or activities implicit in dual militance. On the contrary; party and union compete for the militant's limited time and energies, and the union almost inevitably wins. . . .
>
> In fact, dual militance is really something of a misnomer, given the predictability with which Communist militants in the factories tend to favor trade-union activities. Party leaders regularly complain that even when shop-floor cadres participate in party activities, they bring the union's concerns and perspectives into the sections. This . . . follow[s] logically from several developments . . . (1) the conscious decision, following the rout of the 1950s, to pour the PCI's limited resources into (re-)building a shattered union movement; (2) the trend, starting in the 1960s, toward a more unified union movement that reinforced greater autonomy vis-à-vis the party; (3) the fact that the resurgent militancy of the late 1960s brought more PCI cadres into politics via the unions, rather than vice versa. If their initial socialization came from outside the party, they would obviously be less inclined to see party activity as the most important form of "real" political activity.[120]

Relations between the PCI and the union movement at Fiat swayed between the competitive and the union dominant in the 1970s. Between 1969 and 1974 the union was clearly the primary actor: the party's role was one of mere "support" for union initiatives.[121] Only with the elections in 1975 and 1976 did the PCI regain partial initiative. But relations remain complicated and frequently are extremely tense. The PCI has referred to its affiliated unionists as a "separate body": poorly integrated into the party's activities and reluctant to attend party-sponsored meetings, let alone work out agreements with it. The CGIL's Communist unionists, too, seem to prefer withdrawal and even furtiveness in their dealings with the PCI.

Part of the FIOM's distance from party affairs in Turin is due to its relative weakness compared with the FIM and the UILM, a factor whose importance has already been noted. The 1971 agreement among the three organizations gave the FIOM some 49 percent of the FLM's membership, the FIM 22 percent, and the UILM 28 percent. At the time, the FIOM held 51 percent of all metalworkers' union members in the province.[122] The current organizational affiliations of union delegates similarly deny the FIOM hegemony, as the figures presented in tables 23 and 29 show. Although a large share of Mirafiori's delegates are members of the FIOM, in 1983 its adherents constituted 44 percent of the total. The strong show-

120. Hellman, *Italian Communism in Transition*, 142–43.
121. Interview no. 56, PCI Turin (Secretariat), 9 December 1980.
122. Interview no. 5, FLM Turin (Secretariat), 31 January 1980.

Table 30. PCI Factory Sections and FLM Members at Fiat Mirafiori, 1972–83

Year	Employees	PCI Members	Percentage PCI	FLM Members	Percentage FLM
1972	70,440	709	1	12,556	18
1973	72,540	1,009	1	18,292	25
1974	68,297	1,060	2	18,582	27
1975	69,031	1,238	2	19,273	28
1976	69,747	1,719	2	20,870	30
1977	69,712	1,912	3	20,554	29
1978	70,595	1,889	3	21,477	30
1979	69,520	2,085	3	22,691	33
1980	73,250	2,177	3	22,315	30
1981	n.a.[a]	1,871		17,793	
1982	59,494	1,639	3	12,829	22
1983	51,950	1,410	3	10,486	20

Sources: PCI membership: courtesy of PCI Federation, Turin. FLM membership and number of employees: courtesy of FLM Turin. Figures refer to official end of year.
[a]N.a. = not available.

ing of delegates without any confederal affiliation—still a relatively high 23 percent, despite the provincial FLM's recent decision to push confederal membership among delegates—prohibits dominance by any one organization. If union activities are to continue at Fiat, compromises among the three organizations are essential.

The FIOM-CGIL, and particularly its Communist component, cannot depend on the support of a politically homogeneous work force either. The initial results of an Istituto Gramsci–CeSPE 1980 survey of Fiat workers show that among Turinese employees the PCI strongly outflanked all other parties in response to the question, "If you were to vote tomorrow, for which party would you vote?" It nonetheless did not receive an absolute majority.[123]

The PCI's organizational weaknesses with respect to its core working-class constituency in Turin and Pordenone limited the party's ability to take forceful action to pressure the provincial unions into formally accepting an austerity policy in 1978. "We tried," one Turinese PCI official said bluntly, "but the CGIL in Turin rejected it."[124] Unfortunately, explained

123. The results were PCI, 44 percent; PSI, 11 percent; DC, 4 percent; other parties, 19 percent; other or invalid responses, 14 percent. Because the survey was carried out under the PCI's auspices, it is likely that most unreturned questionnaires were given to non-PCI voters. The proportion the PCI received is thus probably an overestimation. Accornero, Baldissera, and Scamuzzi, "Ricerca di massa sulla condizione operaia alla Fiat," 7.

124. Interview no. 56, PCI Turin (Secretariat), 9 December 1980.

another party functionary, Turinese unionists thought that the party's analysis of the economic crisis and its calls for austerity were simply "maneuvers" aimed at getting the PCI into government.[125] Similarly in Pordenone, the party failed when it tried to pressure organized labor into taking a stronger antiausterity position in 1982. Indeed, unionists refused to allow the Federation to print up a leaflet so critical of confederal recommendations as to appear offensively antiunion. As one Communist unionist dryly remarked, sometimes no help is better than too much.[126] But whatever influence the party wished to exercise, its control over the union movements in Pordenone and Turin was limited. These organizations had already chosen to resist austerity policies and had expressed visible dissent some five years earlier, when the party would have preferred they had not. Autonomous and self-legitimating, they did not need the PCI's support to mobilize their constituents against austerity.

Conclusions

In this chapter I have pulled together environmental and organizational factors that appeared relevant to understanding local labor movement policy orientations. Earlier chapters have shown that the two most important local correlates with union policy orientations resided with the degree of industrial concentration and the type of party system in which labor is inserted. Placing these factors in a short-term historical context—one that referred back to the early 1960s but concentrated on the years since 1968—and analyzing them from the perspective of the organizational agents concerned allowed us to see how they were worked into institutional behavior: how organized labor designed and perpetuated organizational forms that both played off and worked on the material pressures and opportunities around them. Above all, I have been concerned to show how strategy becomes locked into structure, in the form of a relatively autonomous logic of organizational behavior. Once the exceptional shock of the militancy of the hot autumn had generated strategic alterations (in those provinces where militancy did in fact constitute a rupture with earlier rank-and-file behavior), new strategies were perpetuated through correspondingly transformed mechanisms of organizational reproduction. Radicalism became a persistent policy orientation in these contexts, one that

125. Interview no. 69, PCI Turin (Secretariat), 30 January 1981.
126. Interview no. 115, FLM Pordenone (Secretariat), 20 December 1983.

external pressures (from the PCI, for instance, or from the national confederations) could not displace.

Like their counterparts in the national FLM, local opponents of incomes policies were not concerned with short-term issues of individual interest or with immediate wage gains for workers. Rather, they sought to protect the collective and long-term interests of their constituents by defending the workings of their own organizations. Antiausterity proponents were not engaged in wage rebellion; indeed, in Turin and Pordenone effective wage moderation was firmly in place. Incomes policies constituted a threat not because of their wage effects but because of their potential organizational consequences, and it was not the rank and file that rebelled but trade unionists. In a speech given in 1977, on the heels of the national agreement with government that instituted austerity as public policy, a leader of the union movement in Pordenone explained:

> The crisis of relations with the rank and file, it's important to realize, does not emerge when wage demands may appear inadequate, but rather when the union loses its function of using bargaining and conflict in developing coherent responses to the needs of development and change.
>
> Austerity becomes moralistic preaching, and over the long term not very believable, when it is not accompanied by struggle capable of making men and consciousnesses work for the transformation of economic structures and the existing consumerist model of life and the equivalent way of running the state."[127]

127. Federazione prov.le [provinciale] CGIL CISL UIL, "Relazione della Segreteria," Assemblea provinciale dei delegati, Pordenone, 4 febbrario 1977, 13–14, internal document courtesy of CGIL, Rome.

8

Conclusions: Accounting for Union Policy Orientations

This book has shown that the policy orientations of trade unions are best accounted for with reference to the internal logics of organizational behavior that characterize these organizations. To substantiate this argument, I have tested and rejected a number of competing hypotheses drawn from the comparative literature on unions in contempory capitalism. This chapter comments on the analytically most interesting empirical findings of this comparative investigation and then places them in theoretical context. Chart 3 presents the factors that proved relevant in accounting for variations in the policy orientations of organized labor at the provincial level; it should be a useful summary as we review some of the important findings.

Union Relations with the Communist Party

We have found that the political affiliations of Italian trade union officials do not account for their policy orientations in assessing major issues such as austerity, and policy orientations did not coincide with partisanship. More specifically, Communists within the union movement did not constitute a politically compact or homogeneous group. Communists repeatedly divided in their responses to austerity policies in 1978 and 1982–83: austerity pitted comrade against comrade.

Because it did so in the delicate period of national unity, when the PCI was using austerity as its central claim for political participation, one can argue that it prevented the party from entering government for the first time in thirty years. Had there been no opposition within organized labor, the central confederations would probably have formally recommended

Chart 3. Explanatory Variables for Local Policy Orientations

Variable	Moderate	Radical
Political environment	Stable subculture	Competitive party system
Industrial environment	Fragmented	Concentrated
Source of union legitimacy	External (partisan)	Internal (councils, conflict)
Extent of party attention to union	Moderate	High
Dominant working-class social organizer	Communist party	Union movement
Union/party relations	Symbiotic	Competitive
Dominant internal union level	Horizontal (territorial union)	Vertical (category union)
Working-class collective action: impact of hot autumn	Continuous	Interrupted
Union responses to hot autumn	Wary, cautious, halting	Enthusiastic, rapid
Union logic of organizational behavior	Instrumental (emphasis on membership, services)	Symbolic (emphasis on councils, conflict)
Primary mechanism of organizational reproduction	Recruitment of new members	Recruitment of militants, activists, delegates
Degree of union unity	Low	High
Party influence over union delegates	High	Low
Social composition of PCI	Supraclass	Classspecific
Union responses to austerity policies (1978 and 1982)	Reconciled	Opposed

adoption of an incomes policy; this in turn would have given the PCI the final boost it needed to claim government positions. Whether Communist union dissidents knew it or not (and there is every reason to think they did), their opposition to austerity probably cost their party the chance to obtain power. Communist dissidents did not oppose austerity because they intended to foil the PCI's entry into government. Rather, one by-product of opposing EUR in 1978 was to undermine their party's political hopes precisely because those hopes rested on austerity. In effect, Communist union officials set conditions under which the PCI could enter government, conditions too stringent to be met in that era.

This suggests just how inadequate are "transmission belt" notions of union party relations: it obviously is difficult for the party to control organized labor to the extent that Communist unionists are themselves heterogeneous in their policy orientations and effectively act against their own party. A more accurate metaphor for relations between organized labor and the PCI may be "competitive symbiosis."

The local-level research we have reviewed supports this claim in a number of ways. First, we have seen that, regardless of the party's national policies, local Federations appear eager to harmonize their activities with those of the local union movement. Specifically, local Federations did little to redirect union policy where the union movement contested austerity in 1978, despite the political consequences for the party nationally, and they did virtually nothing to mobilize the rank and file against the union in 1982 where the local union's position on altering the wage indexation system failed to coincide fully with the party's national policy. At the local level, relations between the union movement and the PCI, though not necessarily without tension and even occasional conflict, are largely regulated by symbiosis.

Symbiosis, however, occurs on terms set largely either by the party or by organized labor. The degree of union autonomy from local PCI offices varies and appears to be mainly a proximate function of two interacting factors: the proportion of Communist militants active in the union movement in conjunction with the class composition of the PCI's membership. Where the party has successfully enrolled a large proportion of members other than manual workers—where its supraclass strategy has proved successful—it also exercises a quasi-automatic influence over union affairs, thanks to the high proportion of shop-floor union delegates who are simultaneously members of the Communist party. This frees the Federation to devote relatively fewer direct resources to cultivating relations with organized labor than where party membership is monopolized by manual workers but relatively fewer union delegates are Communists.

The underlying basis for both situations—only apparently contradictory—is the existence or absence of a dominant local political subculture. Institutionalized subculturalism provides the basis for party autonomy from the manual working class. Arguably, it is the single most important factor accounting for the long-standing substantively social democratic orientation of the party nationally, an orientation not shared—or at least not to such a degree—by any other Communist party in the West.

Our local-level analysis has confirmed this in a way that other studies have not done by showing that relations between the PCI and organized labor in subcultural environments are characterized simultaneously by considerable party autonomy from union and working-class concerns and a high degree of union dependence on the party. In these settings the party regulates the terms of symbiosis. By contrast, the union does so in settings where the PCI lacks institutionalized mechanisms guaranteeing its own autonomy from trade union and working-class concerns. In areas without a dominant political subculture, symbiosis assumes an overtly competitive tone. And although national union party interactions are not merely an aggregation of local patterns of interaction, the existence of two distinct local patterns of relations is paralleled in national politics.

Third, and equally interesting, we have not observed significant differences in relations between the PCI and organized labor—or, indeed, in the internal politics of the union movement—in Catholic as opposed to Socialist-Communist subcultures. Rather, important differences exist between these organizations in subcultural environments and their counterparts in areas of the country characterized by competitive party systems. This endorses recent research on Italy's political-economic geography that has stressed the differences in the overall social formations between these two kinds of areas and, conversely, the similarities between the two major subcultures.[1] The focus of such research has resided principally with patterns of relations among the market, society, and the political realm, and it has only incidentally offered insights into union/party relations or the inner workings of organized labor. Our voyage through Italian unionism in different environments has extended such research by showing systematically different patterns of relations between the PCI and organized labor in subcultural and nonsubcultural environments and—as I shall detail in a moment—by showing that the very organizational logic of trade unionism itself differs in these two contexts.

How do these findings add up for our understanding of contemporary politics generally? By the mid-1970s, it was not uncommon to hear that political parties were losing their hold over national political life in Italy as elsewhere in Europe and that trade unions were major agents in a broad delegitimation and marginalization of parties, with serious consequences for the polity as a whole. Synthesizing this view, Alessandro Pizzorno observed, for instance: "During the sixties and 1970s the pluralist system of representation seems to have undergone a crisis. The signs of the crisis

1. Arnaldo Bagnasco, *Tre Italie: la problematica territoriale dello sviluppo italiano* (Bologna: Il Mulino, 1977); Arnaldo Bagnasco and Carlo Triglia, eds., *Società e politica nelle aree di piccola impresa: il caso della Valdelsa* (Milan: F. Angeli, 1985); idem, eds., *Società e politica nelle aree di piccola impresa: il caso di Bassano* (Venice: Arsenale, 1984).

are found in the operation of new and unforeseen collective movements or groups, in the decline of the political parties, too weak to be able to integrate their followers in a unitary will, to screen demands, and to propose realistic alternatives for the conduct of the modern polity; and in the consequent excess of tasks that overburden governments, paralyzed by the diffusion of veto powers and the extenuating process of incessant negotiations."[2] The research presented here suggests, however, that it is probably misleading to think of collective movements (such as trade unions) solely as competing with parties for political influence and space. Competition exists, but as we have seen, it is checked by symbiosis. Patterns of local interaction between organized labor and the PCI, for instance, were not necessarily disrupted by the hot autumn. Where they were, the party was already weakly embedded in the working class and subsequently managed to use the growth of union power to its own electoral advantage, an advantage that by the late 1970s almost allowed the PCI to enter government.[3] Local patterns of interaction between organized labor and the party reveal greater elements of symbiosis than of competition, even in nonsubcultural environments where union autonomy is high. Indeed, it is the workings of the party system as a whole that set the terms for trade union autonomy. Even in localities where organized labor gained most autonomy after the hot autumn, unions did not displace parties. Rather, organized labor gained the advantage in setting the terms of symbiosis.

Nationally, too, the Italian party system has proved far more durable and resilient in its responses to the extension of union power than anyone would have predicted in the early 1970s. The recalibration that has taken place since then has allowed central confederations to secure extensive political recognition from the party system. Recognition is, however, double-edged. On the one hand, the parties had to begin taking union policy orientations into account in formulating their own options, and to this extent the scope of their autonomy diminished. On the other hand, however, the very fact that unions deliberately sought recognition from the parties and were unsucessful in purported attempts to displace them

2. Alessandro Pizzorno, "Interests and Parties in Pluralism," in *Organizing Interests in Western Europe: Pluralism, Corporatism, and the Transformation of Politics*, ed. Suzanne D. Berger (Cambridge: Cambridge University Press, 1981), 268.

3. Cf. Marzio Barbagli and Piergiorgio Corbetta, "Partito e movimento: aspetti e rinnovamento del PCI," *Inchiesta* 8 (January–February 1978), 3–46; Stephen Hellman, "Il PCI e l'ambigua eredità dell'autunno caldo a Torino," *Il Mulino* 29 (March–April 1980), 246–95.

meant that the centrality of parties to the political system remained largely intact.

Union Relations with the Rank and File

We have seen that union policy orientations do not necessarily reflect the manifest opinions of the rank and file, imputed or real rank-and-file wage rebellion or economic interest per se, the degree of organizational decentralization, or industrial unionism as such. Rather, local policy orientations are functions of different patterns of organizational reproduction rooted in distinct politicoeconomic settings.

Local union organizations typically stake out their policy positions before receiving systematic information regarding rank-and-file reactions—if indeed they receive it at all—and on the basis of other considerations. If partisan attachments do not account for union policy orientations, neither do overt rank-and-file pressures. We have encountered a high degree of organizational autonomy on the part of even those union offices closest to and in most contact with the work force.

Substantively, we have seen that radical union offices do not necessarily represent radical workers and that trade unions may be more radical than the employees they seek to represent. Such a situation goes against the grain of much thinking about modern trade unionism that, following the lead of Robert Michels,[4] tends to conceive of unions as inherently conservative institutions and, often by implication, of workers as instinctively radical. In the late 1960s, a whole strand of literature on European unionism partook of the view that union bureaucrats were systematically betraying worker militancy. One analysis of relations between Western European union movements and working-class parties in the period after 1968, for instance, proposed that "the conflicts between national leadership of the union and plant-level militants and leaders which arise within the larger framework of the strained relations between unions and parties result from a fundamental contradiction: the top union leaderships seek to retain their power position, based on a monopolizing control of the class in the mediation of the conflict between capital and labor. The union rank and file, on the other hand, tend to take on an

4. Robert Michels, *Political Parties: A Sociological Study of the Oligarchical Tendencies of Modern Democracy* (New York: Free Press, 1962).

immediate confrontation with the employers and the state."[5] In the tradition established by Michels, this interpretation suggests that national labor elites tend toward bureaucratic and substantively moderate behavior, whereas the rank and file's imputed inclination is toward radicalism, toward "an immediate confrontation with the employers and the state." The research I have presented here offers considerable evidence to the contrary.

The surprising moderation of the rank and file in the face of the austerity recommendations we have examined might be considered a function of three factors. First, workers themselves were increasingly confronted with a loss of market power, especially noticeable after 1980, such that the likelihood of achieving significant real wage increases in the short term appeared improbable. Obviously, much would vary according to local labor market conditions, but the core of the FLM's constituency—semiskilled workers in large industry—was probably particularly sensitive to a decline in market power.

Second, however, the union's policy recommendations were themselves so modest as to prove generally acceptable. The Federazione CGIL-CISL-UIL never formally recommended policies that would have entailed a decline in real compensation for most workers. Rather, the policy recommendations, particularly after their modifications by the FLM, but even in their original formulations, suggested at worst that real working-class incomes would remain stationary for some years—at most three, when the next renewal of national labor contracts would inevitably have put wages back on the union's agenda. In the meantime, workers in stronger market conditions knew that subnational, articulated bargaining could be used to induce enough wage drift to make up what they might be losing through national agreements.[6] Until the 1984 modification of the *scala mobile*, the concrete terms of austerity simply were not so bad, especially as the labor market worsened.

Finally, the strategy employed by austerity's opponents in the union movement had the effect of legitimating central recommendations for

5. Rainer Deppe, Richard Herding, and Dietrich Hoss, "The Relationship between Trade Union Action and Political Parties," in *Comparative Analyses*, vol. 2 of *The Resurgence of Class Conflict in Western Europe since 1968*, ed. Colin Crouch and Alessandro Pizzorno (New York: Holmes and Meier, 1978), 182.

6. This is the case even for the eighteen-month freeze of firm- and plant-level wage bargaining that figured in the Scotti accord, given that the clause was not included in any of the union's policy recommendations before the accord itself.

wage moderation. Opponents virtually never challenged austerity outright: certainly not in 1978, with the PCI apparently about to move into government, and only occasionally in 1982. Rather, they sought to clarify and to alter austerity, in order to make explicit the union movement's commitments both to protecting real working-class incomes and to the intricate mechanisms of wage determination that permitted what in other countries would be referred to as wage drift—legitimate and continuous wage bargaining at multiple subnational levels. Ironically but quite deliberately, dissidents helped retain rank-and-file consensus to austerity policies by attempting to modify, not overturn, wage restraint. By using voice rather than resorting to exit,[7] they rendered austerity politically inoperative but economically effective.

It is thus not difficult to account for the overall moderation of the rank-and-file under austerity. More complex and interesting is the behavior of full-time union dissidents, whose activities attest to a theoretically unexpected radicalism in the union movement itself. I have shown that their arguments about austerity were markedly more aggressive than those of the rank and file they represented and that variations in rank-and-file attitudes constitute poor predictors of variations in union responses to austerity. Furthermore, those variants of Michelsian analysis that posit a relation between organizational size and policy moderation[8]—that argue that larger organizations have little need to seek new members through mobilization, militancy, and radical agendas—are also empirically inaccurate for our cases. We confirmed no necessary relation between the unionization rate and policy orientations of local union movements.

We have also seen that explanations focused on rank-and-file wage demands or other economic variables are inadequate to account for union policy orientations. Real wages were not necessarily higher in the areas of the country where the union movement resisted austerity, for instance, and in some areas where it did not, articulated bargaining was continuous and extremely effective in raising wages. Nor was the sheer volume of industrial conflict necessarily higher in those localities where unions resisted incomes policies. The antiausterity union behavior we have observed is not a case of wage rebellion.

7. See Albert O. Hirschman, *Exit, Voice, and Loyalty: Responses to Decline in Firms, Organizations, and States* (Cambridge: Harvard University Press, 1970).

8. Michels, *Political Parties*, 334; cf. Claus Offe and Helmut Weisenthal, "Two Logics of Collective Action: Theoretical Notes on Social Class and Organizational Form," in *Political Power and Social Theory: A Research Annual*, ed. Maurice Zeitlin, 1 (Greenwich, Conn.: JAI Press, 1980).

Confirming this, we have seen that the lexicon of resistance was only marginally about wages as such, and never about wage gains. Italian incomes policies in this period did not collapse along typically British lines, when some unions lead workers (or more accurately, feel pushed by workers) into wage rebellion. In Italy, resistance almost always fell within certain parameters that rendered it acceptable and legitimate: dissidents strove to reinterpret austerity, not foment wage rebellion.

The internal resistance to wage restraint we encountered was, I have shown, less about wages per se than about the right to bargain over wages in the future: it was about the right to control critical resources within the organization. When workers rebel against incomes policies, they presumably do so because such policies are incongruent with market conditions and because they want wage increases. Under many conditions, however, union officials have no pressing interest in wage increases per se. When union officials rebel over incomes policies, they may do so because of their concern with issues of power and legitimacy within their own organizations. The conflicts we have explored were less distributional than normative. They were about the internal rules of the game, about the nature of organizational mission, and about future claims to legitimate inclusion in the processes of decision making. Dissidents had accepted the need to hold wage increases down since the early 1970s, whether as a result of political directives or of market forces. What they could not accept was their own internal delegitimation and marginalization.

Similarly, the decentralization of trade unionism does not in itself generate opposition to incomes policies. Much of the recent literature in political economy has attempted to substantiate such a claim; this book shows that decentralization is neither a necessary nor a sufficient condition for the kinds of internal resistance we have explored.[9] Union offices on the periphery did not necessarily contest austerity; national officials were not necessarily prepared to endorse it. Union centralization is not required for effective wage moderation to occur. Rather, a decentralized labor movement may successfully implement wage moderation if it is suffi-

9. Studies that posit a correlation between the degree of union centralization and the success of incomes policies include Robert J. Flanagan, David W. Soskice, and Lloyd Ulman, *Unionism, Economic Stabilization, and Incomes Policies: European Experience* (Washington, D.C.: Brookings Institution, 1983), especially chap. 11; David Cameron, "Social Democracy, Corporatism, Labour Quiescence, and the Representation of Economic Interest in Advanced Capitalist Society," in *Order and Conflict in Contemporary Capitalism: Studies in the Political Economy of Western European Nations*, ed. John H. Goldthorpe (Oxford: Clarendon Press, 1984), and in general virtually all the literature on neocorporatism.

ciently cohesive, and especially if linkages between full-time officials and shop-floor union representatives are characterized by rather more communication and consensus than bargaining.

Finally, this book has also shown that in Italy the geographic variations to union politics are at least as significant as industrial variations. Plant size alone does not account for the different policy orientations of trade unions. Rather, plant size emerges as a relevant variable only in specific political settings: namely, settings where political subcultures are weak. Thus, radical unions are based in areas of the country characterized *both* by industrial concentration and by competitive party systems; moderate unions, conversely, are rooted in areas of industrial fragmentation and political subcultural dominance. Large plants in the latter areas do not affect the moderate policy orientations of the union offices that organize them; similarly, the numerous small plants in the former parts of the country appear irrelevant to union policy formation.

I have argued above that relations between organized labor and the PCI vary significantly across the Italian peninsula; the same is thus true for the internal politics of organized labor. Although the national FLM guided antiausterity sentiment, only some of its local offices followed the federation's lead. Those that did were joined by their local confederal offices, in an internal cross-union alliance that came to characterize the locality as a whole. In Italy, patterns of organizational behavior are rooted as much in local environments as in industrial characteristics, attesting to the importance of Italy's politicoeconomic geography in shaping the logic of union behavior. Nationally, union federations selectively incorporate those localities whose orientations most coincide with their own, and they exert only limited policy control over the remainder.

The Internal Politics of the Italian Labor Movement

Perhaps surprisingly, the personal inclinations of union functionaries are not very important in determining organizational behavior. We have seen, for instance, that provincial offices of the FLM were all dominated by the hot autumn generation, members of which were generally enchanted with their earlier success. But only certain environments permitted these preferences to be translated into institutional behavior.

Nor does "choice" appear a fully adequate metaphor for describing many of the important strategic decisions union officials made. There had been moments of choice: particular and particularly intense periods of crucial strategic reorganization. For labor movements, these pattern-setting periods are probably most likely to occur around breakthroughs or breakdowns in collective action—around great success or great failure. But once patterns have been set, labor organizations stop choosing and proceed accordingly, on the basis of what quickly become habitual ways of managing themselves and their environments. Choice gets frozen into persistent and highly predictable modes of behavior. Radicals did not choose resistance, but rather felt driven to it by their historically grounded definitions of organizational mission and by the requirements of organizational reproduction. Choices were made, of course, but these were principally choices about how to oppose austerity, not whether to do so. The choice metaphor is not very illuminating when faced, for instance, with a Turinese trade union official whose entire explanation for why the union movement there had fought for amendments to central recommendations in late 1982 consisted of the words: "We were fucking pissed off [*eravamo incazzati*]."[10]

Union groups were concerned to work out the tactics of their responses, not their nature. For radicals, this meant deciding whether to focus on amending confederal recommendations—as the national FLM and the union movement in Turin and Pordenone chose to do—or to repudiate them altogether—as the Bolognese FLM did in 1982. For moderates, choice entailed working on the wording of austerity proposals and devising the most effective mechanisms to gain internal consensus. They aimed mainly at diffusing or heading off opposition as much as possible. The claims of organizational position had already laid out the boundaries of policy orientations, and austerity was conducted within these boundaries. The determining choices had already been made with the responses of various union groups to the hot autumn. The provincial case studies reported in earlier chapters demonstrate that union responses to austerity were functions of their pattern-setting responses to rank-and-file militancy in the late 1960s. If one piece of information could accurately predict union policy orientations throughout the 1970s and into the 1980s, it would be the exact date when a particular union group endorsed the emerging factory councils as the union's own agent on the shop floor. Subsequently, however, the union's logic of organizational behavior became relatively impervious to alteration. Strategies and structures reproduced one another except when subjected to catastrophic failure, and even then they endured in the absence of obvious alternatives.

Built into the fabric of post–hot autumn unionism, dissent over incomes

10. Interview no. 103, FLM Turin (Secretariat), 13 December 1983.

policies and resistance to them were predictable and expected. Opposition was thus anticipated by the central confederations even as they drew up recommendations for austerity. The impact of opposition not only was felt when various union offices responded to central policy proposals, but was written into the original recommendations in the first place. Studies claiming that opposition and resistance were ineffective or of only minor significance[11] fail to recognize that opposition was most effective not after the fact but in preventing certain formal recommendations from emerging at all. The predictability of dissent set limits on what the central confederations could hope to achieve with incomes policies.

Moreover, the predictability of internal and organized dissent suggests that it is probably an error to analyze Italian austerity policies using instruments drawn from the literature on public goods.[12] Problems of public goods concern the opposition of individual and collective interest and focus on unanticipated outcomes. But during the period examined in this book, outcomes were neither unanticipated nor disturbed by the competing claims of individual and collective interests. Rather, outcomes were predictable, the function of rival versions of collective interest. Opponents of austerity were not attempting to protect the interests of individual workers, and individual workers did not rebel over wage moderation. Trade union officials rebelled, and they did so because the Italian labor movement housed competing visions of collective interest, opposed mechanisms of organizational reproduction, and rival patterns of legitimacy.

Local and national union radicalism was largely a function of an institutional pattern of linkages to the rank and file whose integrity union officials desired to protect. These linkages passed through powerful and independent shop-floor union bodies whose daily activities concentrated on bargaining over wages and working conditions and on mobilizing conflict. In such contexts, the legitimacy of organized labor resided largely with its abilities to mobilize the rank and file behind its factory councils. Its continued organizational viability thus depended on its ability to reproduce its factory councils. The institutional interests of union officials in areas of the country dominated by large industry (and without a protective political subculture) hinged on protecting the workings of factory coun-

11. For instance, Marino Regini, "The Conditions for Political Exchange: How Concertation Emerged and Collapsed in Italy and Great Britain," in Goldthorpe, *Order and Conflict in Contemporary Capitalism*, 139.

12. See Mancur Olsen, *The Logic of Collective Action: Public Goods and the Theory of Groups* (Cambridge: Harvard University Press, 1965).

cils. Factory councils gave full-time officials autonomy from the center because they provided the means to bargain and the means to organize strikes. Austerity recommendations threatened this pattern of internal legitimacy and organizational reproduction because they threatened to depress the roles of factory councils and factory bargaining in a process of internal centralization.

Paradoxically, therefore, the evidence shows that those union organizations least directly attuned to actual rank-and-file moderation were also those most fully equipped with the trappings of ostensible grass-roots democracy. Dissidents were attached to firms with highly active factory councils, whose members were elected using blank write-in ballots and were subject to immediate recall. Three factors account for this apparent paradox.

First, delegates were concerned to protect their own roles in the wage-determination process and in collective bargaining generally. These roles were larger, more regular, and more autonomous in large firms where political subcultures were weak. Delegates reasonably feared a centralization of union authority. Although they were prepared to exercise wage restraint (whether thanks to organizational loyalty or to market factors), they wanted a hand in bargaining about what nominal wage increases were to come, they were prepared to say so, and they were able to speak with one voice where they were concentrated in large plants.

Second, factory delegates are largely self-selected: elections are almost always uncontested. In most circumstances, people simply do not want to take on the job, and after the hot autumn phase, organized labor across Italy experienced increasing difficulty in motivating workers to become delegates. The trappings of direct democracy obscure the critical problem of recruitment. Because so few workers are prepared to become activists, union offices in localities dominated by large industry must focus their resources on their factory councils. Because they depend on delegates to maintain contact with the rank and file, communication with delegates comes to replace communication with the rank and file. The priority of these unions is to obtain the consensus of their factory councils. They seek not to bargain with delegates, but to talk to them. Locked into an embrace of communicative reciprocity, union and council seek to defend their own autonomy and scope of tasks even when these tasks become inappropriate to changed business conditions and an increasingly withdrawn and fearful rank and file.

Finally, because delegates are self-selected, a surplus of motivation is usually required, especially in large plants. Delegates are likely to be particularly sensitive to ideological or political concerns, or both, more so than workers generally. This is, I suspect, the least important reason in accounting for the radicalism of factory councils in large industry in areas without dominant political subcultures, despite the considerable public attention it has received in Italy. Regardless of ideological conviction, delegates in these plants had both the incentive and the influence to reject austerity policies, and they had the force to carry their union officials with them, given that the latter's institutional interests coincided with the former's. Those factory councils that mobilized against austerity did so regardless of the sentiments of the rank and file, whose direct control over delegates is slight except in moments of collective enthusiasm. In all but extraordinary circumstances, institutions of direct democracy are as flawed as those of representative democracy when it comes to transmitting accurately the opinions of the rank and file.

This book has focused on conflicts internal to the Italian labor movement. What held labor together despite these conflicts? Why did voice predominate over exit? Three factors account for the surprising extent to which organized labor retained internal cohesiveness despite serious internal conflicts: the existence of cross-cutting cleavages, the structure of internal interdependence, and ideology, both normatively and as a structure of interaction.

First, the structure of the labor movement itself helps explain the tempered nature of resistance. The internal conflicts I have detailed cut across multiple organizational lines. Both dissidents and supporters were found within virtually every component of organized labor: among Communists and Catholics, in the CGIL as well as the CISL, in the FLM and in the confederations. Supporters and opponents of austerity faced each other daily, and each moderated the other. Because they never controlled their own organizational resources, free from moderate contamination, dissidents retained an interest in working within—not against—the larger institutional structures of which they were a part.[13]

Second, and related, the politicization of Italian unionism bred internal interdependency. Because goals at all levels were always informed by general concerns, every level was dependent for resources on all others. In such a context, organizational self-sufficiency was impossible. Factory

13. After 1983 the situation altered: internal conflicts pitted Communists in the CGIL against most of the rest of the labor movement, resulting in the breakdown of the Federazione Unitaria itself in 1984. The Bolognese refusal to keep dissent within legitimate bounds—the decision to ask workers to reject confederal recommendations rather than to approve amended recommendations in 1982—foreshadows this shift in the internal lines of conflict.

councils needed full-time officials to help bargain with management over the technicalities of wage determination and other claims; local full-time officials needed their national offices to step in when bargaining broke down and negotiations were forced to move to Rome, where the Ministry of Labor would step in to help sort out the problem (as happens frequently, especially for large firms); national union offices needed confederal help if wage gains won in industrywide bargaining were not to be wiped out by bracket creep; confederal offices needed everyone to implement an incomes policy. No one level could go it alone.

The structural interdependency of organized labor is a function not just of the informality and lack of institutionalization of the industrial relations system (as the examples above suggest) but mainly of the degree to which the union movement is permeated by ideology and general political goals. If all factory councils wanted were higher wages, they would probably be relatively well equipped to attain them—given favorable market conditions—regardless of whether full-time officials were prepared to help in bargaining. Wage rebellion would be possible if the politics of Italian labor looked like the politics of its British counterpart. But even the lowest levels of Italian unions—the factory councils—are considerably less parochial than their counterparts elsewhere, precisely because this is a highly politicized labor movement. Politicization is intense at all levels: from center to periphery, a vast range of organizational actors aim at goals beyond wage increases and other "material" benefits. Indeed, we have seen that this profound politicization of labor helps account for the competition between major industrial unions and the confederations nationally as well as in various localities.

Politicization is double-edged, however. While it divides, it also unites, creating relations of internal dependency and cohesiveness. Ideological attachments induce higher levels of internal loyalty than would otherwise obtain and thus provide a little normative organizational glue. More important, however, the adoption of a global political strategy at all levels of the organization structures dependency by preventing go-it-alone strategies. Only an internally cohesive and integrated labor movement can realistically hope to work for general social change. An egalitarian wage strategy, for instance, can be pursued by factory councils but quickly runs into limits if the national unions and the central confederations do not do their share: wage differentials may be compressed in the factory only to open up again in national contracts or posttax compensation. In this way, normative and ideological aims come to be structured into the operation of the labor movement and function as factors of internal cohesion. Ironically, if the central confederations thought a narrowing of union tasks at lower levels of the organization was essential to effecting an incomes policy—if they sought to pull the political rug out from under factory delegates and full-time local officials—it was the very politicization of these actors, their commitment to goals of general social transformation, that prevented them from using exit mechanisms of wage rebellion in an era of austerity. Their loyalty was structured into their opposition.

Appendix A

The Field Research

I conducted two sets of interviews for this book. The first ones were carried out between December 1979 and March 1981 and involved 101 persons. Thirty-one of these held positions in Turin or Piedmont, nine in Cuneo, twelve in Modena or Emilia-Romagna, and eighteen in Pordenone or Friuli-Venezia Giulia. Twenty-five interviews were conducted with national officials in the FLM, the three union confederations, and the Federmeccanica. An additional six interviews were obtained with Milanese or Lombardian trade union officials as an informal control on Turinese findings. Of the 101 persons interviewed, eighty-seven were trade union officials or, in a few cases, factory delegates; eleven were officials of the Communist party or related organizations; and three were management representatives.

Interviews took place only on the basis of prior introductions, either from within the union or, where appropriate, through the PCI. Respondents were assured of confidentiality and anonymity. No one refused to be interviewed, and only once did someone request to see questions in writing before the interview. The interviews were unstructured and openended. Topics of discussion varied according to the individual's position in the organization, his length of service, and his expertise. Matters discussed included union organization, collective bargaining, union strategy and policy, local history, relations with political parties and local government, and the 1978 austerity policy. Interviews were as informal as possible: no tape recorder was used, and generally I took as few notes as possible during the interview itself and wrote up a complete record immediately afterward. Discussions ranged from a mere fifteen minutes to three hours. The average interview lasted about an hour.

I made a consistent effort to ask politically delicate or debatable questions of more than one person, preferably across the three organizations. Of the eighty-seven union officials or representatives interviewed, forty-three were affiliated with the CGIL, thirty-five with the CISL, and nine with the UIL. Interviews of representatives of the three unions were roughly proportional to each union's relative strength at each level of the organization (i.e., provincial or regional as well as national). Mainly to preserve anonymity, I have not distinguished among the three component organizations of the FLM in reporting interviews.

I also had many informal discussions with unionists, party officials, and factory militants, generally during meetings or in social settings. In cases where the individual in question had been formally interviewed, occasional remarks were sometimes attached to his individual file.

Interviews were coded as follows: each person was assigned a number based on the date of the first interview. (In rare cases where two or more persons were interviewed simultaneously and only once, the two were given a joint number.) A large number of people were interviewed more than once; in these cases the interview numbers remained consistent, while the date reported is that of the actual discussion cited. The respondent's official union or other position is also indicated. Where the individual's position changed between 1978 and the time of the interview, only the position held in 1978 has been reported (with the prefix ex- as in "ex-FLM"). I have also distinguished members of union Secretariats. Occasionally I have reported no coding information for remarks made by an informant in order to protect anonymity.

Thirty-three additional interviews were held in December 1983 and January 1984—nine in Turin or Piedmont, six in the province of Cuneo, nine in Pordenone, three in Modena, and six with national officials. Five of these were with officials of the Communist party; the rest were with full-time union officials. Almost all of these were persons who knew me from the earlier research. These interviews were generally shorter and concentrated almost exclusively on the 1982 consultazione and the subsequent accord modifying Italy's wage indexation system. Additional issues were discussed mainly to corroborate working hypotheses.

The 1983–84 interviews were coded as follows: each person was assigned a number. New numbers were assigned to people who had been interviewed in the first round in order to indicate the official position the respondent held in November 1982. Again, in cases where the person no longer held the same position, this has been indicated in reporting the interview.

I observed a number of meetings, almost all during the first round of interviewing. These included five FLM, confederal, or other national union or quasi-union meetings. I observed more than two dozen union and Communist party meetings in Turin, six in Cuneo, three in Modena, and five in Pordenone. Except in the case of Pordenone, I attended at least one shop-floor union assembly in each province, on factory premises. A few meetings were held by the Communist party for union or labor-related officials. Approximately 80 percent of the meetings I observed were closed to the public, either officially (as in cases where the press was asked to leave after the introductory address) or de facto. Some were held by one of the three unions and were closed to members of the other two. Shop-floor assemblies generally lasted two hours, and the average time for other meetings was two days.

Although these meetings are rarely referred to in the results reported, observation of them was crucial to the research and served at least three purposes. First, the meetings provided the setting for numerous useful casual conversations and introductions. Second, they allowed intensive exposure to the technical and informal union vocabulary (which, in Italy, goes by the name *sindacalese,* rather as if it were a distinct dialect) and to the various modes of union and PCI analysis. Finally, they acted as an informal check on respondents' reports concerning the processes of union decision making and union/party relations.

Appendix B

Data Sources and Methodology

Strikes

The source of the data is the Istituto Centrale di Statistica (ISTAT), Italy's national statistical body. The data themselves are collected monthly by the local Uffici di Questura (police headquarters). There are no sanctions for failure to report industrial actions. For this reason, the data are subject to problems of reliability.

ISTAT collects three strike indicators: number of strikes, number of strikers, and number of strike hours. These data are published annually in the *Annuario di statistiche del lavoro* (called the *Annuario di statistiche del lavoro e dell'emigrazione* until 1960) and also in the *Annuario statistico italiano* in a less disaggregated form. For table 3, figures for industry for 1950 through 1975 were taken from ISTAT, *Sommario di statistiche storiche dell'Italia 1861–1975* (Rome: ISTAT, 1976). For 1975–78 I consulted the various volumes of *Annuario di statistiche del lavoro*, and I used the relevant volumes of *Annuario statistico italiano* for 1979–80.

ISTAT's definition of industry includes mining, manufacturing, construction, and energy. Analyses of strikes in industry (tables 3, 5, 6, and 12) use ISTAT's classification.

Volume has been calculated by obtaining the ratio of thousands of strike hours per thousand employees in the relevant labor force (see below, under Labor Force); it is the average number of hours each worker struck. Frequency is the ratio between the number of strikes and thousands of employees in the corresponding labor force—strikes per thousand workers. Duration is the ratio between thousands of strike hours and thousands of strikers—strike hours per striker. Finally, size is the ratio between number of strikers and number of strikes—the average number of strikers per strike. The original figures on strike hours, number of strikers, and size of the relevant labor force are available in thousands only.

The three strike indicators—strikers, strikes, and strike hours—are also published annually by ISTAT for the Italian metalworking industries. For tables 9 and 10, they have been taken from the various volumes of *Annuario di statistiche del lavoro e dell'emigrazione, Annuario di statistiche del lavoro*, and for 1979–80, from the *Annuario statistico italiano*. These data are not available for each of the provinces.

For table 12, provincial figures on thousands of industrial strike hours were published for the years from 1958 to 1965 in ISTAT's *Annuario di statistiche provinciali*. Between 1965 and 1974 they were published in the *Annuario di statistiche del lavoro*. Publication of provincial figures ceased after 1974. The figures for 1975–80 were generously made available by ISTAT, Rome. The analyses of provincial labor conflict cover the four industrial sectors indicated above. I calculated volume by dividing thousands of strike hours by the size of the relevant work force, also in thousands (see below, under Labor Force).

Since 1975, ISTAT has also collected national figures for all three strike indicators and provincially for strike hours on what are classified as *conflitti estranei al rapporto del lavoro*. These refer to strikes over international and political issues, previously not included in ISTAT's figures. The national figures are available in ISTAT's annual publications, as above; the provincial figures were generously made available by ISTAT, Rome.

Electoral Data

The electoral data used in the correlation analysis between the PCI's electoral strength and unionization (reported in chap. 2) refer to the national Camera dei Deputati results of 1953, 1958, 1963, 1968, 1972, 1976, and 1979. For years when no elections were held, assumed values of partisan strength were linearly extrapolated from the two proximate elections. For the years 1950 through 1952 separate values for the PCI and the PSI are not available, and I excluded these years from the analysis.

The data were taken from PCI, Ufficio Elettorale, *Elezioni politiche del 3–4 giugno: prima documentazione sui risultati delle elezioni della Camera dei Deputati e del Senato della Repubblica* (Rome: PCI, 1979), and from PCI, Ufficio Elettorale e di Statistica, ed., *Il PCI nelle elezioni e nel Paese, 1946–1976* (Rome: PCI, 1977), both generously made available by the PCI, Rome.

Unionization

The national unionization figures used in the correlation analysis in chapter 2 reflect membership in the industrial unions (mining, manufacturing, construction, and energy) of only two of the three major Italian labor confederations, the CISL and the CGIL. (This definition of industry corresponds to ISTAT's but not necessarily to that used by the confederations.) The UIL has been unable to make available its historical series. Figures for the CISL and the CGIL have been published, for 1950 through 1977, in Guido Romagnoli, ed., *La sindacalizzazione tra ideologia e pratica: il caso italiano, 1950/1977*, Centro Studi Nazionale CISL Firenze (Rome: Edizioni Lavoro, 1980), vol. 2, table 2.2. Data for 1978 and 1979 were generously provided directly by the organizational offices of the national CGIL and CISL. For 1978 and 1979, I have classified the following unions as industrial: for the CGIL: FILTA, FILZIAT, FILCEA, FILLEA, FNLE, FIOM, and FILPC; for the CISL: FIM, FILTA, Federchimici, FILCA, Federlibro, and Federenergia.

The figures in table 15 on industrial unionization rates in 1981 in four provinces and nationally also include the UIL. A number of mergers within the CISL and the CGIL had occurred since 1979. The unions classified as industrial in 1981 are as follows: for the UIL: UILIAS, UILTA, Monopolio di Stato, FeNEAL, UILM, UILSP, UILPEM, UILCID, FILE, and FILSIC (as of 1981, FILSIC is the sum of FILAGC, Spettacolo, and USAIBA); for the CGIL: FILZIAT, FILCEA, FILLEA, FIOM, FILPC, FILTEA, and FNLE; for the CISL: FAT, FILTA, FIM, FLAIE, FLERICA, FILCA, and FIS.

Labor Force

Labor force statistics in Italy are complicated by the lack of a uniform postwar series. In 1959 ISTAT initiated its quarterly survey of the labor force. The classification used was thoroughly revised in 1977 to bring Italian figures in line with those of the European Economic Community. The entire series from 1959–76 was then reestimated by ISTAT, and the results for 1959 through 1978 were published in ISTAT, "Una metodologia di raccordo per le serie statistiche sulle forze di lavoro," *Note e Relazioni*, no. 56 (July 1979). For 1979–80, I have consulted the relevant *Annuario statistico italiano*.

A second source on labor force statistics is the national accounts statistics, giving figures for the years 1951–70, available in ISTAT, *Sommario di statistiche storiche dell'Italia, 1861–1975*. To construct a uniform series on non-self-employed blue- and white-collar workers in industry, I regressed the 1959–80 series against that covering 1951–70, above. Estimated values for the period 1951–58 were thus produced that were consistent with the later time series. The strike analyses reported in chapter 2 use this reconstructed series, 1951–80.

Provincial labor force figures are not available on an annual basis. To calculate the annual volume of industrial conflict for the four provinces between 1958 and 1980, I used census figures for 1951, 1961, 1971, and 1981 for those years; missing values were linearly extrapolated. The national strike values used in comparison with the provincial figures reported in table 12 were obtained using the same labor force series.

With the 1981 census, employees in consumer durable repair shops were reclassified into the tertiary sector rather than falling under industry, as had previously been the case. CeSPE (see below) recalculated the 1971 data to render them compatible with those from 1981. The figures for 1951 and 1961 have not been reelaborated; hence provincial industrial employment is slightly overestimated through 1971. In consequence, the volume of industrial conflict for all years before 1971 is slightly underestimated in table 12. Nationally, the underestimation is about 10 percent, since these repair shops employed some 80,000 persons in 1971. Comparing the original census results with the reelaborated figures for the four provinces, the differences were: Turin, 535,947 versus 516,936 (3.5 percent); Cuneo, 72,929 versus 69,267 (5 percent); Pordenone, not available; Modena, 110,139 versus 103,353 (6 percent).

The sources for the census figures were: 1951, reported in ISTAT, *Annuario di statistiche provinciali, 1959* (Rome: ISTAT, n.d.), table 25; 1961, reported in ISTAT, *Annuario di statistiche provinciali* (Rome: ISTAT, 1974), vol. 13, table 88; 1971 and 1981, reported in Aris Accornero, Fabrizio Carmignani, and Nino Magna, "La geografia industriale tra due censimenti," *Ricerche CeSPE*, supplement to *Politica ed Economia*, no. 6 (June 1982): 42–43.

For the analyses of strikes reported in tables 5 and 6 I ascertained the size of the labor force in the metalworking industries by examining the Ministry of Labor's series on blue-collar workers, disaggregated by industrial sector, available in ISTAT's *Statistiche del lavoro,* for the years 1950 through 1979. The data are collected quarterly. For 1978 and 1979, figures include only blue-collar employees in firms with at least fifty employees. Values for these two years were reestimated in the following manner: the last five observations (1973–77) for the series were compared with ISTAT's series on the size of the non-self-employed blue- and white-collar industrial labor force. The values for 1978 and 1979 in the Ministry of Labor's series on blue-collar employees in the metalworking industries were increased so that the difference between them and ISTAT's series corresponded to the average difference over the preceding half-decade.

Since the size of the labor force in the metalworking industries includes only blue-collar employees, I also constructed a series on national blue-collar industrial employees for comparative purposes. These were used for tables 5 and 6. Data from 1950 through 1979 are available in the Ministry of Labor's *Statistiche del lavoro,* various years. Values for 1978 and 1979 were reestimated in the manner described above. Before 1965 the series covered fewer industrial sectors, so that figures for 1950–64 are not uniform with those for 1965–77. Again, these earlier years were increased by the average difference between this series and ISTAT's on non-self-employed industrial employees over the years 1965–70. Because the comparisons between the volume and frequency of industrial conflict in the metalworking industries and in industry as a whole were based on ratios referring only to manual employees, the values are artificially inflated and should be considered only in relation to one another, not in relation to the more accurate values that use the size of the non-self-employed industrial labor force as a whole.

Methodology

All statistical analyses were conducted using the Statistical Analysis System (SAS), version 79.5, as installed on the IBM 370 at Cornell University.

Index

Library of Congress Cataloging-in-Publication Data

Golden, Miriam, 1954–
Labor divided.

Bibliography: p.
Includes index.
1. Trade-unions—Italy—Political activity—History—20th century. 2. Trade-unions and communism—Italy—History—20th century. 3. Partito communista italiano—History. 4. Labor policy—Italy—History—20th century. I. Title.
HD6712.G66 1988 322'.2'0945 88-47726
ISBN 0-8014-2200-0 (alk. paper)